Doing and Writing
Action Research

Doing and Writing
Action Research

Jean McNiff & Jack Whitehead

Los Angeles | London | New Delhi
Singapore | Washington DC

First published 2009

SAGE Publications Ltd
1 Oliver's Yard
55 City Road
London EC1Y 1SP

SAGE Publications Inc.
2455 Teller Road
Thousand Oaks, California 91320

SAGE Publications India Pvt Ltd
B 1/I 1 Mohan Cooperative Industrial Area
Mathura Road, Post Bag 7
New Delhi 110 044

SAGE Publications Asia-Pacific Pte Ltd
33 Pekin Street #02-01
Far East Square
Singapore 048763

Library of Congress Control Number: 2008935899

British Library Cataloguing in Publication data

A catalogue record for this book is available from the British Library

ISBN 978-1-84787-174-9
ISBN 978-1-84787-175-6 (pbk)

Typeset by C&M Digitals (P) Ltd, Chennai, India
Printed in Great Britain by TJ International Ltd, Padstow, Cornwall
Printed on paper from sustainable resources

Mixed Sources
Product group from well-managed
forests and other controlled sources
www.fsc.org Cert no.SGS-COC-2482
© 1996 Forest Stewardship Council

Contents

Acknowledgements

We wish to thank the following for their reading of the manuscript, in whole or part, and for their insightful responses that have contributed greatly in shaping the book into its present form.

Sally Aston
Pamela Austin
Margie Childs
Mark Cordery
Alette Delport
Chris Glavey
Dot Jackson
Maria James
Tobeka Mapasa
Ana Naidoo
Ray O'Neill
Julie Pearson
Christo Pienaar
Jane Renowden
Alex Sinclair
Paul Webb
Rita White
Lesley Wood

We wish to thank our editor at Sage, Patrick Brindle, for his support and kindness throughout.

Introduction

This book is about doing and writing action research. It is written for practitioner-researchers studying on initial and continuing award-bearing courses, and their supervisors and providers, and it responds to several needs.

The first need stems from the commitment of many governments to arrange for widening access to higher education and the accreditation of initial training and continuing professional learning in the workplace. Some professions, such as chiropody, insist that their members should engage in ongoing learning; and some, like teaching, aim to create an all-masters or, in higher education, an all-doctorate profession. However, these aims need to be placed in context, especially regarding issues of maintaining quality. If high quality is to be maintained, the aims can be realised only through the deep commitments to achieving quality by the people in question, as well as through the provision of appropriate resources and supports to help them do so. The book addresses these issues of quality. It raises key questions about what is involved in producing a quality report, such as, 'What does a report look like at a specific level?', 'How do you write one?' and 'How is its quality judged?' Also, given the increasing demand by practitioners for courses offering accreditation for workplace-based learning, there is a parallel demand for supervisors and tutors to support those practitioners' studies, which also involves supporting the production of reports. This can be problematic, because, sometimes, existing higher education or workplace-based personnel are required to teach on award-bearing courses without appropriate preparation in higher degree supervision themselves. 'I have marked my student teachers' MA assignments', said a schools-based mentoring teacher recently. 'I had to learn the job on the job. It has inspired me to go on and get my own masters.'

The second need stems from the growing popularity of action research, especially the view communicated in this book, of the practitioner, individually or with others, studying their practice and showing how they hold themselves accountable for it. This again becomes a matter of quality, in relation to producing reports that demonstrate originality, rigour and significance, generally recognised as the criteria for the accreditation of higher awards and degrees. It is also, however, a matter of politics, in relation to what is said in the public domain and who is allowed to say it. Too often, action research is still seen only as a powerful means for professional development, but not as a means of knowledge creation or theory generation. This view is frequently promoted both by the professions themselves, and also by the still traditionalist Academy, whose purposes are served by fostering a view of practitioners as capable of telling good stories but not of creating knowledge, and by not putting in place the means to enable practitioners to be recognised as competent theorists. Practitioners are encouraged to 'tell their stories' but are not required to offer explanations and critical analyses of those stories, which, on Foucault's (1979) analysis, is a means of keeping them in their place as products of a power regime. Simply 'telling our stories' continues to position practitioners as capable of offering descriptions, but not explanations (theories) of why they do what they do. Furthermore, practitioners frequently collude in their own subjugation. They say, 'Don't tell me about theory. I am happy just telling my story', a sign perhaps of the invisible all-pervasive disciplinary power of elitist forms that keep people quiet. While democracy may be alive and well in relation to the rhetoric of widening participation, it continues to struggle in relation to the deep epistemological apartheid that is a feature of many contemporary knowledge systems.

This has implications for you, as a practitioner, whether you are studying or supervising on an accredited programme. You need to become proficient in debates about knowledge and knowledge creation if you are to have a voice in those debates. It is no use leaving it to someone else, because there is no one else. However, if you are to speak for yourself, you need to know what you are talking about, and how to say it. If you are to produce a report that will be agreed by the academy as of high quality, you need to know what this involves and how to achieve it. This book will help you do so. It will help you to produce a high quality action research report that will stand, on its own terms, alongside the best reports in other research traditions, and contribute to a knowledge base where all voices are represented, and demonstrate its capacity for social and cultural transformation.

ABOUT WRITING

The book is about doing and writing action research. The two are indivisible, contrary to much public opinion that says you do the action first and then you do the writing. Writing is itself a form of action. Finding ways to improve your capacity for writing is itself a form of action research – you research your practice of writing. Doing action research therefore becomes multi-layered: it is about improving the quality of practice in the workplace, and also about improving the quality of the practice of writing, at the workplace of your desk, about your action in your other workplaces.

We take the view, with Derrida (1997), that writing is 'the inscription of a communicated idea' (in Deutscher 2005: 9), a making external in a recordable form that which is internal. Writing can take the form of letters and words, film and video, performance, cave paintings, graffiti, or thinking. When you write you make your physical mark. You also make your political mark, your mark of symbolic power, in that you claim the right to make your mark, a right that is too often claimed only by those sufficiently privileged to know already how to do so and what kind of mark is acceptable in the dominant system of knowledge. You claim your own kind of distinction (Bourdieu 1984), in different ways. In your writing, you write your life, as a person who can make a quality contribution to the world.

The aim of this book therefore is to help you to produce an account that will be understood immediately, so that the originality, rigour and significance of your work will be properly appreciated. It is about communicating the quality of your work through ensuring the quality of the text itself. Medium and message are inseparable, and quality in one reflects quality in the other.

DISTINCTION AND SYMBOLIC POWER

These issues are key in relation to whether practitioners' research will be respected to the extent that it will command academic legitimation, especially in the form of funding. Currently, most government money, allocated from exercises such as the Research Assessment Exercise in the UK, or its successor, and their equivalents in other countries, goes to top education research institutions, often working from a social sciences perspective, that tend to focus on doing research into education using traditional forms of scholarship. Practitioner groups often find it difficult to secure strong funding because the funding system leans strongly in the direction of the establishment, not surprisingly since it is created and maintained by the establishment. Derrida (1997) notes that it is difficult to overturn a hierarchical system when one is forced to abide by the rules of the hierarchy itself. So if you wish to get recognition, you have to produce a report that will meet the criteria of the establishment, albeit in its own way. You have to produce a report that will immediately impress your reader through its originality, rigour and significance, and its capacity to explicate these issues. Too often practitioner-researchers think that a reader will see immediately what they are getting at, without any further explanation, which is seldom the case. The first thing a reader knows about you is what they see on the page. So if you do not explain to your reader what you wish them to read, or present yourself as not well disciplined through careless referencing or vague language, your reader will assume that you are unaware of the importance of these things, and reject your work, or, worse, read someone else's. This is serious. To get accreditation and subsequent recognition, you must present yourself as a person who knows what they are talking about, with confidence, and with the authority of your own experience and scholarship.

This book goes some way to helping you to do this. It will not replace the sheer hard work of studying and writing. You have to work with the ideas themselves in order to write. The book will give you advice about how to make a fire, but you have to make your own fire if you are to set anyone's imagination alight. You can do it. The book gives you ideas about how you can do it and supports for the process.

ABOUT US AUTHORS

We authors, Jack Whitehead and Jean McNiff, have been working and researching together for almost 30 years. Between us we have supported nearly 50 doctoral programmes, hundreds of masters programmes, and countless workplace-based programmes. The written accounts of practitioners now make up a globally influential knowledge base (see www.actionresearch.net and www.jeanmcniff.com), to which you can contribute through writing your report. You and we can continue to exercise global influence through making our marks, for a more peaceful and productive world, in which everyone's voice may be heard. We hope you will participate in this most joyous and worthwhile project. It does mean effort, tenacity and courage, but so does anything worthwhile, and life is short.

Be confident that you can contribute to the many conversations of humankind (Geras 1995) going on around the world, about how we can all show how we hold ourselves accountable for our work and our lives. Please contact us for further information about how to contribute. We promise that we will respond, perhaps not immediately, but we will.

We thank you for reading this book.

Jean McNiff: please contact Jean at jeanmcniff@mac.com

Jack Whitehead: please contact Jack at edsajw@bath.ac.uk

PART I

What is Written in an Action Research Report?

This part deals with the question 'What is written in an action research report?' It contains Chapters 1, 2, 3 and 4.

Chapter 1 asks, 'What is special about action research reports?' It outlines some key features that distinguish action research from traditional research. The chapter deals with some theoretical issues that are basic to action research and that you may wish to refer to as you work your way through the more practice-based chapters that follow.

Chapter 2 asks, 'What goes into an action research report?' and outlines the main contents of a report.

Chapter 3 asks, 'What does an action research report look like?' and engages with issues of the form of a report.

Chapter 4 asks, 'How do you produce a quality report?' and deals with issues about the practicalities of writing.

Each chapter gives ideas about which criteria are important for the different aspects, how you can achieve the criteria, and how your work will be judged.

What is Special about Action Research Reports?

This chapter explains what is special about action research reports, and how they are different from traditional research reports. This is because action research is a different kind of research from traditional research, so their forms of reporting are also different. To write a good quality action research report, you need to appreciate what the differences are, and what action research involves that makes it different.

Furthermore, action research is not just about professional education, or about doing projects (which is a stance adopted in many mainstream literatures), though these aspects are important. It is more a philosophical stance towards the world, an attitude of enquiry that enables people to question and improve taken-for-granted ways of thinking and acting. Writing a high quality report means appreciating these deeper issues, and showing your understanding in your writing. This involves using a certain kind of language, including some key concepts and key words.

This chapter sets out the main points you need to know, and is organised as follows:

1. Speaking the language: key concepts and words.
2. What is action research, and what is it not?
3. How is action research different from traditional research?
4. What is special about the content and form of action research reports?
5. How is the quality of action research reports judged?
6. Summary.
7. Checklist of reflective questions.

Note: This chapter deals with theoretical issues that are basic to action research, which you may wish to refer back to as you work your way through the more practice-based chapters that follow.

SPEAKING THE LANGUAGE: KEY CONCEPTS AND WORDS

To speak with authority about action research, which is part of the broader field of educational research, you need to develop confidence in using a certain form of academic language. This involves specific elements, the most important of which are these:

1. Key terminology.
2. The values and logics of practice.
3. Ideas about theory.

Key terminology

All professions use specific concepts and terminology in their discourses. Car engineers speak about combustion chambers and wheel axles. Educational researchers speak about ontology, epistemology, methodology, and social intent. There is nothing difficult about these words. Here is what they mean.

- **Ontology**: This refers to a theory of being, how we see ourselves (different from cosmology, which is to do with one's worldview). You need to think about your ontological stance in action research, because how you see yourself influences how you see other people. Do you see them as an 'It', separate from you, or a 'You', an integral part of your lifeworld (Buber 1970)?
- **Epistemology**: This refers to a theory of knowledge (what is known), including a theory of knowledge acquisition or creation (how it comes to be known). Questions arise about whether you come to know only through reading books and listening to other people, or whether you can generate your own knowledge. Do people have to be told, or can they think for themselves?
- **Methodology**: This refers to a theory of how things are done. Many traditionalist researchers see research as the application of a fixed set of methods to the study of a particular situation in order to achieve a definite solution, whereas action researchers tend to see research as a creative process of trial and error, working their way through and arriving at a 'best for now' position.
- **Social intent**: Research is always political, because it is done for specific reasons and purposes in a social context. Why do research in the first place? What do you hope to find out? What will you do with what you find out? Educational action research is even more political, because it means destabilising the way you think, and this has consequences for how you act.

The concepts are interlinked, and permeate other discussions, as demonstrated now.

The values and logics of practice

It can be useful to think of practice – what we do – as influenced by, and influencing (1) a values base (what we value), and (2) a logical form (how we think). Values, logics and practice are mutually influencing: what we believe in and value influences how we think; how we think influences what we believe in; and values and logics influence, and are influenced by, our practices (see Figure 1.1).

The situation is not entirely straightforward, because different people think about values and logics in different ways. Here are some of the problematics.

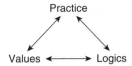

Figure 1.1   The interrelationships between practice, values and logics

- **Values** refers to what we value, what we hold as good. However …

    o Some people speak about values as abstractions, such as 'justice' and 'freedom'. They say, 'I believe in (this thing called) justice' or 'I believe in (this thing called) freedom'. They

    o Other people see values as embodied in what they do. They don't just talk about what they believe in. They do it. They practise justice and freedom in the way they live. So the abstract values come alive in real-life practice.

- **Logic** refers to how we think. There are different kinds of logic because people think in different ways (contrary to popular opinion that says there is only one form of thinking and therefore only one kind of logic).

    o Some people think in terms of structures and boxes. They see end points, one-dimensional linear tracks, and only one correct form of thinking. The aim is to achieve closure and final answers. This is a one-track view that stems from Aristotelian thinking. It informs a technical rational view that is the basis of many contemporary practices such as the organisation of labour and a cult of efficiency (Callahan 1962).

    o Some people think in terms of 'both–and': you can aim to be tidy but are constantly in a muddle, or you can have great visions, but not have the time to achieve them. This is a dialectical view that contains the idea of contradiction. It stems from the work of the dialectical theorists, including the Marxist philosophers such as Ilyenkov (1977).

    o Other people think in terms of unbounded open spaces. They see moving horizons and fluid multi-dimensional forms, and different ways of being and doing. This is a dynamic inclusional view that emphasises 'being' rather than 'having' (Fromm 1978). It has been refined most recently in the work of Rayner (2008), who speaks about inclusionality as awareness of the dynamic and transformational nature of relationships in co-creative spaces.

- **Values and logics** are not fixed categories:

    o The things people value usually change over time; what you choose to do at 16 may change once you get to 40.

    o The way you think also tends to change; you learn to see things in a more mature way over time.

However, if you see the idea of 'values' and 'logics' as abstractions, they can become fixed categories. Some people speak about love and justice all their lives, yet seldom achieve a way of living that is loving or just.

These issues are especially important when writing about practice, because, in action research, practice can be understood as trying to realise one's values, and this involves periodically taking stock of what we believe in and how we think. Action research reports need to make the point consistently that doing action research is problematic because the underpinning thinking is problematic, especially about values and logics.

Figure 1.2   Person pointing at a 'thing' 'out there'

All these ideas are interlinked. The values and logics of practice are deeply linked with issues of ontology, epistemology, methodology and intent. The whole pattern takes on the form of a dynamic, self-recreating constellation of forms that are also influenced by context.

Ideas about theory

A third key concept is theory, which is interrelated with the ideas above.

Sometimes people get worried about the word 'theory', for no reason. Broadly speaking, 'theory' means 'an explanation'. When you say, 'I have a theory about something', you are saying, 'I can explain how and why that thing works as it does'. If you say, 'I have a theory about people who wear red shoes', you are saying, 'I can explain how and why some people wear red shoes' or 'I know why people who wear red shoes act in the way they do'. Your knowledge informs your theory: to explain something, you have to know about it.

There is no one kind of theory, though some of the literatures try to persuade you that there is. Different people have different views, especially about the relationships between knowledge, theory and practice. Here is how they differ.

- Some people take a spectator stance and see themselves as separate from everything else. They see knowledge and theory as things 'out there'. They see practice in the same way, something separate from themselves, which they implement (Figure 1.2). They see everything as objects; that is, they 'objectify' things, or reify them (turn them into things).
- Other people see knowledge and theory as 'in here', embodied in the practice. 'Practice' and 'theory' become 'practice-theory', two sides of the same coin and in a dynamic relationship with each other. You, the researcher, are also in dynamic relation with other people and with your entire environment.

So, with these ideas in mind, let's move to a discussion about what action research is and what it is not.

WHAT IS ACTION RESEARCH?

Doing action research involves several things, including:

1. Taking action: what you do in your practice to improve something.
2. Doing research: how you find out about and analyse what you do in your practice, to see whether something has actually improved.
3. Telling the story and sharing your findings: telling others what you have done and how you have done it, and why it is important. You make a claim to knowledge that you have done or learned something that has influenced processes of improvement.

It also involves appreciating that:

4. Ideas about taking action, doing research, and telling stories also need to be problematised. Below we spell out some of the problematics.

Lawrence Stenhouse wrote (1983) that 'research is systematic enquiry made public.' Action research lends a new dimension, because it is about processes of improvement, and making claims that something has improved. Stenhouse's idea may therefore be extended as 'Action research is systematic enquiry undertaken to improve a social situation, and then made public.'

Taking action

There are different kinds of action, including everyday action, social action, and educational action. Here is how they are different.

- **Everyday action**, such as watching television or doing the shopping, is about doing mundane things.
- **Social action** is about acting with social intent, doing things in order to influence someone somewhere. This is one of the kinds of action involved in action research. According to Weber (reported in Schutz 1972), social action is action that 'by virtue of the subjective meaning attached to it by the acting individual (or individuals), takes account of the behaviour of others, and is thereby orientated in its course' (Schutz 1972: 29); in other words, individuals act according to how they perceive their relationships with other people. Taking social action involves using personal energy to achieve the intent. This can transform into collective social energy when people come to understand how their actions actually do influence new thinking and action (see Example 1.1).

Example 1.1
An example of people taking social action in South Africa (1976) can be found at http://overcomingapartheid.msu.edu.

- **Educational action** is the most important kind of action in action research. Educational action goes beyond (but still includes) social action, because it is inspired by the kind of life affirming energy that gives a sense of wellbeing, a sense that our lives are worthwhile. There is a relationship between what you do when you enhance the quality of your own life experience, such as when gardening or listening to music, and what you do when you try actively to influence other people's thinking so that they also come to appreciate their life experiences as life affirming and worthwhile.

Doing research

The aim of all research is to generate knowledge, something that was not known before, and to demonstrate the validity, or believability, of this knowledge. This means offering descriptions, explanations and analyses for what is done and how it is done. The process of offering descriptions, explanations and analyses is called generating theory. The most significant kind of knowledge in research is original knowledge, not just the recycling of existing knowledge but the creation of knowledge that has never been thought of before. (This is a key distinction between masters and doctoral level research.)

Doing action research

The 'research' of action research is about offering descriptions, explanations and analyses for action.

- Descriptions show the situation as it is and as it unfolds, what you are doing.
- Explanations contain the reasons and purposes for actions, why you did what you did and what you hoped to achieve and your awareness of the significance of what you have done. They also contain a claim to knowledge, that you have found something out that was not known before.
- Analyses say what the significance of the research is for new learning and new discourses.

As an action researcher, you hope to claim that you have found new ways to improve your learning, so that you can contribute to improving your personal and social circumstances. This has involved rigorous processes of observation (watching what is going on), reflection (thinking about whether it is good and why, and how it can be improved if necessary), and monitoring and data gathering (keeping track of what you and others do). It has involved testing your provisional claims to knowledge (asking other people to look at your work, listen while you explain why you think it is good, and give you feedback about whether you need to rethink some aspects). In this way you have created new knowledge of your practice, and you can explain the significance of your research for the new learning and growth of yourself and other people.

Differences of perspective in action research and traditional research

This action research stance is different from traditional research. In much traditional research, a researcher stands outside a research field and observes, describes and explains what is happening 'out there' (Figure 1.2). The aim is to test a hypothesis and to produce knowledge and theories about an existing situation, with a view to generalising the research findings, which can then be

origin, nature and use of theory. We deal with this idea shortly. First we discuss ideas about multimedia, which is an area of special importance.

Multimedia forms of representation

New digital technologies are enabling action research reports to get closer to communicating the nature of professionals' practices than words on a page. A key idea is that video data can communicate the explanatory significance of flows of energy with values in practitioners' educational influences in their own learning and in the learning of others.

Video data are especially important, because many practitioners resist engaging with traditional forms of research. This has nothing to do with not being able to engage with abstract propositions. It is more about how people's own experiences give meaning to their lives, and how these meanings can be distorted when they appear in traditional journal articles and books. Plain text cannot adequately communicate the value-laden flows of energy of practitioners as they seek to give meaning and purpose to life. If you look at Mary Roche's PhD thesis (at http://www.jeanmcniff.com/MaryRoche/index.html) you will see how she communicates the meaning of her work with children through the use of multiple videoclips. Mary and others are addressing Elliot Eisner's (1997) call to develop new forms of representation to communicate understandings of educational practices. These ideas are especially relevant to the next section, about why an issue is studied.

Why is it studied? (This involves matters of social intent)

Traditional research aims to show a causal relationship between variables in a situation – 'If I do x, then y will happen.' The aim is to produce results that will test and explain a given hypothesis. Explanations can then be applied to any and all like situations. The idea is to apply theory to practice, and ensure that the practice fits the theory. Propositional theories are usually grounded in factual and procedural knowledge, from an objectified stance. The main kinds of questions the researcher asks are, 'What is happening here? How can it be explained?' The quality of the research is judged by the rigour of its methods, and whether an analysis of the data (often statistical) produces sufficiently robust evidence to justify its replication. The wider purpose of this kind of research is to predict and control the future.

Action research is conducted by researchers who wish to improve their personal and social situations. They focus first on improving their learning by asking, 'How do I/we learn how to improve? How do I/we offer explanations for what I am/we are doing?' They improve their capacity to do research, and create personal practical knowledge. Theory is embodied within their practices, and is generated through their practices. The quality of the research is tested by:

- how rigorously it has been conducted
- the validity of the new knowledge, by showing the researcher living their values, which become a means to judge the quality of the research
- whether it has been tested against the critical evaluation of others.

This kind of enquiry can take the form of action-reflection cycles, where:

- people observe what is going on
- think about how they can improve it
- act
- gather data to show the transformational nature of their actions
- test and modify their existing thinking and practices
- communicate the significance of what they are doing
- try new ways of acting, which lead to a new action-reflection cycle.

This becomes evaluation in action. The overall intent of the research is to learn. The purpose of the research is to improve the future by acting on the present.

Where the practitioner is in the research

We said on page 12 that in much traditional research, a researcher stands outside a research field and observes, describes and explains what is going on; whereas in action research, the practitioner-researcher positions themselves as the research field, within a social context, and observes, describes and explains what is going on in their own learning, in relation to themselves and the social context. This means that the 'I' studies their own 'I', in relation with other 'I's' who are doing the same.

This has implications for what counts as theory, and raises issues about different forms of theory.

Forms of theory

To repeat, 'theory' broadly means 'an explanation.' Action research enables you to give an explanation for your actions and how you give meaning to your life. You claim, 'I know what I am doing and I know why I am doing it.' You claim that you can offer a personal theory of practice. Because you are alive, and your practice is living, this becomes your living theory of practice. You are living theory in action. Your living theory may change as you develop new insights; you and your theories are dynamic and transformational, because you are developing within a developing context. This view is different from a traditional view of theory as a set of propositions, as set out by Pring:

> 'Theory' would seem to have the following features. It refers to a set of propositions which are stated with sufficient generality yet precision that they explain the 'behaviour' of a range of phenomena and predict what would happen in the future. (Pring 2000: 124–5).

Example 1.8

Look at the video-clips at of Jane Renowden speaking about how she generates her own living theory of accountability, and the significance of her research for her personal and professional life.

(a)   http://uk.youtube.com/watch?v=yND2Ra7vdhQ
(b)   http://uk.youtube.com/watch?v=QSK1lI3sMVE
(c)   http://uk.youtube.com/watch?v=kBOKMlVPDRo
(d)   http://uk.youtube.com/watch?v=sIpJsXyhvm4
(e)   http://uk.youtube.com/watch?v=tg42056St-0
(f)   http://uk.youtube.com/watch?v=VllNe1NjQYQ

The idea of 'living theory' is well established in the literature, so it is important to differentiate between 'theory', which refers to propositional forms of theory about the way things are, and 'living theories', about practitioners' personal theories of practice. You do and live theory through your practice.

These ideas inform the content and form of action research reports.

WHAT IS SPECIAL ABOUT THE CONTENT AND FORM OF ACTION RESEARCH REPORTS?

Action research reports are special in both content and form. To appreciate what they look like, let's consider first some ideas about writing.

We said in the Introduction that 'writing' is about 'making a mark' to communicate a message, whether on a page, screen or a mind (Derrida 1981; see also Deutscher 2005: 11). In semiotics, the study of signs and symbols in communication, 'sign' refers to what is communicated, and 'signifier' refers to how it is communicated. The message may be about an idea, a feeling, an instruction, or a piece of news. Todorov (1990) says that 'discourses' may be better than 'writing' because communication happens through discussion. Writing is a way to make a message public through using one's voice (questions arise about who speaks and who is listened to). So writing has two roles – what is communicated, and the means of its own communication.

Most writing can be classified into different categories, called genres, such as poetry, narrative, or drama. Each genre has its own traditions and rules about the content and form of the writing (Barry 2002). A love letter would not usually take the form of a formal essay nor would a philosophical argument be presented as a handbook.

Here is an excerpt about what traditional writing in philosophy should look like:

> Contemporary philosophical writing is largely impersonal and technical in style. It proposes definitions, makes arguments, criticizes other arguments, corrects previous infidelities and imprecisions in a position, and situates it all in a context of issues current in the discipline. ...

The writing of philosophy is now measured by professional standards. Those standards specify that, even where a text is not yet presented in a clear, impersonal and argumentative form, it should, in principle, be translatable into one. (Mathien and Wright 2006: 1, 3)

The book you are reading also contains many philosophical ideas. It shows philosophy in action, used for social improvement; the multimedia evidence base shows people doing philosophy, not just talking about it – see especially Mary Roche's (2007) thesis at http://www.jeanmcniff.com/MaryRoche/index.html

Many experimental writers do cross the boundaries of genres, but most writers tend to stay within genres that are recognised through an existing body of work (the canon) that communicates the rules, norms and standards of the genre, and the writer picks these up by example. In action research, these rules often get broken. You can experiment with the form you use, including your use of multimedia. Dadds and Hart (2001) speak about 'methodological inventiveness', the need to develop new forms in communicating research, while recognising that the work will be judged by academic standards:

[As supervisors of higher degree studies], we have shared our unease, paradoxically, when practitioner researchers chose to go 'out on a limb', wondering if they would depart too radically from the academic criteria on their Masters' course and fail to achieve the quality standards set by the institution. More importantly, we have also shared a common sense of inspiration when practitioner researchers have reached out for exciting, unorthodox ways of doing and reporting their research and, as a result, taxed the mind of the academy, demanding new thinking about what constitutes legitimate practitioner research at Masters' level. (Dadds and Hart 2001: 8)

So, while you can experiment, your content and form must fulfil the criteria of quality research, especially in terms of demonstrating their originality, rigour and significance. These issues are addressed in later chapters.

Action research reports tell a story, about how and why the research was undertaken, and what new knowledge was discovered or created. Many stories mix genres. Larter (1987) presents his work as a dialogue. Spiro (2008) uses poetry and creative writing. Many reports include visual metaphors, such as pictures and diagrams, and others include multimedia, while candidates with difficulties in writing may submit tape-recorded reports. Furthermore, there are different kinds of story.

Different kinds of story

Stories are distinctive because they contain, among other things, people, actions, a plot and a script. The plot has a visible form, an architecture. This architecture is sometimes linear, where the action goes from start to finish, as in a Bauhaus building, and sometimes it is dynamically transformational, where different elements emerge at different times, as in Gaudí's cathedral in Barcelona. Sometimes the narrative uses flashbacks and future projections. One scene transforms into another scene, to communicate the moving picture of the story.

This idea of dynamic transformations distinguishes action research reports from traditional reports, which follow rules about two-dimensional transformations, where the scenes are linear and follow a specific sequence. These are rules about conforming to an established order. The rules of action research are about communicating the creative nature of the research. The transformations involved are multi-dimensional, generative and dynamic. They are rules of creative design, showing disciplined enquiry through a creative form.

All these issues inform decisions about how the quality of action research reports is judged.

HOW IS THE QUALITY OF ACTION RESEARCH REPORTS JUDGED?

This section sets out how your report is judged. It deals with these issues:

1. What is judged?
2. Who judges it?
3. How is it judged?

What is judged?

Research aims to generate knowledge. The object of an enquiry is the researcher's claim to knowledge; the purpose of the research is to test the validity of the claim and articulate its significance. Therefore, judges want to see whether you have: (a) made a claim to knowledge; (b) tested its validity so that it does not appear simply as your opinion; and (c) explained the significance of the research. These are three standard criteria. So you need to be clear about:

a. What making a knowledge claim means.
b. What validity means and what is involved in testing the validity of a knowledge claim.
c. What the significance of a knowledge claim means.

Also,

d. You need to be clear about which criteria and standards you are speaking about – criteria and standards of practice (this section); criteria and standards of research (p. 27); or both.

What a claim to knowledge means

A claim to knowledge means that you say you know something. If you say, 'Today is Friday', you are saying, '[I know that] today is Friday'. We make knowledge claims all the time without realising it. Knowledge claims can be small – 'Here is the bus stop' – and large – 'The Prime Minister has said that today will be a public holiday'. The evidence for a knowledge claim is sometimes observable: you can see the truthfulness of the claim 'It is raining' by looking out of the window. You cannot however see the truthfulness of the claim 'I have toothache'. This business of demonstrating the validity of knowledge claims is often the grounds for vigorous debates about what counts as knowledge and who counts as a knower.

What the validity of a claim to knowledge means

The idea of validity means that something is true, and can be believed. When people say, 'That's a valid point,' they mean that the point is relevant, meaningful and believable.

When you make a claim to knowledge you say you know something to be the case. This means it has to be demonstrated as valid, i.e. it can be believed. In practical terms, it communicates that you have done what you say you have done. The well-known paint advertisement slogan, 'It does exactly what it says on the tin', is a claim to knowledge whose validity can be tested by seeing whether the paint sticks as well as you expect. The claim you are making and testing in your report is that you have improved what you are doing and you know how and why you have done so.

What the significance of a claim to knowledge means

When you say that what you know is significant, you are saying that it has meaning, for yourself and other people, and should be recognised as such. You need to spell out what the significance of your work is, so that it can be taken seriously and pronounced legitimate in the public domain. Issues of validity and legitimacy are always linked; this was a key theme in the work of Foucault (1980), who emphasised the always–already relationship between knowledge and power. You need to have confidence in the significance of your work if you expect others to do so.

You are therefore also claiming that you have achieved identified criteria and standards in your research. These include both criteria and standards of practice (below) and criteria and standards of research (p. 27).

Criteria and standards of practice in action research

In action research you explain how you have achieved specific standards in your practice, grounded in your values and commitments. Your practice shows these values in action, through your commitments to the following (drawn from Winter 1989):

- **Improvement**: You try to live your educational values of, for example, justice, freedom, inclusion and independent thinking in your practice.

- **Learning**: You learn from doing the action research, with and from others.
- **Collaborative enquiry**: You take other people's ideas into account, while taking responsibility for your influences in learning.
- **Risk**: You appreciate that nothing is certain. You go on the journey nevertheless.
- **Reflexive critique**: You deconstruct your thinking in light of new learning from experience.
- **Dialectical critique**: You understand how you and your circumstances have been influenced by history and culture.
- **New beginnings**: You understand that the end of one action reflection cycle will become the beginning of a new one.

You explain how you have addressed all these issues and have made judgements about how well you have done so.

Who judges it?

Your work is judged by different people looking for specific things and using specific standards of judgement (standards of judgement refers to how something is judged). They want to see whether you can test and establish the validity of your claims to knowledge. These people are:

- Yourself: you judge the quality of your work on an ongoing basis.
- Other people:
  - Your critical friends and validation groups, who make formative assessments on an ongoing basis, and give you critical feedback about possible modifications.
  - Your assessors and examiners, who make summative assessments and final recommendations about your accreditation.

How is it judged?

An action research report is judged in relation to how well it demonstrates an understanding of the processes involved in testing the validity of a knowledge claim. These processes include showing understanding of:

a. What the validity of a claim to knowledge involves.
b. Which criteria and standards are involved in doing research.
c. How academic judgements are made about the quality of research.

What showing the validity of a claim to knowledge involves

Showing the validity of a claim to knowledge involves two validity checks. The first relates to your capacity to test the validity of your knowledge claim against your personal criteria and standards of judgement. The second relates to how well you communicate it so that other people can test it in relation to objective criteria and standards of judgement. These processes are known as personal validity and social validity.

Personal validity

Personal validity begins with articulating the values that guide your work. These become your criteria, what you expect to see; for example, do you demonstrate justice, can you produce examples of you acting fairly? The validity of your claim is in the extent to which you have realised your values, or at least tried. Your values come to stand as both criteria and standards of judgement.

Social validity

It is not enough only to say that you have lived your values in your practice. You have to test the claim against the critical feedback of others, and they need guidance about what to look for. If you tell them to look for examples of your values of justice and freedom in your practice, they will look for this, and make judgements accordingly.

They do this deliberately and rationally, according to identified procedures that enable them to reach intersubjective agreement, such as those set out by Habermas (1976), as follows.

- Is the claim comprehensible? Does it make sense to the reader?
- Is it truthful? Is the researcher telling the truth? Do they provide a firm evidence base against which to test the claim?
- Is it authentic? Does the researcher demonstrate their authenticity by showing, over time and through interaction, that they have committed to living as fully as possible the values they explicitly espouse?
- Is it appropriate? Does the researcher show that they understand how historical and cultural forces form a normative background to the claim?

Here is the original text from which these ideas are drawn:

I shall develop the thesis that anyone acting communicatively must, in performing any speech action, raise universal validity claims and suppose that they can be vindicated (or redeemed: *einlösen*). Insofar as he [sic] wants to participate in a process of reaching understanding, he cannot avoid raising the following – and indeed precisely the following – validity claims. He claims to be:

1. *Uttering* something understandably;
2. Giving (the hearer) *something* to understand;
3. Making *himself* thereby understandable; and
4. Coming to an understanding *with another person.*

The speaker must choose a comprehensible expression (*verständlich*) so that speaker and hearer can understand one another. The speaker must have the intention of communicating a true (*wahr*) proposition (or a propositional content, the existential presuppositions of which are satisfied) so that the hearer can share the knowledge of the speaker. The speaker must want to express his intentions truthfully (*wahrhaftig*) so that the hearer can believe the utterance of the speaker (can trust him). Finally, the speaker must choose an utterance that is right (*richtig*) so that the hearer can accept the utterance and speaker and hearer can agree with one another in the utterance with respect to a recognized normative background. Moreover, communicative action can continue undisturbed only as long as participants suppose that the validity claims they reciprocally raise are justified. (Habermas 1976: 2–3)

Demonstrating validity also shows certain commitments, grounded in your values (see Polanyi 1958), and these come to act as your criteria and standards of research, as follows.

Criteria and standards of research

You show a commitment to the following:

- **Rigorous research**: You test the validity of your ideas within a disciplined methodological and epistemological framework.
- **Scholarly enquiry**: You hold your ideas against the ideas of people in the literature.
- **Truth**: You go through rigorous validation procedures, and do not expect people simply to take your word for it.
- **Your personal knowledge**: You see your claims as worthy of merit.
- **Courage and tenacity**: You get your claim validated and legitimated through informed debate.
- **Provisionality**: You believe that you are right, but you acknowledge that you may be mistaken.
- **Living values in practice**: You are prepared to stand up for what you believe in.

Making academic judgements

Your report also has to address criteria of academic validity, as set by the accrediting higher education institution. Although these vary among institutions, they tend to include the following:

- The work contains a claim to knowledge and makes a contribution to knowledge of the field.
- The work demonstrates an ability to undertake an educational study or enquiry in an appropriately critical, original and balanced fashion in a particular subject.
- The work demonstrates an understanding of the context of the research.
- The work shows improvement in the practice described, or explains what may have constrained improvement.
- The work is written in an appropriate form.
- The work contains material of peer-reviewed publishable merit.
- The work is error-free and technically accurate with a full bibliography and references.

(These criteria are adapted from the University of Bath 2008)

These are generic criteria, and important. We refer to them as appropriate in different chapters, and as relevant to the levels of achievement expected at different levels. These levels are different in undergraduate, masters and doctoral levels, and are explained in Chapters 6, 7 and 8. As well as observing these institutional criteria, you can also ask your reader to judge your work in terms of your own criteria and standards. These issues are also addressed in the relevant chapters.

SUMMARY

This chapter has covered the following points. Doing action research is about taking action in the workplace, finding out about how and why it has been successful (or not), and sharing findings through research stories. It involves thinking about underpinning logics and values, and being aware of what counts as theory. Action research is different from traditional kinds of research in terms of its epistemologies and methodologies, and is communicated using different forms of representation. The main aim of action research is to make a claim that you know how and why you have improved your practice, and to test the validity of the claim through rigorous validation procedures.

? CHECKLIST OF REFLECTIVE QUESTIONS

Here is a checklist of reflective questions. These should help you to focus on and develop confidence in the key points in the chapter.

Am I confident in using academic language?

- Do I use key terminology such as 'ontology', 'epistemology', 'methodology' and 'social intent'?
- Do I show that I am clear about the relationship between practice, values and logics?
- Do I communicate my understanding of the difference between 'theory' and 'living theory'?

Do I show that I know what doing action research involves?

- Am I clear about what kinds of action are involved in action research?
- Do I explain the relationship between action, research, and telling the story?
- Do I demonstrate appropriate kinds of commitment?

Do I show my understanding of what is studied, how it is studied and represented, and why it is studied?

- Do I make clear the centrality of theory, and how theory can emerge from within the action?
- Do I show my understanding of the importance of articulating the significance of my action research?

Do I communicate my understanding of 'validity'?

- Do I articulate the difference between personal validity and social validity? Do I say by which social criteria my story may be judged?
- Do I show that I appreciate the kinds of academic judgements that will be made about my work?

If you can say 'yes' to all the above, you are well on your way to achieving an outstanding piece of action research and writing an impressive report.

Now let's turn to the practical business of writing, specifically what goes into an action research report (Chapter 2), what it looks like (Chapter 3), and how it is written (Chapter 4).

What Goes into an Action Research Report?

This chapter explains what goes into an action research report, and how the content will be judged. It addresses these questions:

1. What are the criteria for the content of an action research report? What goes into the report?
2. How do you achieve these criteria? What standards are expected?
3. How will the content of your action research report be judged?
4. Summary.
5. Checklist of reflective questions.

Bear in mind, however, that, although there are expectations about what an action research report should contain, each person's report is unique, written from the author's individual perspective. You need to meet the expectations, but also have the confidence to write a report that is yours and yours alone.

Before we begin, here is a story to set the scene.

WHEN ACTION RESEARCH GETS STUCK

We authors, Jack and Jean, attended a practitioner research conference recently. About 15 practitioners presented their work, and told their stories of practice. Notably, the stories were mainly descriptions of action: 'I did this, I did that.' There was little explanation: 'I did this because …' or 'I did that in order to …' There was little awareness of the need for explanations in terms of why the practitioner took action, what they wanted to achieve, or an understanding of the potential significance of the work.

This is when action research gets stuck, when practitioners stop at the level of offering descriptions of action, without also offering explanations for the action, or saying that they understand the significance of what they have done; and often without using an appropriate form of communication. Claims are made without explaining why they should be believed. The kinds of explanatory and critical frames we are referring to are essential, however, because it is the ability of practitioners to show that they are capable of explaining what they are doing that turns everyday stories into research stories. Practitioners show how and why they hold themselves accountable for what they are doing as educational agents whose work is judged in relation to stringent standards of accountability in practice, research and communicability.

This chapter deals with these matters. It explains what goes into an action research report, so that it is not seen as stuck, but gives strong explanations for why practitioners do what they do and how they justify it for their moral accountability and professional credibility.

Now to the content of action research reports.

WHAT ARE THE CRITERIA FOR THE CONTENT OF AN ACTION RESEARCH REPORT? WHAT GOES INTO THE REPORT?

This section contains the following:

1. Criteria for judging the quality of an action research report.
2. How to frame your report to achieve this quality.
3. Examples to show the criteria in action.

Criteria for judging the quality of an action research report

When we speak about criteria, we say what we expect to happen. If you go to a five-star hotel, you expect excellent service and beautiful surroundings. Your expectations for a five-star hotel would be different from those for a three-star hotel, where you would expect different standards of service and elegance. The criteria are the same but the standards are different.

The expectations for an action research report are different from the expectations of a traditional report, though both would maintain high academic standards. The expectations are as follows.

a. An action research report tells a story. This is a real-life story and is about:

   o What you know and how you have come to know these.
   o Your explanations for what you know and how you have come to know these.
   o Your analysis of the significance of your story for your own and other people's learning.

b. The story told is an original story; it has never been told before. It is the story of your learning, as you tried to improve your practice, in order to influence your social circumstances. This involves reflecting on what you have done and producing evidence to support what the story says.

c. The story contains critical engagement with a range of issues to do with demonstrating and testing the validity of your story, including the generation of evidence, to show that you have done what you say you have done. This involves analysing what you have done, and the quality of the evidence, and articulating its significance, especially about whether you are living your values in your practice, and testing your ideas against the ideas of others, including key writers.

Stories that fulfil these criteria become real-life theories of practice. They qualify as theories because they contain descriptions and explanations arising from reflection on what you are doing, and your critical analysis of its significance. Your report will therefore be judged in the following terms.

- How thoroughly do you describe the processes involved (what happened and how it happened)? For example, 'This morning I got up early and ran for the bus.'
- How clearly do you explain to your reader the processes involved (how reflection leads to explanations for practice, why it happened and what for)? 'This morning I got up early because I had an interview, and ran for the bus so that I would be on time.'
- How critically do you analyse the significance of what you are doing? 'This morning I got up early because I had an interview, and ran for the bus so that I would be on time, which in itself was an achievement, given my state of fitness.'

The base line is that your work will always be judged in terms of how well you weave together your descriptions, reflective explanations and critical analyses. The more advanced your programme of studies, the greater the shift from descriptions of action to reflective explanations and critical analysis. A rough guide as to what is expected at different levels is as follows:

- At undergraduate/workplace level, you give mainly descriptions of action (what happened), with some reflective explanations (reasons and purposes), and perhaps some critical analysis (articulation of its significance). You can find a workplace report on p. 17.
- At masters level, you give descriptions of action within a framework of reflective explanations for the action, with some critical analysis. You describe the events, say why you believe things happened and for what purpose, and analyse their significance. You can see an example of a masters dissertation at http://www.actionresearch.net/values/gsgma.PDF, where, in his enquiry into 'The Ethics of Personal Subjective Narrative Research', Geoff Suderman-Gladwell (2001) reflects on the nature of an ethical framework that underlies a University Research Ethics Board and its acceptance of a policy statement on 'Ethical Conduct for Research Involving Humans'.
- A doctoral thesis offers a critical analysis of both descriptions and explanations for the action, and demonstrates the researcher's capacity to reflect on their learning and to comment on the originality, rigour and significance of the work. You can see an example of a doctoral thesis at http://www.actionresearch.net/janespirophd.shtml, where Jane Spiro explains how she has arrived at a notion of *Knowledge Transformation*, through understanding the story of herself as creative writer, creative educator, creative manager and creative educational researcher.

All levels expect high quality communication. The report is judged in the following terms: the story is understandable, authentic, truthful, and told in a critically reflective way. This involves demonstrating the skills of writing for a reader (see Chapter 4).

These criteria also apply to reports that involve multimedia representations and visual narratives. These are not simply descriptive narratives, as, for example, on a video of a guide to a Paris. They are explanatory narratives, where the actions are explained and analysed. Joy Mounter (2007) includes video-clips of her work with 6-year-old pupils in answering her question, 'Can children carry out action research about learning, creating their own learning theory?' You can access this account at http://www.jackwhitehead.com/tuesdayma/joymounterull.htm together with three video-clips in Appendix 11. Joy explains her educational influences in learning, and why she does what she does in relation to supporting her pupils' learning.

How to frame your report to achieve this quality

Different frames, different voices

Working with these descriptive, explanatory and critical frameworks means that an action research report will contain multiple layers of increasing complexity, where each layer involves a different 'voice' and perspective. To illustrate these ideas, try doing the following thought experiment about how to frame the report.

Imagine seven framed pictures of different sizes, ranging from small to very large. In your mind, lay them all flat on a table. Place the pictures on top of one another, so that the smaller ones fit within and on top of the larger ones.

Now imagine yourself as the subject matter in each of the pictures (Figure 2.1). The content in each picture is you, your 'I', and each is alive, like the pictures in the Harry Potter movies. Each person speaks for themselves, and they all speak with one another. Each has a different job and their own voice, and what each has to say is equally important.

The job of the different 'I's' is as follows, in order of increasing analytical complexity.

Frame 1 – your actor-agent 'I'

The 'I' in Frame 1 is an actor-agent. Their job is say what they have done as they took action in their workplaces to improve the quality of their learning and practice in their efforts to address a problematic social situation, and asked questions of the kind, 'How do I improve my practice?' They give descriptions of the action: 'I did this, I did that. This happened, that happened.'

Frame 2 – your explanatory 'I'

The 'I' in Frame 2 is your explanatory 'I'. Their job is to explain what is happening in Frame 1, to say why it is happening and for what purpose. They say, 'I did this because …' (they give reasons), and 'I did this in order to …' (they give purposes).

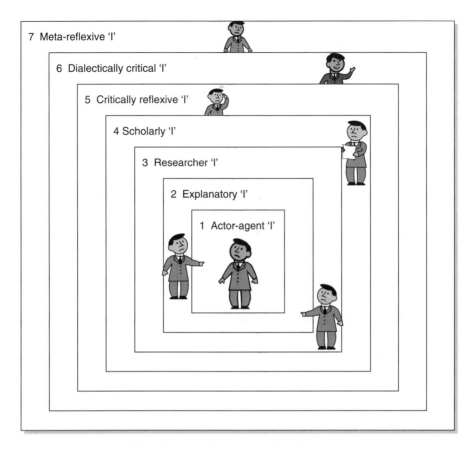

Figure 2.1   The relationship between the different 'I's in a report

Frame 3 – your researcher 'I'

The job of your researcher 'I' is to show how your claims about what you have done (descriptions of action), and your reasons and purposes (your explanations), are tested rigorously and shown to be valid. They do this by reflecting on the quality of the action in Frame 1, and on the quality of the explanations in Frame 2. This involves gathering data from the action and producing an evidence base against which the validity of the claims may be tested.

Frame 4 – your scholarly 'I'

The job of your scholarly 'I' is to test the validity of your claim against the values base of your practice, and other people's, as communicated through the ideas of key writers. This involves engaging critically with the literature and saying what you incorporate in your thinking, and what you disagree with that you wish to challenge.

Frame 5 – your critically reflexive 'I'

The job of your critically reflexive 'I' (Winter 1989) is to show how you are aware of your own biases. This involves the ideas of deconstruction and decentring (Chapter 8). It also involves understanding how our thinking is influenced by the 'norms' of a culture, and appreciating the validity of other people's opinions. In addition, it encompasses understanding that other people may see themselves as more important than us.

Frame 6 – your dialectically critical 'I'

The job of your dialectically critical 'I' is to show how you appreciate that you are in a context that is shaped by historical, cultural, economic and political forces. This means appreciating that it may not be possible to do everything you wish to do, and recognising that you may need to negotiate and compromise. How you achieve this is part of your action enquiry.

Frame 7 – your meta-reflexive 'I'

The job of your meta-reflexive (or meta-cognitive) 'I' is to look at all the other 'I's' together, and offer an analysis of the significance of the entire action-reflection process. The significance would be in terms of what this process contributes to your continuing learning, and how your learning may contribute to the learning of other people.

All the 'I's' in the different frames speak in harmony. Although they are all entitled to speak, they should not cut across one another, but complement what the others have to say. They are like an orchestra, each instrument playing in harmony with the others (Glavey 2008). This is not to say that conflicts do not exist. It is to say that the harmony that informs our practices and reflections carries hope for the future of humanity. Achieving harmony means that we do not gloss over difficulties we encounter in our enquiries, but face them honestly, and include our responses in the narrative.

Standing outside the frame – your editorial 'I'

Your job, as a writer, is to conduct the orchestra, to ensure that all the different voices speak harmoniously, and to produce a text that the reader will experience as comprehensible, authentic, truthful and appropriate. As your different voices speak, you reflect on the quality of how they all fit together, and you become a critical editor of your own work. Your different voices constitute your text. Your job is to make sure that the text itself is coherent, with no slippages or omissions.

Examples to show the criteria in action

Here are three examples to illustrate how the different voices work together, and move from description to critical analysis.

Example 2.2: A story of practice

This story is told by Jean, when she was working with a masters group in South Africa.

One of the early module assignments had the title, 'Give a critical analysis of a paper you have read'. Before doing the assignment, we had to be clear about what a critical analysis entailed, so we did the following.

We broke into small discussion groups, and worked through the following tasks:

- **Task 1**: Each group took a particular event in the news. At that time, the security guards' strike was in full swing, and one group took this as their topic.
- **Task 2**: They said what was going on, to offer a descriptive account. Participants described what some of the security guards were doing: they refused to maintain a presence in banks and public spaces. There was one story about how the guards themselves were looting premises.
- **Task 3**: Participants explained why this was happening. They explained that the security guards were underpaid and overworked, and how their contracts had not been honoured. They gave reasons and purposes for the guards' action.
- **Task 4**: They had to think whether this event had any historical precedents, how it was being reported in the press, and whether these factors had a bearing on what was happening, as well as on their own thinking as course participants.
- **Task 5**: Participants said whether or not they agreed with the action. Some did and some did not. Some had been personally affected because security for their institutions had been withdrawn. They gave a critical commentary on and analysis of the situation.
- **Task 6**: They reflected on their own analyses, and checked what was influencing their decisions. Was a member of their family a security guard? Had their lives been affected by the strike in a particular way?
- **Task 7**: They said whether the exercise had been helpful in enabling them to analyse their learning, and see how they could extend their critical capacity. The focus shifted from analysing the story to analysing the need for critical analysis.

We then brought these understandings to the task of doing a critical analysis of a scholarly paper. Each person asked a range of questions (addressing the issues above though not necessarily in the order presented):

- Which paper have I chosen?
- What is the main issue in the paper?
- What is the story of action in the paper?
- What reasons and purposes are given for the action?
- How do I analyse the story of action?
- How do I analyse the explanations for the action?
- Do I agree with the action taken?
- Where do I ground my judgements about the action and the explanations for the action?
- Am I aware of why and how I am making these judgements?
- Can I comment critically on my own stance? Am I prejudiced? If so, in what way?
- What have I learned about what I need to do in relation to my own learning and my capacity for critical analysis?

- When I write my report, will I tell a story that appeals to the audience? Will I tell it clearly and unambiguously, drawing out the key features above? Will I make sure that I produce an error-free document?

The task turned from a simple overview and commentary on the paper to a critical reflection on the significance of one's own learning for improving practice and contributing to social wellbeing.

Example 2.3: Commentators' review of a football match

The same kind of increasing analytical complexity happens when commentators review a football match they have just watched on television. Usually the panel of four or five commentators contains some ex-professional footballers, and often the manager of a club. These panels tend to follow the same processes outlined above:

- They say which match they have watched: the match was between Manchester United and Liverpool.
- They give a description of the action: Manchester dominated the match; they scored three goals.
- They offer explanations for the action: Liverpool were not on top form today; two of their players had been ill; they were playing away from home.
- They compare what they have just seen with their own knowledge of other stories in the football canon (the archive of stories): when Manchester played Chelsea three years ago, the result was that …
- They give a critical analysis of the action: both teams did their best, but it was clear that Manchester were superior because all their players were on top form and they were favourites to win, which gave them an emotional edge.
- They comment on their own analysis: 'Listen, you have to appreciate that I played for Manchester in the 1980s, so I am obviously prejudiced!' or 'I think we should be more sympathetic to Liverpool, because they have had a rough time in recent months'.
- They present their analyses in a form of language that is appropriate to their topic and the context. They speak the language of football. They speak knowledgeably, sincerely, truthfully and appropriately. These criteria act as standards for judging the validity of what they say, and their credibility in saying it.
- They explain the significance of their interactions together for their own learning and for improving the quality and status of the game.

Example 2.4: A critically reflective multimedia account

At http://www.jackwhitehead.com/aerictr08/jwictr08key.htm you can see the same process in action through multimedia. First you can access the notes for a keynote presentation by Jack Whitehead (2008a) on 'Combining Voices in Living Educational Theories that are Freely Given in Teacher Research'. The script includes references to multimedia example of practice. It also includes sections that comment on the significance of the contents of the presentation itself, as well as its multimedia form. You can also access the full videoed presentation at mms://wms.bath.ac.uk/live/education/JackWhitehead_030408/jackkeynoteictr280308large.wmv. The experience of engaging with these self-referential presentations communicates clearly how experience and meaning are integrated. This integration is a key aspect of action enquiries that aim to show how we link our experiences and the meanings we offer for those experiences. In this presentation, Jack shows how he is in harmony with his life-affirming energy and values. It has taken him several years to re-channel his responses of anger and embarrassment described towards the end of the presentations into the flow of life-affirming energy he expresses in the video-presentation.

Summary of this section

So far we have commented on the expectations (criteria) for an action research report, and the different layers and voices involved. We now look at how these aspects are taken into account in the construction of a report.

HOW DO YOU ACHIEVE THESE CRITERIA? WHAT STANDARDS ARE EXPECTED?

The issue now becomes, how do you build up the layers to produce an action research report, so that it reads as a seamless whole?

This section explains how you can do it.

Creating a critically reflective account

Step 1: Description

The first step is to describe the action, which gives you a descriptive story.

A descriptive story

I got up early, had a good breakfast, and left the house. I ran for the bus, and got into the office in good time.

Step 2: Explanation

Now add a layer that gives explanations for the action in terms of reasons and purposes.

An explanatory story

I got up early, because I had an interview and I wanted to be calm for the day and not hurried, so that I could be at my best for the interview. I had a good breakfast in order to be well set up in myself. I always go to work by bus, leaving my car at home as my contribution to sustaining the environment. This morning I ran for the bus and got into the office early, pleased that I had made a good start to this important day.

Step 3: Research

The descriptive story of action has transformed into an explanatory story of action. The description has been embedded within the explanatory layer. Now it needs to turn into a research story. This means seeing the action as a means of finding out something you did not know before. It involves monitoring the action, gathering data and generating evidence from the data in order to ground a knowledge claim.

So now add a research layer to the story.

A research story

I am a journalist. I recently recovered from a long illness that left me disoriented and without a real sense of purpose. I felt so down that I could not continue my full-time employment.

Three weeks ago I decided that I was going to re-organise my life to make it more purposeful and meaningful. I also decided to monitor my progress in my daily diary so that I would have a record that I could look back on and remember, and perhaps write a self-help book that others in similar situations may find useful. To give my project credibility, I decided to turn it into a research project. This would involve generating an evidence base in which I would ground my claim that I had learned how to recover from depression and how to create a fulfilling and productive life.

To monitor my actions and my learning I decided to keep a written journal and also a video diary. I would be able to show the process of my recovery, and the re-emergence of my sense of self-affirmation. I also kept field notes, and held conversations with critical friends, whose opinions I actively sought about whether or not I was succeeding in my actions (getting better). I also produced a quality research report (did I give explanations for how and why I was getting better?). Some of my data extracts show the ongoing improvement in my attitudes.

My field notes contain the following:

- 5 December 2007: conversation with Jo about the breaking story in London. Said I would go with her to interview the minister responsible. Offered to act as her assistant. Not fit enough yet to do the interview myself. Early days but getting there.
- 6 December 2007: organised a crew to film the interview. Booked equipment, contacted crew, organised food for the trip. Good to be back on the job, confidence growing through interactions.

I finally decided to apply for a part-time job. On the day of the interview, I got up early so that ... and so on.

Step 4: Scholarship

This story has become a research story, showing how the descriptions and explanations can be grounded in an evidence base. This prevents your story being seen as fiction. Now, to qualify for an academic award, it needs to demonstrate scholarship, which means engagement with the literatures, to show the process of testing the knowledge claim against the ideas of key thinkers.

Here is how the story can turn into a scholarly account.

A scholarly account

I am a journalist. I recently recovered from a long illness that left me disoriented and without a real sense of purpose. I felt so down that I could not continue my full-time employment. During my really bad days I read a few self-help books (Chopra 2004; Dainow 1997) and these helped me to understand what was going on, and how I could transform my situation.

Three weeks ago I therefore decided that I was going to re-organise my life to make it more purposeful and meaningful. Foucault (1990) also emphasises the need to care for the self. He says that caring for the self is a way of demonstrating the will to power, the will to self-affirmation. We need to care for ourselves first if we are actively to care for others.

I also decided to monitor my progress in my daily diary so that I would have a record that I could look back on and remember the experience, and perhaps write a self-help book that others in similar situations may find useful. To give my project credibility, I decided to turn it into a research project. From my studies in journalism I was familiar with a range of research methods, as set out for example in Cohen et al. (2007). This would involve generating an evidence base in which I would ground my claim that I had indeed learned how to recover from depression and how to create a fulfilling and productive life … and so on.

Step 5: Critical reflection

The report now needs to develop a focus on critical self-reflection, what Winter (1989) calls reflexive critique. This is when you think carefully about what you have done and why you have done it, so you can show the processes of your learning. This reflection process enables you to make critical judgements about your actions and research, and about the quality of your report.

Here is an example of critical reflection in action.

A critically reflective account

I am a journalist. I recently recovered from a long illness that left me disoriented and without a real sense of purpose. I felt so down that I could not continue my full-time employment. During my really bad days I read a few self-help books (Chopra 2004; Dainow 1997) and these helped me to understand what was going on, and how I could transform my situation. As I reflect on my situation now, from the perspective of a survivor, I understand the long journey I have made to full self-recovery, and what it has cost in terms of personal discipline; yet I also understand how difficulty can lead to unexpected personal triumphs (Frankl 1959; Todorov 1999).

Three weeks ago I therefore decided that I was going to re-organise my life to make it more purposeful and meaningful. Foucault (1990) also emphasises the need to care for the self. He says that caring for the self is a way of demonstrating the will to power, the will to self-affirmation. We need to care for ourselves first if we are actively to care for others.

I also decided to monitor my progress in my daily diary so that I would have a record that I could look back on and remember the experience, and perhaps write a self-help book that others in similar situations may find useful. To give my project credibility, I decided to turn it into a research project. From my studies in journalism I was familiar with a range of research methods, as set out for example in Cohen et al. (2007). This would involve generating an evidence base in which I would ground my claim that I had indeed learned how to recover from depression and how to create a fulfilling and productive life.

As I reflected on my evidence base, I became aware of the importance of gathering relevant data. In my research diary, I found episodes that did not seem to relate to the matter in hand, for example, an account of a walk in the park. On reflection, and to help me with later stages of my research, I have learned to focus only on those data that tell me something about what I want to find out and how I can do that … and so on.

Step 6: Dialectical critique

This refers to the process of stepping outside the research, and locating it within your changing understanding of the historical, social, economic and political contexts in which it has been done, and to think about the significance and implications of the work for personal, social and cultural transformation. This process draws on Derrida's (1997) ideas of deconstruction, where your previous stable perceptions of the social world are destabilised. This involves first destabilising your own logics and values. It also means bringing the same critical capacity to making judgements about the quality of your report, to see whether you are communicating normative assumptions through your use of language (see Chapters 4 and 8).

Here is an example.

A story of dialectical critique
(We pick up the story in its final paragraphs)
… As I reflected on my evidence base, I became aware of the importance of gathering relevant data. In my research diary, I found episodes that did not seem to relate to the matter in hand, for example, an account of a walk in the park. On reflection, and to help me with the later stages of my research, I have learned to focus only on those data that tell me something about what I want to find out and how I can do that.

I can now also point to the fact that I had to learn how to challenge my previously held assumptions about what it means to be a disabled person within a normative culture of able-bodied people. Prior to my illness I had taken my health for granted. Having experienced the social marginalisation that illness can bring, I have learned to have greater compassion for others who are also less than their best, and I now bring this new understanding to my writings as a journalist. I have also come to understand the historical and cultural processes involved in Othering, which include trying to make the Other invisible (Alford 2001), and positioning the Other as deviant (Said 1978). I see how powerful such assumptions can be in social practices, and how they can be used to perpetuate and reinforce an existing social order.

Step 7: Meta-reflexive critique

This refers to the capacity to reflect on the process of reflection and analysis itself, and appreciate how making meaning is part of everyday experience. Schutz (1972) explains the importance of not separating meaning from experience, which is an error of some forms of traditional research and their means of communication. In this case, reports are presented only in propositional form, ignoring the in-the-moment nature of living processes. Integrating meaning and experience is like being in a hall of mirrors, where one reflection reflects back the reflection to the person whose reflection is being represented. Meaning and experience are integrated, each part containing the other parts, and each part capable of making new meanings from and with the other parts.

Here is an example of meta-reflection in action.

A meta-reflexive account

… I can now also point to the fact that I had to learn how to challenge my previously held assumptions about what it means to be a 'disabled' person within a normative culture of able-bodied people. Prior to my illness I had taken my health for granted. Having experienced the social marginalisation that illness can bring, I have learned to have greater compassion for others who are also less than their best, and I now bring this new understanding to my writings as a journalist. I have also come to understand the historical and cultural processes involved in Othering, which include trying to make the Other invisible (Alford 2001), and positioning the Other as deviant (Said 1978). I see how powerful such assumptions can be in social practices, and how they can be used to perpetuate and reinforce an existing social order.

What has writing this story meant for me? Through writing this story I have been able to reflect critically on how the writing process has enabled me to understand what is involved in mental and physical destabilisation, and how it is possible to turn potentially life-destructive experiences into life-affirming ones. Writing the experience has been both cathartic and transformational. I have interrogated my self-perceptions, and I understand better how I am author of my own life and in control of how I interpret my life experiences. I have healed myself, through the process of making explicit what was previously hidden. I am now able to make my full contribution to my life, and, through my writing, enable others to do the same.

The end of my story is that I was offered the job, and resume full-time work on Monday.

What we see in this example is how a text can transform from descriptions of action into an explanatory story, then into a research story and a scholarly account, and finally into a text that shows critically reflective commentary on the learning generated through the process, and insights into how those processes can influence personal understandings within the existing culture.

We said above that you are not expected to address all these criteria except at doctoral level. Chapters 6, 7 and 8 set out the criteria for different levels. Regardless of level, however, your work will be judged in relation to whether you have achieved certain criteria and standards, and these are spelled out now.

HOW WILL THE CONTENT OF YOUR ACTION RESEARCH REPORT BE JUDGED?

This section sets out:

1. What contents examiners expect to see in your report.
2. How you can fulfil examiners' expectations.
3. Standards used in judging quality in the content of an action research report.

Remember that we are speaking about the content of a report in this chapter. In the next chapter we speak about its form, where the expectations will be different.

What contents examiners expect to see in your report

When external examiners judge an action research report, they are instructed to assess the work in terms of specific criteria. Although there are variations, most universities specify the following (remember that different levels of accreditation assess the fulfilment of the criteria at different levels of depth). These criteria appear also on p. 27.

- The work contains a claim to knowledge and makes a contribution to knowledge of the field.
- The work demonstrates an ability to undertake an educational study or enquiry in an appropriately critical, original and balanced fashion.
- The work demonstrates an understanding of the context of the research.
- The work shows improvement in the practice described, or explains what may have constrained improvement.

- The work is written in an appropriate form.
- The work contains material of peer-reviewed publishable merit.
- The work is error-free and technically accurate with a full bibliography and references.

(Adapted from the University of Bath 2008)

This means that you have to produce an original text that does the following:

- You make a claim to knowledge and show its significance for your field.
- You demonstrate the validity and originality of your claim by showing your critical understanding of the processes involved.
- Your claim is about improvement in learning, practice and research, within your context.
- You explain how and why the practice has improved, or not.
- You communicate your ideas in an appropriate form.
- You communicate the significance of your claim through an appropriate form of language that qualifies it to enter the public domain.
- Your text is error-free and technically accurate with a full bibliography and references.

We deal with all these aspects across this and the next two chapters. In this chapter we focus on the first three questions, which are about the content of your report, so let's look at these more closely.

How you can fulfil examiners' expectations

Ask yourself whether your work meets the following criteria.

Does your work contain a claim to knowledge and do you show its significance for your field?

Your should be able to say:

The claim you make through doing your action research is that you have improved your practice. This began by improving your learning. Both these aspects happened because you learned how to do research into your practice. You can say that you know something now that you did not know before. Your claim is original because no one else has improved your practice, so no one else has made the claim before. You know that you have improved your practice and you know how you have done it. You learned from the experience of asking, 'How do I improve what I am doing?' and investigating your practice.

Do you demonstrate the validity and originality of your claim by showing your critical understanding of the processes involved?

Your should be able to say:

You demonstrate the validity and originality of your claim by showing how you experienced yourself as a living contradiction when your values were denied in your practice (Whitehead 1989). You took action to address the issue, in an attempt to live your values more fully. You systematically monitored the situation and gathered data to show how things developed, and you generated evidence whose validity you tested against identified criteria and standards of judgement, and against the critical feedback of others.

Does your work show improvement in learning, practice and research within your context, or give reasons for lack of improvement?

Your should be able to say:

Your claim is that you have improved your practice by improving your learning. You have learned how to do things better. You judge your work in terms of your values. You have come to live your values of, for example, justice, freedom, kindness and independent learning more fully than before. If so, you are moving towards what you understand as the good, when what you value becomes real. Improvement can be understood as realising the good (what you value) in present practice while recognising that it could also be better. You show that you have inspired others to investigate their practices, so you have exercised your educational influence in their learning. You have encouraged them to think for themselves, and make independent choices. If you have not succeeded in influencing improvement, you can say why, showing, perhaps, how your context constrained your efforts. For example, Erica Holley (1997) shows how she influenced the writings of one of her students and includes a dialogue in which this influence was worked on by the student. She also shows how she made a creative response to the constraining influences of government policies on appraisal.

In addressing these criteria, you are in fact demonstrating an improvement in knowledge, skills and research capacities, as follows.

You can claim an improvement in knowledge
You now know, and can articulate the following better than before:

- Understanding of your values.
- The reasons and purposes of your research.
- Your subject knowledge.
- What counts as evidence, and particular standards of judgement.
- Issues of context, and how this may help or hinder your efforts at improvement.

You can claim an improvement in skills
You can do the following better than before:

- How to take educational action in your workplace.
- How to influence your own learning and the learning of others, and inspire them to improve it.
- How to monitor and research your practice.
- How to negotiate, delegate, be personally effective, and plan strategically.

- How to do research and tell the story.
- How to evaluate and negotiate your criteria.

You can claim an improvement in research capacity

You have greater capacity in the following than before:

- Undertaking independent enquiries and bringing them to successful completion.
- The sustainable renewal of practice, and influencing organisational learning.
- Research capacity; you know what is involved in doing research.
- Explaining how and why research should be understood as good quality, especially in terms of its originality, rigour and significance.

You have done all these things, and can say so, as your original claim to knowledge of your field.

Standards used in judging quality in the content of an action research report

Remember that your examiner will approach your text with the following in mind in relation to its content:

- I am anticipating that the text will show, through its content, how the author has achieved the institutionally-mandated criteria for an academic report.
- I am anticipating that the text will tell a story of educational action and learning that is comprehensible, authentic, truthful and appropriate for its context. I am therefore anticipating that, when I read the text, I am going to see that the ideas are comprehensible, that the writer is authentic, that the story is truthful, and that the writer is aware of the need for appropriate content, given that we are both in a context that has certain expectations of an educational enquiry.

You can also ask your examiner to judge your report in relation to your own standards of judgement, about how you dealt with issues of practice and the exercise of your educational influence for organisational learning. Some examples that show how practitioner-researchers have done this are as follows:

- Mary Hartog's (2004), 'A Self Study of a Higher Education Tutor: How Can I Improve my Practice?', available at http://www.actionresearch.net/hartog.shtml
- Bernie Sullivan's (2006) 'A Living Theory of a Practice of Social Justice: Realising the Right of Traveller Children to Educational Equality', available at http://www.jean mcniff.com/bernieabstract.html
- Catríona McDonagh's (2007) 'My Living Theory of Learning to Teach for Social Justice: How Do I enable Primary School Children with Specific Learning Disability (Dyslexia) and Myself as their Teacher to Realise our Learning Potentials?', available at http://www.jeanmcniff.com/mcdonaghabstract.html

All explain how they would like their examiners to judge their work in terms of what they, the authors, see as the most significant contributions of the work.

You can do the same. You could claim that your work demonstrates certain aspects, as set out below, and ask that these be used to judge its quality. You would therefore claim that you are demonstrating different kinds of validity through your work. You do not have to use all these ideas, but you should be able to state the principles involved when you make your own judgements.

Your standards of judgement could include the following (the ideas of content validity, process validity and democratic validity are from Herr and Anderson 2005; see also Chapter 8 for ideas about forms of validity).

- My report (dissertation, thesis) gives descriptions and explanations for improvement in my workplace. I can therefore claim content validity for my work.
- My report shows the processes involved in influencing this improvement. I am claiming that I understand what I have done and how I have done it. I am claiming process validity for my work.
- My report shows that people have come to respect one another and have developed dialogical practices. I am claiming democratic validity for my work.
- My report shows how I have influenced learning, and enabled people to come to know in their own way, so that they can take responsibility for their own decisions in future. I am claiming catalytic validity (Lather 1991) for my work.

It is possible for you to claim these different kinds of validity, but you must explain to your reader what you mean by your terms, so that your reader will see the significance of what you are doing.

SUMMARY

This chapter has looked at what goes into an action research report, how the criteria will be achieved, and how the report will be judged. We have looked at how to build up the increasingly complex layers of critical analysis, so that a descriptive story can transform into a research account that demonstrates rigour and scholarship. We have also considered the kinds of validity you can claim for your research, and how this can be done.

 CHECKLIST OF REFLECTIVE QUESTIONS

Here is a checklist of reflective questions that will help you to focus on the key issues of the chapter.

Am I clear about what goes into an action research report?

- Do I show that I know the difference between descriptions and explanations?
- Do I articulate my understanding of the need for theoretical analyses?
- Do I communicate the significance of what I am doing?

Does my action research story demonstrate levels of increasing theoretical complexity?

- Do I tell the reader what these levels are, and what the relationship is between them?
- Do I communicate the dynamic and organic nature of this relationship?

Do I understand the kinds of academic judgements that will be made on my work?

- Do I explicitly address these criteria?
- Do I articulate how my work demonstrates originality, rigour and significance?
- Do I say what my standards of judgement are, i.e. how I wish my work to be judged?

If you can do all these things, the content of your action research report will be judged as of outstanding quality.

We now turn to Chapter 3, and consider issues about how the form of the story communicates the content, and how both content and form need to be commensurable.

3   *What Does an Action Research Report Look Like?*

In Chapter 2 we looked at the content of an action research report, *what* is written. In this chapter we discuss its form, *how* it is written. The form of the report is as important as its content, because the content is communicated through the form, so the form becomes the content. The same process happens elsewhere. A 'staged' wrestling match becomes a performance (Barthes 2000); the moves are already scripted, so the performance becomes the content. In dance and music, technique communicates the message. Visual poetics does the same: in Lewis Carroll's *Alice's Adventures in Wonderland* the poem about the mouse's tale is in the shape of a long tail. The message – what is being communicated – is carried through the medium – how it is communicated. The best texts are those where form and content blend into one.

This chapter explains what the form of an action research report looks like, and how it communicates its messages. Your job as a writer is to organise the ideas in your text in such a way that your reader will understand, through its presentation, what you are getting at. This involves appealing to their aesthetic appreciation as much as to their cognitive capacity.

The chapter is organised as follows:

1. What is distinctive about an action research report? What does it look like?
2. How do you achieve the criteria? How do you write an action research report?
3. How is your action research report judged in relation to its form?
4. Summary.
5. Checklist of reflective questions.

Again we emphasise that each writer produces their own unique report. Examiners expect to read a report that demonstrates the author's capacity to write their story in their own way. Although we are presenting some key ideas to help your writing, you should trust your judgement in producing a report that will reflect back to you the authentic explanation of your learning. So let's now consider what is distinctive about the form of an action research report.

WHAT IS DISTINCTIVE ABOUT THE FORM OF AN ACTION RESEARCH REPORT?

In this section we set out the criteria for writing an action research report. These refer to the key formal features of the text. By 'formal' we mean elements of form – organisation, structure and uses of language. These are:

1. The form of the text is commensurable with the form of the research.
2. It is initially a writerly text that transforms into a readerly text.
3. The form of the report communicates its underpinning logics and values.
4. It shows processes of deconstruction.
5. It uses a narrative form, and you are the main actor in the story.
6. It is transformational and catalytic.
7. It demonstrates methodological rigour.

The form of the text is commensurable with the form of the research

We said in Chapter 1 that traditional research and action research are different. Broadly speaking, traditional research is about abstract ideas, and aims to predict and control practices, whereas action research is about real life and aims to improve practices. Improvement involves transformation, from one state to an improved state, so this needs to be demonstrated through a transformational form that communicates real life processes. The following sections explain how this can be done.

An action research report is initially a writerly text that transforms into a readerly text

Barthes (1970) speaks about readerly and writerly texts. A readerly text speaks about a subject matter with authority and according to its own specific rules. It positions the reader as a receiver of its meaning. The reader is not expected to interpret the text in any way other than how the text intends. A set of instructions or a manual is a readerly text. So is an encyclopaedia, a calendar and a bank statement. They tell you what the facts are. A readerly text tends to be easier for a reader because they do not have to work out for themselves what it is about. The author tells them.

Writerly texts involve the reader in the living co-construction of the text, which can be demanding. The author sees the reader as a real-life creative thinker who makes meaning of the text. The text becomes a live document, a mediating experience between the minds of the writer and the reader.

Todorov (1990: 42) recognises that different readers will respond differently: 'two accounts dealing with the same text will never be identical'. His model (Figure 3.1) shows how this happens.

Figure 3.1   The stages of a text's itinerary (from Todorov 1990: 42)

The text you are reading is a readerly text that began life as a writerly text. The first drafts were wordy and untidy, and then order emerged as we engaged critically with what we were trying to communicate, and refined endlessly. Most writers go through this process, which can be laborious, but seems to be part of successful writing that is accessible and enjoyable for the reader. In *Critical Intellectuals on Writing* (Olson and Worsham 2003), different authors explain their writing processes, which are usually far from smooth.

We authors, Jack and Jean, have seen, time and again, that the drafts of an action research account are writerly texts, where the practitioner-researcher works out ideas. The writer produces a text where the values and understandings emerge in the course of the writing. After the initial draft, most writers come to appreciate that their reader needs some kind of framing device, through which they make sense of what they are reading. This is when the writer stops writing for themselves and begins writing for their reader. (This has implications for supervision practices in higher degree studies, and the need for patience while candidates sort out their ideas, as well as demonstrating faith that they can do it.)

Communicating successfully through writing, however, can be problematic, because it depends largely on whether the author and reader share the same logics, values and epistemologies, as we now explain.

The form of the report communicates its underpinning logics, values and epistemologies

In Chapter 1 we looked at how a practice is underpinned by certain logics and values. The way we think (our form of logic) and what we value (our values) work together to influence the way we know and the way we come to know (our epistemologies). These in turn influence how we act (our practices) (see Figure 1.1 on p. 9).

Consequently, if we think and come to know in divisive ways (use divisive epistemologies), we are likely to practise in ways that divide and fragment. If we develop living epistemologies (forms of knowing in an open and relational way) we will come to practise in ways that encourage nurturing relationships. This idea is key to the form of an action research report, because it also contains the idea of deconstruction (see below).

Example 3.1

This example shows Alan Rayner speaking about different kinds of epistemology and their forms of representation. The video-clip, accessible at http://www.youtube.com/watch?v=yVa7FUIA3W8, shows Alan demonstrating the ideas of inclusional and exclusional forms.

You need to appreciate that there are different kinds of logics, values and epistemologies. Certain views, especially in higher education, maintain that there is only one form of logic, one set of values, and one kind of epistemology. This is not the case. These views are part of the western intellectual tradition, which values propositional forms of logic and one-directional thinking, and encourages conformity and analytical fragmentation. This form of thinking stemmed from Aristotle, who said that a thing had to be either–or, not both–and. This became known as the Law of the Excluded Middle, and has real-life consequences. If you are not a 'perfect type', you are seen as not normal, and, because few people are 'perfect', they become Other. Many theorists, including Butler (1999), argue that 'the ideal' is a dangerous mythology and leads to exclusive societies (Young 1999). However, propositional logics remain dominant, especially in academia, though things are changing.

On the other hand, the underpinning values and logics of action research are living, inclusional and emancipatory. Action researchers tell freedom stories about how they have found ways to take action to improve their situations. This involved deconstruction and becoming critical. These are stories of real life, underpinned by logics and values that are also living, the properties of real-life people.

Example 3.2

Video-data enable us to see the expression of life-affirming energy in our educational relationships, and to include such flows of energy as explanatory principles in our accounts. In the video-clip, accessible at www.youtube.com/watch?v=MBTLfyjkFh0, Jack includes a re-enactment of a meeting with a Senate working party on a matter of academic freedom. These kinds of performance texts enable practitioner-researchers to produce action research reports that include visual representations that look like the lives we live in our daily practices.

These new forms of dynamic narrative and multimedia representation are different from traditional forms. They also have significance for how action research reports are judged. Examiners need to develop their own understandings, so that examining can become a process of democratic evaluation. This means that candidate and examiner negotiate their standards of judgement, which may seem a radical step for some examiners, but essential in establishing the real quality of research accounts.

An action research report shows processes of deconstruction

The term 'deconstruction' (Derrida 1997) means questioning anything that is taken for granted to check for its validity and reveal its hidden foundations. This applies especially to normative messages communicated through the culture. 'Normative' implies both normal, and also what should be the case. When a neighbour says, 'My husband is very good – he does the washing up', you can see her acceptance of normative assumptions about gender roles. Deconstruction can be difficult because we are born into a culture that teaches us to think in certain ways. It means interrogating assumptions about thinking while using the same form of thinking that we are interrogating, which involves continually shifting perspectives.

In social life, deconstruction means questioning how people are categorised in terms of race, skin colour, gender, age, capacity and looks, as well as questioning the system of categorisation itself. Often we learn to categorise ourselves, digging into self-made holes from which we cannot, or do not want to, escape. It also means questioning the historical, social, economic and cultural practices that have led to our present situations.

In literary studies, deconstruction means that seeing a text representing a reality 'out there' shifts to seeing the text itself as a construction of the author's thinking, so 'reality' itself becomes problematic (Norris 1989). When a text demonstrates the capacity to reflect on itself, it has ironic validity (Lather 1991). The best action research reports demonstrate this capacity.

Example 3.3

The following example shows Eden Charles deconstructing his thinking, accessible at http://www.youtube.com/watch?v=EcfZE_z-C_w. Speaking about his PhD work, he says:

> In this clip I am recounting an experience from a working trip to Sierra Leone to my research supervisor, Jack Whitehead. I went not long after the end of the devastating civil war there. I think that this clip contains something of the living dynamic of my Ubuntu way of being. I am speaking about people who have gone through the most horrific of experiences and who will live with the consequences of that for the rest of their lives. I am not dwelling on the horror of the tragedy of that civil war, even though I am visibly moved by it. Instead I am praising the humanity of the women rather than condemning or dwelling on the evils. I am also demonstrating my connection with the women in Sierra Leone and seeing, feeling themselves as part of me. Despite living and working in Europe I feel and not just understand the oneness of our condition. My values of humanity, my ontological and political urges are provoked and I am filled with generative passion to engage in work that can bring about a better situation. I carry this spirit into my work as a consultant in which I see it as a site for being a positive influence on restorative processes of reidentification characterised and enabled by a guiltless recognition. (Charles 2007: 162)

These ideas about deconstruction are important for writing your report, because it means that you will no longer have specific rules to guide your writing or demonstrate the validity of your work, so you will have to create new ones. Lyotard explains this dilemma for the postmodern writer, which includes action researchers:

> A postmodern artist or writer is in the position of a philosopher: the text he [sic] writes, the work he produces are not in principle governed by preestablished rules, and they cannot be judged according to a determining judgement, by applying familiar categories to the text or to the work. Those rules and categories are what the work of art itself is looking for. The artist and writer, then, are working without rules in order to formulate the rules of what will have been done. (Lyotard 1984: 81)

Action research reports are narrativized accounts, and you are the main actor in the story

When you tell your action research story you explain three things: (1) what you have done and how you did it (the story of the action); (2) how you investigated what you did and why you did it (the research story); and (3) why your story should be taken seriously (its significance). You ground your story in the literature, so it becomes a scholarly account, and you show how you can critically reflect on what you have done.

This section explains how this content is communicated. The most appropriate form for an action research report is narrative. However, narrative itself takes different forms for different purposes (see also p. 55). Key points to consider are voice, style and progression.

Voice

In action research, people speak for themselves. You are the main actor in your story, while working with others who tell their stories. It becomes a community of storytellers. This is different from traditional research reports, where one person speaks on behalf of others. In action research reports, all people speak for themselves. The stories are first-person 'I' stories. Stories that tell about communicative action often become 'I~we' stories. This is also different from traditional research stories that speak about 'the researcher' as a third person. There are implications, because you have to show that yours is a true story, not your opinion or wishful thinking. This means producing an evidence base, and interrogating how you have deconstructed your thinking so that you are not misled by your own biases.

Example 3.4

Chris Glavey (2008) writes about his concerns that young people were not considered by some school authorities as able to speak for themselves. He writes about 'bringing people to voice', rather than 'giving them a voice' because he believes that all people have a voice, which they are often prevented from using. Chris also speaks about the collaborative nature of his research, and how the young people he was working with often asked, 'Chris, how is **our** thesis coming along?'

Style

The style of the narrative is personal and speaks about learning, unlike traditional reports that speak mainly about the subject matter. The style of writing should be user-friendly but not chatty, and should position the reader as an intelligent companion who is also involved in deconstruction, especially deconstructing your report to see whether you have engaged seriously with your own processes of reflexive and dialectical critique.

Progression

The progression of the story is transformational. We explain this idea further in the next section. It is a transformational story that communicates the underlying connections between the characters in the story, and the connections between the author and reader. Bateson (1979) speaks about the need to develop the capacity to see all things as connected. An action research account makes these hidden connections explicit, between experience and meaning, and between the different aspects of the story.

Example 3.5

Máirín Glenn (2006) shows the interconnectedness of her practice and theory in the abstract to her PhD thesis:

> Through my research I have developed my capacity for critical engagement, especially in relation to critiquing many normative practices in dominant forms of education; specifically in terms of their underpinning technical rational ontologies and epistemologies of fragmentation. My original contributions to knowledge are to do with how I show that I can account for how I have transformed my own erstwhile fragmented epistemologies into holistic and inclusional forms of knowing and practice. From the grounds of my research-based practice, I am able to make my original claim that I have developed my living theory of a holistic educational practice, through collaborative multimedia projects, and I ground my evidence in the multimedia narrative of my research account.
>
> A distinctive feature of my research account is my articulation of how my ontological values of love and care have transformed into my living critical epistemological standards of judgement, as I produce my multimedia evidence-based living theory of a holistic educational practice. Through working with collaborative multimedia projects, I explain how I have developed an epistemology of practice that enables me to account for my educational influence in learning.

It is transformational and catalytic

An action research report communicates the generative transformational capacity of the research (see Chomsky 1957 for the origins of this idea). Every thing contains its own potentials for new forms: a bulb transforms into a flower, a caterpillar into a butterfly. People have generative capacity for an infinite number of new practices, and each can be an improvement of itself. The enquiry never ends, because each 'satisfactory' ending contains new beginnings.

These ideas have implications for systemic influence because one aspect has the generative transformational capacity to influence new developments. There are implications also for action researchers. Practitioner-researchers can act as catalysts, to influence others to improve what they are doing: but in action research the catalyst itself changes as part of the changing system. Action research has catalytic validity, therefore, when systemic change happens. This is seen also through the transformational form of the text, where each step acts as a catalyst for, and transforms into, the next step. This is part of the methodological rigour of action research.

It demonstrates methodological rigour

Methodology refers to the way you design and do your research and test the validity of your findings. Your report communicates the systematic nature of the research, as it emerges from seeming chaos. Most researchers experience times of confusion when nothing makes sense. Law (2004) speaks about mess in human enquiry, and Mellor (1998) says that the methodology is in the muddle. Writing a report can also involve periods of intense frustration when the ideas do not come right. However, if you have faith in your own personal knowledge, things do come right, most of the time.

The rigour of your methodology is in how one aspect transforms into another. This process can be interpreted in different ways. For example, one view of history sees things as 'one damn thing after another', where things happen in a linear sequence leading to closure. A more critical perspective says that circumstances at one point generate actions at the next. History therefore becomes a transformational process of catalytic moments, where the present holds consequences for the future. This is also the nature of action research. When you ask, 'How do I improve what I am doing?' you are unleashing a set of catalytic possibilities.

The ideas so far set out are some of the main features of the form of an action research report. You may find other features that are equally important. The question now becomes, how do you do action research and how do you communicate the process in your report?

HOW DO YOU ACHIEVE THE CRITERIA? HOW DO YOU WRITE AN ACTION RESEARCH REPORT?

This section sets out how to write an action research report. Remember that you can use multimedia forms of representation, e.g. when you include multimedia excerpts within your written report, as the examples so far have demonstrated, or you can write a report that takes a multimedia form itself, as Ray O'Neill does at http://www.ictaspoliticalaction.com For his PhD thesis, Ray wrote a conventional linguistic text that referred to his multimedia base (O'Neill 2008), and produced a web-based thesis that showed a PhD thesis as a form of living communicative action.

Let's begin with a basic action plan.

The action plan below shows the main steps in doing action research. The plan also provides a basic framework for writing your account. When you write your proposal (Chapter 5), you explain how you are planning to conduct your research, so you write your action plan in a way that shows how you intend to take action in the future: 'This is what I hope to do and this is how and why I aim to do it'. When you write up your research, you tell the story of what you have done, in the past tense: 'This is what I did and this is how and why I did it'.

A general framework for a report therefore looks like this:

- Introduction to the research report
- The research story:

  o What was my concern?
  o Why was I concerned?
  o How can I show what the situation was like initially?
  o What could I do? What did I do?
  o How did I gather data to show ongoing developments?
  o What did I find out?
  o How could I show that any conclusions I came to were reasonably fair and accurate?
  o How could I articulate the significance of my action research?
  o How did I modify my ideas and practices in light of my evaluation?

- Conclusion

You can also organise your ideas and text into parts or sections. This is useful for a longer text such as a PhD thesis. An example is the contents page of Whitehead and McNiff's (2006) *Action Research: Living Theory*, which gives an account of our action research.

Introduction
Working with the Text

PART ONE   BACKGROUNDS AND CONTEXTS

Chapter 1   Background to our Research: Reasons and Purposes
             (What are our concerns?)

You can find further examples of using action reflection steps as the framework for a report in McNiff (2008a) at http://www.jeanmcniff.com/aera08/JM_AERA08_Paper_final.htm, and McNiff (2008b) at http://www.jeanmcniff.com/cagedbird.htm

This kind of framework is appropriate for reports at all levels, from foundation to doctoral degrees, and contains everything in the different writing frames set out in Chapter 2, which are:

1. Action – a largely descriptive story of the action.
2. Explanation – an explanatory layer offering explanations for the story of the action.
3. Research – you show how the validity of the story was tested.
4. Scholarship – you strengthen the validity of the claim through linking it with existing ideas.

5. Critical reflection – you learn from the action-reflection.
6. Dialectical critique – you make judgements on the quality of your action, your research, and your own thinking.
7. Meta-reflection – you say how doing and writing your action research has developed your learning and contributed to the learning of others.

The more advanced your studies, the deeper you will go into the different levels.

Now let's take a more detailed look at what the action-reflection steps involve. We have used the questions as chapter and section headings. You can do the same if you wish.

Writing an action research report

Introduction to the research report

The following points go into your introduction:

- Tell the reader what the research is about. State your claim to knowledge, and give a brief overview of how you will test its validity. Say why you have chosen an action research methodology.
- Say that the report is about yourself and your learning, so it is written in the first person. Your 'I' is at the centre of the enquiry.
- Introduce yourself to the reader. Say who you are, where you work, and anything special about your circumstances that led you to do the research.
- Say briefly what the main findings of the research are, and what their potential significance could be.
- Give a brief overview of the chapters ahead.

Now tell your reader that you are going to write your research story.

Your research story

The contents of your story are as follows. Note: you may also use the headings below as chapter headings, as we have done in the book mentioned above.

What was my concern?

This section says what the research was about, and contains the following points.

- Say what you wanted to investigate. This is your research issue: the state of relation-ships in your organisation, or creating online learning environments. It could have been a problem, or something you were interested in, or an evaluation of your present situation.
- Say that you were studying your practice in the contexts where these issues were happening, in order to find ways of improving the situation.
- Explain that you were concerned because you were experiencing yourself as a living contradiction as your values were being denied in your practice (Whitehead 1989).

Perhaps organisational structures, or established ways of working, were preventing you from realising your values; perhaps you were denying them yourself, because you were acting in ways that were contrary to what you believed in. Say that you undertook your research to find ways of realising your values more fully.

- Now articulate your research question.

Your research question

You formulated a research question in relation to the identified concern. Your question took the form: 'How do I improve ...?' You can use different words, but the underpinning idea is that you were trying to find a way to improve something. For example:

- How do I help to improve the relationships in my organisation?
- How do I encourage people to use this new technology?
- How do I create better online learning environments?

A special point: the problematics of 'I' and 'we'

Sometimes you may be involved in a collaborative project, where your 'I' turns into 'we'. Take care when writing up this kind of project. If the project was genuinely a collaborative project, and the voices of all participants are heard, then you can probably use 'we'. If it is your voice only, and you are speaking on behalf of others, clarify whose ideas are whose, and ensure that you are representing others appropriately. In most reports, 'we' refers to the action in the workplace, while 'I' am the one who reports what I am learning through the action 'we' took in the workplace. 'My' learning is grounded in my interactions with other 'I's'.

Why was I concerned?

This section deals with the reasons for your concern, and why it was a concern. It discusses issues of values and contexts.

Values

We said that values are the things you value, such as friendship and kindness. In traditional reports, values tend to be spoken about as abstractions. Raz's *The Practice of Value* (2003) speaks about values in an abstract way. In action research, which is about living people and real life, values become manifested as how we do what we do. If we act with kindness, we live the value of kindness. If we involve everyone in public debates, we act democratically. Values are living practices, not only words. Your job as writer is to show how you lived your values so that they became practices and did not remain at the level of words.

Your values inspire and provide the reasons for your research, as well as its purposes. They also act as the basis for your conceptual frameworks. The ideas you espouse, such as justice and freedom, and the literatures you read about these ideas (for example, Arendt 1977 about justice, or Berlin 1969 about freedom) stem from your values.

Contexts

Set out what your research contexts are. These can be as follows.

Personal contexts   Say who you are, where you work, what your working conditions are like. Say anything special about you. Were you forcibly retired at the age of 60? Did you fail your exams because you are dyslexic? What does your reader need to know about you? Do not write your life story, just enough to let the reader see the relevance of your personal contexts.

Locational contexts   Say where your research took place – in a hospital or union building. Describe anything special about the place. Perhaps it was geographically remote, or in an area of social disadvantage. Give any special details that will help your reader understand the context: perhaps insufficient resources or a history of institutional bullying?

Research contexts   Outline what the literature says about your field of enquiry. Show how you incorporate other people's ideas into your own thinking, as well as critique them. You cannot agree or disagree with them unless you explain why the ideas are relevant, and this means showing that you have read them. Do not simply drop names. Bassey (1999: 6) cautions against what he calls 'genuflection', 'sandbagging' and 'kingmaking', which are practices designed to look good, pad out the writing, or shore up an author's weak scholarship.

Policy contexts   Say what the current policy is in your area. What is the policy around rescue services, or emergency waiting times, or urban planning? Do you have to meet targets, or produce outcomes? These may be important contextualising features.

Any other specially relevant contexts   Do you work with offenders or young people at risk; or in a botanical gardens or zoo? Are you deaf, or especially gifted in a particular field? If so, say so. Help your reader understand why information about your contexts is central to the research.

Combining values and contexts

Now combine these ideas about values and contexts. They provide the background to your research and give reasons for why you took action. Say what you hoped to achieve, and whether you were in a position to do so. This means talking about your research goals. It may not be appropriate to say, 'I wanted to change the situation', because the only things we can ever change in a sustainable way are our own thinking or behaviours. It is more realistic to speak about influencing others' thinking and practices.

These aspects then act as the basis for:

4. Making judgements about the quality of your report in relation to its form.

Here are some further ideas.

Engaging with your own thinking

Explain how you have reflected on and tried to improve your learning and actions. You do not have to pretend that you got everything right, or even that things turned out well. It is, in fact, important to explain the uncertainty, as you tried to make sense of an ever-changing scenario.

Try to show your reader how you made sense out of chaos. Quote from your reflective diary. Give comments from your critical friends to show how you learned through interaction with others. Explain how your thinking evolved through critical reflection and led to new learning. Be brave in explaining that you came to appreciate that you sometimes had to change your mind, because your data were showing you things you would rather not have seen.

You have hundreds of ways to show that you engaged critically with your own thinking – how this sometimes led you down blind alleys and sometimes got you on the right track. You may also wish to say how you brought order from chaos in writing your text.

Engaging with the thinking of others

This means engaging with the ideas of key theorists in the literature. An action research report does not require a chapter dedicated specifically to a literature search, but you must show that you have read as widely as is expected by the level of accreditation you are seeking. You should aim to engage with the literature throughout, not only in specific places. Chapter 7 develops these ideas.

Engaging with the literature means you can show how you have been inspired by the ideas of others, and how you are testing the validity of your ideas in relation to theirs. You can see how the thinking of key authors has inspired us, Jack and Jean, in our writing. We have tested the appropriateness of our thinking, for example: about capacity for knowledge creation in relation to Chomsky (1986); about personal knowledge and values in relation to Polanyi (1958); about validity and social criteria in relation to Habermas (1976, 1987); and about social betterment in relation to Said (1994a). These are some of the hundreds of authors whose work we draw on to inform our own.

Remember that 'the literature' refers to books and scholarly papers, newspaper reports and visual and oral communications through film, video and radio. We have spoken throughout about the usefulness of multimedia representations.

rm of your report, it is your responsibility to explain how and why ideas of others in your own thinking, or not, and give reasons.

aging with the thinking of the social formation of which you are a part

A major focus in your research report is dialectical critique. This is where you locate your action research within its social and cultural context. It means understanding and analysing the different social, economic, political and cultural forces that have shaped the context. In South Africa you would comment critically on how previous apartheid regimes have left a cultural and psychological legacy of inequality and oppression. These have strengthened your emancipatory intent. In Palestine and Israel you would comment on the struggle for competing rights, and show how you have developed inclusional practices in response.

You also need to show how your thinking has developed within specific contexts. Bourdieu (1990) says we are born into a *habitus*, the cultural and social context with its normative behaviours and epistemologies. Our thinking is influenced by the epistemological traditions of our culture, and by cultural expectations that are outcomes of the thinking of people who have also been influenced by those cultural expectations. The best action research accounts are those where the writer comments on how they have freed their own thinking so that they can take action to influence the thinking of others and create new futures. Tsepo Majake (2008b) explains how he moved beyond victim-age, and Zola Malgas (2008) shows how she has developed an in-house staff development programme that is grounded in critique.

These elements of critical and balanced judgement act as the basis for making judgements about the quality of your report, in relation to its form.

Making judgements

Your examiner judges the form of your report in terms of the following expectations:

- I am anticipating that the form of the text is going to show how the author has achieved the institutionally-mandated criteria.
- I am anticipating that the form of the text will contribute to its comprehensibility, authenticity, truthfulness and appropriateness. Therefore, I am anticipating that, when I read the text, I am going to see, through the form, that the ideas are comprehensible, that the writer is authentic, that the story is truthful, and that the writer is aware of the need for an appropriate form of writing, given that we are both in a context where certain conventions of form are already in place.
- I am anticipating that the form of the text is going to be commensurable with its content. I am not anticipating that I will read a traditional form, as in scientific reports.

You can also ask your examiner to judge your report in relation to your own standards of judgement (see the examples of Mary Hartog, Bernie Sullivan and Caitríona McDonagh, on p. 45), about how you have addressed the institutional criteria identified above; and in relation to those aspects which you consider most meaningful for your practice, something like this.

- My report (dissertation, thesis) shows my capacity for transforming my thinking, as communicated through my writing, and I am therefore claiming transformational validity for my text.
- My report manifests its underlying logics and values through its form. I claim that I have shown formal validity for my report.
- My report uses a narrative form, and I am the main actor in my story. I have included a valid account of my research, and am claiming narrative validity for my report.
- My report shows processes of deconstruction. I demonstrate my capacity for reflexive and dialectical critique by deconstructing my own thinking, and am claiming reflexive validity for my report.
- My report is transformational and catalytic. I have shown the transformational processes involved in my research. I claim catalytic validity for my report.
- My report shows methodological rigour. I have shown all the processes of doing research, including ideas about establishing the validity of my claim to knowledge and the significance of the work. I am claiming methodological validity for my report.

SUMMARY

This chapter has looked at the form of an action research report. It has discussed the key formal features, and how these can be incorporated into an action plan. The action plan, which addresses questions of the kind, 'How do I improve my practice?' can be used to write up your report, as well as for producing an action plan (Chapter 5). The form of the report is judged in relation to specified academic criteria, as well as the demonstration of critical engagement with your own thinking and with the literature.

CHECKLIST OF REFLECTIVE QUESTIONS

?

Here is a checklist to remind you of the key formal features of your report. Check that you have covered all the following elements, regardless of level.

Does my report take the form of a readerly text?

- Do I speak directly with my reader?
- Do I anticipate that my reader will bring their own interpretations to the text? Do I explain carefully how I wish the text to be interpreted?

Does my report manifest its underlying logics and values through its form?

- Do I appreciate my reader as a thoughtful, creative person, and have I produced a text that does not talk up or down to them?

(Cont'd)

- Have I used an inclusional and relational form in my writing?
- Do I write in a way that communicates my thinking as open and transformational? Do I show how one idea transforms into another? Do I show that my research adopted a cyclical form? Do I explain that the research project outlined in this report is part of my lifelong enquiry?

Does my report use a narrative form, and do I explain why I am the main actor?

- Do I tell a good story? Is it a research story? Have I included all the aspects of content, as set out in Chapter 2?
- Do I use a transformational narrative form, where one episode is a transformation of the thinking involved in previous ones?
- Do I position myself at the centre of the research, so I ask questions about me in relation with others? Do I show how I resist investigating their practices, and focus on getting my own right first?

Does my report show processes of deconstruction?

- Do I explain how I have decentred myself so that I appreciate the contributions of others to my learning?
- Do I show that I have deconstructed my thinking, and have problematised issues rather than taking them for granted?
- Do I come across as a thoughtfully critical person, who is able to see how the research is located within a social, economic, historical and political context? Do I see the bigger picture and speak about the possible influence of my research on those wider contexts?

Is my report transformational and catalytic?

- Do I show that the form of my report shows processes of transformation? Do I explain how an initial question can transform into a powerful claim to knowledge?
- Do I show how the report has the potential to influence my own and others' learning?

Does my report show methodological rigour?

- Have I included all methodological aspects? Have I explained the procedures involved in transforming data into evidence?
- Do I produce a robust evidence base to show how I have tested the validity of my claims?
- Do I show the processes of validating my knowledge claims against the critical feedback of others?
- Do I appreciate the significance of my research, and why I need to place my report in the public domain?

If you can demonstrate all these elements, you will produce a high quality report.

We now move to Chapter 4, which discusses practical issues of writing.

Producing a Good Quality Text

The Writing Process

This chapter sets out what you need to do to produce a good quality text. The research focus shifts from *doing* to *writing* action research. The question still takes the form, 'How do I improve what I am doing?' but now asks, 'How do I write a quality text that readers will enjoy? How do I communicate the originality, rigour and significance of my research?' Achieving this means appreciating what is involved in producing a quality text, producing it, and then evaluating its quality in relation to appropriate standards of judgement. The text now moves from talking about the signified, to becoming the signifier; it moves from what is being spoken about, to the process of speaking itself.

The chapter addresses these issues:

1. What are the criteria/features of a good quality action research text?
2. How do you produce a good quality text in order to achieve the criteria?
3. How is the quality of the text judged?
4. Summary.
5. Checklist of reflective questions.

WHAT ARE THE CRITERIA/FEATURES OF A GOOD QUALITY ACTION RESEARCH TEXT?

As noted in Chapter 1, your research report fulfils Stenhouse's (1983) idea that 'research is a systematic process of enquiry made public', and the extended idea that it is about improving practice. You are placing your report in the public domain, so it now belongs to your readers as much as to you, and they will also make judgements about its quality, especially in terms of its originality, significance and rigour. These give your report social validity and legitimacy, which can lead to an academic qualification. You therefore need to know what readers are looking for, and make sure you give it to them.

General readers are looking for several things, and will judge the work accordingly. These include the following criteria:

- Is the work readable?
- Is it well structured?
- Does it speak to my experience?
- Is it fiction or fact? How can I tell?
- Is it interesting?
- Does it hold my attention?
- Is the form of language appropriate?
- Do I feel inspired after reading it?

Academic readers are looking for the same things, and more. As noted, they are hoping to see that the work:

- Contains a claim to knowledge and makes a contribution to knowledge of the field.
- Demonstrates critical, original and balanced engagement.
- Shows understanding of the research context.
- Shows improvement in practice described, and if not, explains why not.
- Is written in an appropriate form.
- Contains material of peer-reviewed publishable merit.
- Is error-free and technically accurate with a full bibliography and references.

In Chapters 2 and 3, we looked at criteria relating to the content and form of the text. In this chapter we look at issues of writing the text itself, which raises issues of communicability. Communicability involves the criteria of social validity (Habermas 1976) combined with criteria of textual validity. They look like this:

1. **Comprehensibility**: Is there clarity in expression, structure of the text and use of language?
2. **Authenticity**: Does the author tell a story that shows over time and through interaction how they have established their authenticity in showing a commitment to live the values they explicitly espouse?
3. **Truthfulness**: Are the research claims justified, to show that this is a true story and not a work of fiction?
4. **Appropriateness**: Does the author show awareness of the values base and biases of the normative background, especially how cultural and historical forces have contributed to the present context?

Let's look at what is involved.

Comprehensibility

Making something comprehensible involves key practices, most importantly to remember that you are writing for a specific market and its readers. This means using a form of language that will appeal to that market and structuring the text so that the meanings are clear. Always write for a reader. In your first drafts, perhaps you write more for yourself as you work out ideas (you write a writerly text), but ultimately you have to write for a reader (a readerly text). They will confer validity on your claims and legitimacy on the text, so get them on your side by writing for them. Put a photo of your reader on your computer, perhaps in cap and gown, to remind yourself that you are writing for them, not you. Comprehensibility relates to your logic. We follow Marcuse in understanding logic as a mode of thought that is appropriate for comprehending the real as rational (Marcuse 1964: 105).

Readers in general look for writing they can enjoy and that speaks to their experience. Therefore the writing has to be comprehensible and clear in expression and the use of language, the structure of the report, and presentation of the text. It involves practising the skill of writing. Do not think good writing will come overnight, even if you have lots of talent.

> 'Talent alone cannot make a writer,' said Ralph Waldo Emerson, more than a hundred years ago. And how right he was. While talent does help ... success in writing, particularly writing for which you will be [recognised], depends mostly on market analysis and commitment to satisfying market requirements. (O'Reilly 1994: 1)

Here are some key aspects involved in achieving clarity of expression, clear structure, and fluent presentation of the text.

Clarity of expression

Be aware of the language you are using, and speak directly to the reader's experience. Many people think that an academic report needs to be written in 'Sunday best' language, which is not necessarily the case. Everyday language is perfectly acceptable for an academic report. This does not mean trivialising the language or the ideas; it means speaking directly, with minimal fuss, aware that you are speaking to an educated reader who knows the field, and who wants to hear what you have learned or your particular contribution. It is your responsibility to tell them, clearly and to the point.

Writing an academic report means using a form of language appropriate for an academic reader. They would expect to see your use of professional terminology, and engagement with scholarly debates. This can have implications for some researchers who need to switch language codes for different places. It sometimes means changing a workplace dialect for an academic dialect. It is your responsibility to learn the received dialect, which happens to be an academic dialect.

Minimalist form

Speaking directly involves a minimalist form of language, which means writing in a plain, uncluttered way. Avoid using words such as 'highly' or 'extremely', unless you are using them to make a point, and take out every 'very'. Avoid hyperbole, the kind of exaggeration that invites exclamation marks. Do not write 'It was fantastic!!!' or 'This was the best thing ever!'

Do not use two words when one will do. In 'This was a very beautiful and pleasant house,' take out 'very' and choose between 'beautiful' and 'pleasant'. 'This was a beautiful house' says what you mean in a way that does not overburden the reader. Your reader has a limited concentration span and patience, so do not smother them with words (in the sentence you have just read we took out the initial 'Bear in mind that ...'). Be ruthless in editing (see below). If a word does not earn its keep, it has to go.

Avoid expressions that say you know it all. Avoid 'surely' and 'obviously'. What is obvious to you may not be obvious to anyone else. Avoid self-congratulatory comments: 'I believe I am demonstrating something that no one else has thought of before ...' Yes, maybe so, but your reader will not warm to you. Avoid rhetorical questions: 'So how is this to be demon-strated?' They tend to frustrate even the most patient reader, who wants to hear your ideas, not answer empty questions.

In brief, avoid preciousness, which can be distracting and irritating. Go for a plain, simple style, written with authority and discipline.

Clarity of structure

Derrida spoke of a text as a 'heterogeneous, differential and open field of forces' (Derrida 1986; cited in Deutscher 2005: 33). Achieving clarity of struc-ture means organising your material so that your reader can easily find their way through this open field of forces. You can achieve clear organisation through pedagogical and textual devices, such as the following.

Signposts

Signposts usually take the form of headings and subheadings. Editors talk about 'A', 'B' and 'C' headings to denote sections and sub-sections of the text. These are usually given different weightings and fonts, and use devices such as typefaces, capitals, italics and bold, like this:

> THIS IS AN 'A' HEADING
> **This is a 'b' heading**
> *This is a 'c' heading*

If you use a software programme such as Word, your headings may already be built into the programme. It is up to you to choose a headings system, but once you have chosen it, stick with it so as not to confuse your reader.

You can use other devices such as boxes or shading, margin notes and visu-als. Keep it simple. Signposts provide a means of navigating the text, so avoid using a system that is so complex that the reader needs a codebook to work out what the signposts mean.

Advance organisers

These are devices that orient the reader by giving an advance summary of the text, its key features and significance, and anything special to watch out for. Advance organisers are often combined with end-of-text summaries. The reader should be able to read the advance and post summaries, and see imme-diately what the text is about. Using these devices means: 'Tell them what you are going to do, do it, and then tell them what you have done'. Remember that you are writing a pedagogical text, so it is your responsibility to walk with your reader through the text, and not let them get lost.

Correct grammar

Correct grammar involves correct spelling, punctuation, sentence construction, paragraphing and use of words. Many books are available to help. You should invest in a good dictionary and thesaurus. You can find a lot of information on the internet, such as the difference between 'each other' (two people), and 'one another' (more than two people). Study the literature to see which publications use single or double inverted commas. Watch how writers use sentences to communicate one idea at a time, and build these sentences into separate paragraphs to communicate sets of ideas. See how they develop an argument through the skilful use of text. If you find it difficult to use correct grammar, do your homework and find ways of improving (see the academic criterion about error-free and technically accurate presentation). If you lack confidence around these issues, perhaps because you are dyslexic or if English is your second language, find expert help through a professional copy-editor or first language speaker. Remember that it is not the responsibility of your supervisor to correct your language. You have chosen to do this programme of study, so it is your responsibility to find expert help where necessary. Experts usually charge for their services, so it is a matter of what you are prepared to do to achieve your degree. (But watch out for plagiarism or getting someone else to do your work for you – see below.)

Avoid repetition

Often in a text, less is more: understatement can be better than overstatement, especially in academic texts. Say what you have to say once, and leave it at that. Avoid repeating favourite quotations. Keep a list of quotations in your notebook and tick them off once you have used them. It is easy to forget which ones you have used in a lengthy text, so be systematic. Also, avoid repeating favourite individual or strings of words, such as 'it would appear that …'.

These are a few techniques from a vast repertoire of writing skills that make a text comprehensible to the reader. The best way is to practise the skill of writing (see below). This involves reading the work of successful people in the field for technique as well as content, noting what they do (and do not do), and following their lead while developing your own style (but do not copy).

We now look at the second criterion for effective communication.

Authenticity

This criterion refers to your capacity to tell a story that shows over time and through interaction how you have established your authenticity in showing a commitment to live the values that you explicitly espouse.

Authenticity refers to the idea that people can trust you to be the same person tomorrow as you are today in the sense of expressing values that help to constitute your identity. We are continuously changing, as are our contexts, yet we can show our authenticity through time and interaction by showing that we are genuinely committed to living as fully as we can the values we claim to believe in. Through what you write and how you write it, you can show that you are genuine, someone who does what they say they are going to do. This can be difficult, because the only thing your reader knows about you is what they read on the page, so you need to reassure them that they can believe what you say through your form of writing and presentation. Specifically, people need to know that you can be trusted in your actions, research and scholarship, as follows.

Can your actions be trusted?

Explain how you can be trusted in terms of your actions, how you did what you did with good intent and with the motivation of contributing to other people's wellbeing. This means you would spell out your values near the beginning of your story, and show how, over time, you did your best to live them in practice. You talk about your commitments, and you also show them in action.

Can your research be trusted?

Show that you can be trusted in terms of your research and capacity for methodological rigour. This involves giving explanations for your actions, and producing a strong evidence base to back up your claims. It involves showing how you gathered data, tested these rigorously, linked them with your research question and aims, and analysed these in a disciplined way. You need especially to engage with disconfirming data, which told you things you did not want to know, and explain how you took action accordingly. You need to show how you searched your data for key pieces that you could turn into evidence. When you make your claim to knowledge, you need to justify it, and not expect people simply to believe that it happened as you say it did.

Can your scholarship be trusted?

Show that you can be trusted in your scholarship. Honour all academic conventions, and put your references in good order. When you cite a person's name, make sure that it is relevant to its context, and is not simply decorative. Also show that you have read the work in question. On p. 60 we mentioned Michael Bassey's (1999) point about avoiding 'kingmaking', 'genuflecting' and 'sandbagging'. It is easy to pretend that you have read widely by picking up names and giving summaries you have read elsewhere. Some readers may be fooled some of the time, but over the length of a report, an experienced reader will pick up whether or not the researcher actually has read those works.

Authenticity means showing how you are authentic through your writing. Do you write with passion and conviction, with the authority of your own experience? Do your words ring true? Do you show that you are confident in your ideas, or do you cover up by waffling? It is of course possible to mislead people through skilful technique. Groucho Marx was famous for saying that once you have convinced people that you are sincere they will believe anything you tell them. Remember that your reader is experienced and has developed an ear for a text, as a wine taster develops a nose, so they will raise questions about any writing they do not consider authentic.

This brings us to the next point about how you show that you are telling the truth.

Truthfulness

Claims to knowledge are also called 'truth claims', so your report needs to show that you are telling the truth about what happened. This is especially relevant to data gathering and analysis, and the production of evidence to test your claims to knowledge.

The processes of establishing the validity of a truth claim are as follows:

- The claim is grounded in a question identified at the beginning of the research. This is usually about how you can live your values more fully in practice: 'How do I live my values of freedom?'
- You explain why the question is important.
- You monitor the action and gather data to show the research context, especially about how freedom is or is not being practised. You keep your data in your data archive.
- You try out new freedom-oriented practices, and gather more data to show yourself and others in action.
- You ask critical friends and validation groups to scrutinise your data in relation to your research question. All offer critical feedback. You try to get triangulation – comments from at least three different points of view.
- You check the relevance of the data against your original values. They enable you to select pieces of data that show how the research question is being addressed.
- You identify those data that can now stand as evidence. Again you subject this evidence to the scrutiny of critical friends and validation groups. If they agree that the evidence is relevant and meaningful, you can use the evidence base to test the validity of the emerging claims. So validation meetings comprise several processes, including: (a) listening to the research account; (b) scrutinising the data; and (c) agreeing (or not) the validity of the knowledge claim.
- You explain the significance of your research for educational influences in learning.

Processes such as these demonstrate the methodological rigour of the research. It is a question of establishing the validity of the claim to knowledge through establishing the validity of the evidence base.

These processes apply to multimedia representations, the same as to linguistic ones. A visual narrative would have to demonstrate validation procedures. Examples are available to show good quality writing with visual narratives, including video-data. Most multimedia work uses video-data to create an evidence base, but new work is emerging where a complete thesis can take multimedia form (O'Neill 2008, accessible at www.ictaspoliticalaction. com). An archive of further examples can be found at http://www.actionresearch.net

Establishing the truthfulness of a claim within an academic context involves testing it against the literature. Key writers come to act as virtual critical friends (real if you contact them). Research that is about creating the conditions of freedom would involve virtual critical friends such as Berlin (1969), Foucault (1980) and Hampshire (2000). Engaging with the literature lends credibility and authority to the report, and strengthens your credentials as a researcher.

Appropriateness

Appropriateness refers to your awareness that you and your situation are influenced by values, including those that underpin flows of historical and current economic, political and social forces.

It is essential to talk about your values, which ground and drive your research. Sometimes people are not aware of their values, or even that they have values. Some people think that values refer only to socially acceptable ones, but cruelty is as strong a value as kindness, and the desire for power can be stronger than a love of peace. Try writing down the values that inspire your life, or talk with a critical friend about why you do the work you do, and what is rewarding about it.

Most of us experience ourselves as a living contradiction when our values are denied in our practices (Whitehead 1989). We can use our research as a means of overcoming the contradiction. This is often the starting point of an action enquiry. You ask, 'How do I improve this situation here?', understanding that the way to improve a social situation is first to improve your own thinking and learning.

It is important to appreciate that your espoused values can also be the outcomes of persuasion, often through the media. Marlin (2002) explains how propaganda can become an art form to persuade people to believe things they actually don't believe in. The experiments of Milgram (1973) show this in practice. People tortured others, against their better judgement, because they were persuaded that they were doing the right thing. You are also subject to these forms of persuasion, through the messages you receive from the culture. You therefore need to show that you have developed your capacity for critical thinking.

This involves deconstructing what you say. What do you communicate when you refer to patients as 'them'; or say, 'It's either this or that.' How do others feel when you say 'No' to their ideas; and what do you communicate when you say about disabled people, 'It's not their fault.' Your report will communicate, through your use of language, whether or not you live your espoused values.

These are some of the criteria that your reader is expecting from the form of language of your report. The issue now is, how do you write this kind of language?

Here are some ideas about how you can do so.

HOW DO YOU PRODUCE A GOOD QUALITY TEXT?

Here are some ideas about how to produce a good report. These include logistical issues, such as finding time and space to write, as well as editorial issues such as drafting and proofreading. They also include coping strategies when things go wrong. The most important strategies are as follows:

1. Planning and getting organised.
2. Drafting.

3. Inviting critique.
4. Editing.
5. Proofreading.
6. Coping with difficulties.
7. Understanding legal issues.

Planning and getting organised

Planning your writing programme involves thinking about logistical issues, including time, space and resources, and textual issues about what the final product will look like.

Planning and organising: logistical issues

Dealing with the logistics of the physical activity of producing a text means spending time thinking about how, where and when you are going to write.

When does the writing start?

Many people believe you can leave the writing of the report until all the data have been gathered in. This is not the case. You should begin the writing from the start of the research, for example by keeping a reflective journal, and doing pieces of practice writing about issues. Get into the habit of producing progress reports. These and other writings can act as data about your own learning and actions, and may find their way into the final report.

Decide when you write. Some people maintain a regular schedule, and recognise themselves as 'morning' or 'evening' people. Other people find that they have to discipline themselves when the ideas do not flow. Try to maintain regular contact with your text; if you leave it for several days, you will forget what you have written, and waste time getting back in touch with it. Try to spend at least half an hour every day working with the text, and thinking about the ideas.

Finding a place to write

Some people need their own space to write. For others, this is not practical – because you probably share a living space with other people, so your writing space needs to be negotiated. Ask people to clear a space for you at certain times. J.K. Rowling tells how she wrote much of her early Harry Potter books in cafés because she had no other space. Alan Titchmarsh, the famous TV gardener turned author, was reputed to write his books in a garden shed. Some people do their writing sitting up in bed. We authors, Jean and Jack, do a lot of writing on planes and trains and while waiting in airports. The main thing is to find a space where you can write, and just do it. Do not use lack of space as an excuse not to write.

Planning and organising ideas

Writing a successful text means being in love with your topic because you are going to live with it for a long time. Organise your ideas by thinking about the issues that grip your attention. This takes discipline: it is generally easier to daydream than think constructively. If you are struggling to get the ideas right, think about them last thing at night and let your mind do the rest. In the morning the ideas usually come right. Organising your ideas may take several days or weeks, but they will eventually come right if you have faith in your own capacity to make sense of your experience.

Drafting

Many people mistakenly believe that their first draft is the final version. Sorry, it does not work like this. You may need about ten complete drafts before you have a final document. Even the most experienced writers will produce multiple drafts as they are writing. For every paper or book we have written, at least 20 more have gone in the bin.

The first draft is where you work out the ideas. This will probably be a lengthy text because you may not stop to edit and reduce the word length until later. This stage is like putting everything you have on the table, and sorting out where things go, what you are going to keep and discard. Your later drafts refine the ideas, and get to the point. The first draft of the book you are reading was far different from its final form, and a lot of paper has been recycled. Your drafts will become more focused and relevant as you engage with the advice of critical friends and with the ideas.

Inviting critique

Critique is essential to sorting out your ideas. Getting other people's responses to your thinking and writing will help you move forward, as well as reveal flaws in your arguments or errors in your writing. Talk with your critical friends, and listen to what they have to say. If they suggest that your ideas are mistaken, don't get defensive, but listen and learn, and rethink. If they point out a flaw – perhaps you have not properly tested the validity of a claim – look again and rewrite. It is better to rewrite before submitting your document, when an examiner may possibly reject the work. Share your text with colleagues at intervals, and ask for critical feedback, but don't expect them to respond immediately. Respect their time and commitments, as they respect yours.

Editing

Editing is where you read your text with a dispassionate critical eye, to see if it makes sense and reads well. If anything in your text does not make sense to you, it is not going to make sense to a reader either. Make sure that every sentence relates to the others, that the ideas are coherent and the argument is clearly expressed, and that words are used to their best advantage. This means you have to read it to yourself many times, and each time make sure that every word counts. Edit with a critical eye. This can be hard for writers, many of whom are often reluctant to throw out ideas, yet it is part of the discipline of becoming a writer whose work readers will want to read. Take out all repetition, frilly words, pretentiousness and other redundancies. Keep focused, to the point, and speak in a language that your reader will understand. You can of course experiment with different genres or style. Researchers sometimes use poetry or drama in their works, but they also make clear to the reader how these different genres should be engaged with and understood.

Proofreading

Proofreading is where you make sure that your manuscript is error-free and technically accurate. This means reading critically to spot any errors in grammar, including spelling, punctuation and syntax, and making sure that you obey the conventions of academic scholarship. Check that your references in the text match those in the bibliography. Make sure the dates match and that you have all the names of the authors in the bibliography. Citations such as 'Brown et al.' may appear in the text, but all authors' names must be written out in full in the bibliography. Check your references against your text multiple times. This is serious. In a doctorate, the regulations of most institutions maintain that a thesis may be passed with minor modifications, which means up to about six errors in the manuscript. Too many errors may mean that the thesis will be recommended for revision. It is in your own interests to proofread thoroughly. If you cannot proofread yourself, engage the services of a professional proofreader to do it for you. Their job is to work with your text as a text, not in terms of the concepts or ideas, and ensure that all the technicalities of presentation are correct.

Coping with difficulties

Sometimes people get tired of writing, or lose faith in what they are doing. This is understandable because producing a lengthy text takes time and sustained effort. So you need to develop ways to deal with the situation. When you run out of ideas or get lost in trying to sort them out, stop trying to write and do something else. Have confidence in your tacit understanding that you know what you want to say, and let your mind do the rest. This can take time, sometimes days. Do not try not to relax. Even the most experienced writers acknowledge that they have to stop from time to time to let things settle in the mind. Many postmodern writers say that you don't write the text so much as let the text write itself. However, don't pretend that you are stuck when in fact you don't want to work. Good writing stems from a small amount of talent and a large amount of hard work.

The experience of not knowing what to say next is often called 'writer's block'. If this is your experience, get to know what fires you up to the extent that you want to say something. You can:

- read an article
- view a picture
- listen to someone speaking
- or utilise any other stimulus.

all of which makes you want to say something because you are:

- angry
- enthusiastic
- sympathetic
- or experiencing any other emotion that makes you want to speak.

Then, as soon as you feel that you want to get back to writing, sit at the desk or the computer and work at it. Bring all your discipline to the task, and just stick with it until it comes right, as it will. This is the sheer hard slog and determination involved in being a writer.

Understanding legal issues

When you produce your report and put it in the public domain, it becomes part of the social order, which is run according to certain laws. One of those laws deals with intellectual property. A person's ideas are their property, as much as their car or house, and original ideas must not be used without permission or acknowledgement. Using someone's ideas without acknowledging the source is plagiarism, and you must be aware and careful.

It is sometimes difficult to know where one person's thinking leaves off and another's begins. Sometimes we, Jack and Jean, work with an idea rapidly, and it develops through our interactions. When we produce an idea jointly we acknowledge this. When an idea was created by one or the other, we also acknowledge this.

When you use someone's idea you must acknowledge your intellectual debt. Cite their names in your text and give the source where you found the idea, plus the page reference. Learn how to cite references properly – there are plenty of books on this topic. Always check that the reference in the body of your text is also in your bibliography. If you miss out a reference you will jeopardise the quality of the report and could be penalised.

Do not use any part of a text that has already been published without giving its source. Doing so amounts to cheating. This also applies to material from the internet. Sophisticated programmes are now available to help examiners detect whether the material exists elsewhere, but for your own integrity, you should never cheat. This applies also to using your own work again. Sometimes people use material from a previous assignment in a current one. This is unethical and dangerous. If an examiner chose to go through the entire record, as sometimes happens for quality assurance purposes, and they find that a candidate has used the same material for aspects of different assignments, that candidate could be disqualified. Plagiarism of any kind can carry severe penalties, so be aware.

At the end of the day, it has to be accepted that some candidates do cheat and get away with it. Most people, however, produce original work whose ownership and quality they can stand over, which is how it should be. We should all be proud of what we do.

HOW IS THE QUALITY OF THE TEXT JUDGED?

Your reader judges your text in relation to the general and academic criteria on p. 70, demonstrated by your communication of ideas through the use of language. If you show that you can do this, you can claim several kinds of validity for your text, including:

1. Rhetorical validity.
2. Ironic validity.
3. Catalytic validity.
4. Educational validity.

Rhetorical validity

All texts aim to communicate something; most aim to persuade a reader to believe something. Your text does this. You are hoping to persuade your reader that they should validate your claim to knowledge and give you your award. You are presenting your work as your truth; in Foucault's (1980) terms, your text communicates your system of knowledge – what you know and how you come to know it.

The art of rhetoric can be both overt and subtle. It can be used in educational ways, when people are persuaded to think for themselves; and in colonising ways, when they are persuaded to do things against their better judgement. Your text aims both to persuade (demonstrate rhetorical validity) and also to educate (demonstrate educational validity), so you need to use language in a way that ensures that independent and valid judgements are made about it.

You therefore need to make explicit what you are trying to communicate, first in relation to your practice (your standards for judging the quality of your practice), for example:

• My research demonstrates the realisation of love at work (Lohr 2006).
• I transform my values of care into my living standards of judgement (Charles 2007).
• My work shows how I have enabled marginalised children to speak for themselves (Cahill 2007).

You also need to set out how you have done this (your standards for judging the rhetorical validity of your text):

• I show, through the use of language, that my account is comprehensible, authentic, truthful and appropriate to its context.

- My writing demonstrates, through the use of language, my capacity to exercise my educational influence.
- I use textual devices to clarify any ambiguities in my account.

Ironic validity

This idea, made popular by Lather (1991), has been a feature of textual analysis at least since the 'linguistic turn' of the mid twentieth century (Norris 1989), when philosophers such as Derrida (1997) began to make clear that language was socially constructed, and used to achieve specific human interests. Foucault (1994) especially asked how it was possible for the subject (person) to tell the truth about itself. The question arises, how is it possible to reflect on the use of language while using that form of language? Critical analysts such as Said (1991) explain how literature can communicate the norms and values of a culture so that what is said becomes taken for granted; and Wittgenstein (1953) explains how people use different 'language games', with unspoken norms. Consider this conversation:

> A: It's rather cold in here, don't you think? That window's open.
> B: Yes, it is.

B refuses to play the language game that A has initiated. Wittgenstein says that most people play language games for specific purposes, and Chomsky (1991) says we often do so for our own ends.

To overcome colonising practices, says Derrida (1997), it is necessary to make the familiar strange, to see things through critical eyes. This means putting yourself in the other's shoes, and recognising yourself potentially as Other to the other (Buber 1970). In terms of your text, it means putting yourself in the shoes of your reader. Your reader is looking for your awareness of how you may be communicating normative assumptions, your capacity to deconstruct your own thinking, and your explanations for how you are doing it.

You therefore need to explain how you have done this (your standards for judging the ironic validity of your text), for example:

- At this point in my narrative I need to step back and comment on the way in which I have spoken about my practice.
- In saying that I adopted a management perspective to my work, I need to clarify that my understanding of management is of collaborative working practices.
- While I am maintaining that my claim to have improved my practice is justified, I am aware of the need to produce authenticated evidence to test the validity of my claim, and to show how I have subjected it to rigorous critique, on the assumption that I may be mistaken.

Catalytic validity

Catalytic validity (Lather 1991) is about how you can re-orient and refocus your research so that you can understand reality in order to transform it, a process Freire (1973) termed 'conscientization'. Catalytic validity involves both a recognition of the reality-changing impact of the research process, as well as consciously channelling this impact so that participants gain self-understanding and self-determination through their involvement. Whitehead and Huxtable (2008) have explored the catalytic validity of the living educational theories of self-study researchers in improving practice and in creating a new epistemology of educational knowledge.

Educational validity

'Educational' in this book means a practice that aims to encourage others to think for themselves, and make wise choices about how they should act. This means using language in a transparent way and setting out explicitly what you think is the significance of your work, and the significance of your capacity to communicate it. Doing this is not arrogance, but a sign of how you hold yourself accountable for judging your capacity for educational validity (Chapter 9).

You need to explain how you have done this (your standards for judging the educational validity of your text), for example:

- I have used a form of language in my practice that encourages people to take responsibility for their own choices.
- I have shown through my text how I have communicated my capacity for critical deconstruction.
- I have used a self-reflective form of language in my report to show my capacity to communicate the educational significance of my work.

These issues emphasise key themes: the tentative nature of knowledge claims; the need to test them to establish their validity; and the need for reflexive and dialectical critique (Winter 1989), which informs the ironic validity (Lather 1991) of your text. Your reader is hoping, throughout, to read a mature, self-reflexive account that demonstrates your capacity to engage thoughtfully and energetically with your own thinking, and show how this has enabled you to become more critical and considerate in your practice.

SUMMARY

This chapter has looked at some of the technicalities of writing as a means of communication. We have considered how the generalist and academic criteria of good quality writing can be achieved to ensure its comprehensibility, authenticity, truthfulness and appropriateness. We have looked at the practicalities of producing a text, and how it will be judged in terms of its originality, significance and rigour.

CHECKLIST OF REFLECTIVE QUESTIONS

Here is a checklist to remind you of the main ways in which you can make your text accessible to your reader.

Is my text comprehensible?

- Do I take care in clarity of expression? Do I use a minimalist form?
- Is the structure clear? Do I provide signposts and navigational devices?
- Do I use correct grammar and avoid repetition?

Do I come across as authentic?

- Do I show that I as a person, and I as a researcher and scholar, can be trusted?
- Do I take care to communicate the values base of my research and show how I am trying to live them in my practice?
- Does my text demonstrate my originality, while observing traditional academic criteria?

Am I truthful? Can people believe me?

- Do I show, through my methodology and my evidence base, that my knowledge claims may be believed?
- Do I include appendices to supplement the evidence base, to show that my evidence is trustworthy? Are my data signed and dated? Do I include ethics statements and other devices to show that I have minded other people's wellbeing?

Is my text appropriate for the social and academic context I am in?

- Do I explain how my work is grounded in my values, which may be different from the values of my institution or community?
- Do I explain that I am interrogating my own and others' normative assumptions?
- Do I show how I have learned the importance of speaking for myself?

Is my text of a high technical merit?

- Can my reader see that I have produced a tightly structured, well-argued text through my disciplined attention to detail?
- Have I checked for errors, and ensured that my bibliography is accurate?
- Have I produced a clean text that is visually appealing and that my reader will want to read?

Do I claim, implicitly or explicitly, different kinds of validity for my text?

- Do I say that I have achieved, for example, rhetorical, ironic, catalytic and educational validity?
- Do I show that I am at ease with these ideas?
- Do I select from the different kinds of validity the ones that are right for me?

If you have done all these things, you have probably produced a text that is a pleasure to read.

Now to Part II, where we look first at writing a proposal (Chapter 5), and how you can go on to write your action research according to different academic levels (Chapters 6, 7 and 8).

PART II

How is an Action Research Report Written?

This part deals with the question 'How is an action research report written?' It contains Chapters 5, 6, 7 and 8.

Chapter 5 asks, 'How do you write an action research proposal?' It explains how to write a proposal, and gives examples.

Chapter 6 asks, 'How do you write an undergraduate/workplace-based action research report?' It explains how to write one, and gives an example.

Chapter 7 asks, 'How do you write a masters action research report?' It explains how to write one, and gives many examples from real-life dissertations and theses.

Chapter 8 asks, 'How do you write a doctoral action research report?' It explains how to write one, and gives examples from real-life doctoral theses.

Each chapter gives ideas about which criteria are important for the different levels, how you can achieve the criteria, and how your work will be judged.

5 Writing an Action Research Proposal

When you write a proposal, you say what you intend to do in your research, how you are going to do it, and why. You tell your reader what they need to know to let them see that the research plan is feasible, and that you have the capacity to carry it out. This means that you have to plan and design your research in advance, and write it out as a blueprint for your project. This chapter will help you to do this.

The chapter is organised as follows:

1. What goes into a research proposal?
2. How do you write a proposal?
3. How is the proposal judged?
4. Examples of research proposals.
5. Summary.
6. Checklist of reflective questions.

Remember that your research project and your research proposal are different things. Your research project is about how you hope to find out about what you do, and your proposal sets out how you intend to do this. Your proposal will be judged in terms of (1) how well you plan and design your research, and (2) how well you communicate the processes involved, in relation to (3) the expectations of the level of accreditation you are aiming for.

Here is what is involved in writing a proposal.

WHAT GOES INTO A RESEARCH PROPOSAL?

This section contains advice on:

1. Planning your research project.
2. Designing your research project.

Writing a proposal is a practical exercise that involves planning and designing. You plan and design your research project in the same way as you plan and design your garden project or walking tour. It is a feasibility exercise that lets you take stock of logistical aspects in terms of the availability of resources, as well as your capacity to bring the project to successful completion. Because your research is about knowledge creation, your reader needs to know what knowledge claims you intend to make and how you are going to make them. A proposal for an academic award will be judged according to different standards at the different levels of undergraduate, masters and doctorate.

Planning your research project

Planning involves identifying what you hope to do and why, what resources you need to enable you to do it, and whether you have access to them. It lets you take stock both of availability of resources, and your capacity to do the job.

Think about the following.

What do you hope to do and why?

Be fairly clear about your reasons and purposes in advance. New ideas will emerge during the course of the project but you need to have a strong sense beforehand about the rightness of what you are doing.

Getting a picture of the overall shape of your project involves saying what you want to do, why you want to do it, and what you hope to achieve. These three aspects must be included in an academic report, which is about knowledge creation, and involves descriptions, explanations and analyses, as follows.

Say what you want to achieve

Here are some of the things you may want to achieve:

- You wish to improve your practice.
- You want to encourage others to evaluate what they are doing.
- You are aiming for systemic influence.

State your reasons

Here are some of the reasons you may have for wanting to take action:

- You wish to improve your practice because it could be better in identifiable ways.
- You want to encourage others to evaluate what they are doing because you feel that self-evaluation is important for organisational success.
- You are aiming for systemic influence because you believe that people can influence one another as a form of social betterment.

State your purposes

Here are some of the purposes you may have for your action enquiry:

- You wish to improve your practice in order to make your work more effective.
- You want to encourage others to evaluate what they are doing, so that work standards will rise in your workplace.
- You are aiming for systemic influence so that a culture of enquiry will develop.

All these aspects need to be written into your proposal, regardless of academic level.

What do you need to enable you to do your project?

Logistical aspects include the following:

- **Costs**: Are any costs involved? Include obvious costs such as postage, and hidden costs such as sending work out if necessary. Will you have a contingency fund for unexpected costs?
- **Time**: Will you have time to do your project? Will your family and friends give you space? What about work–life balance?
- **People**: You will inevitably involve other people as research participants, critical friends and validation groups. Have you access to them? Will they be willing to help?
- **Permissions**: You will have to clear all ethical matters before you begin. Will you get these permissions? Are there any possible difficulties? This is especially important when planning to use multimedia, where you will not have control over your visual narratives when they are made more public through channels such as YouTube.
- **Resources**: Have you access to the resources you need? These include a library, money to purchase books and equipment, a good supervisor, conversations with professional groups, and anything specific to your context. If you are using multimedia, you will need the necessary technology, such as a good computer, camera and recording equipment.

Have you the capacity to carry out your project?

Readers want to know:

- Have you access to the necessary resources?
- Have you a good sense of the overall conceptualisation of your project? Have you a broad understanding of the issues involved and how they can be addressed?
- Do you know (roughly) where you wish to go and how to get there? Talk about your methodology to show that you know how you are going to conduct the enquiry and gather data and generate evidence. Say what kind of knowledge claim you hope to make and how you are going to test its validity.
- Have you read sufficiently to get you started? Do you know which literatures you need to access to help you advance your thinking? You would set out some of your conceptual frameworks, i.e. the overall concepts that will frame your study.
- Do you have the stamina and commitment to maintain a prolonged study schedule? This means explaining that you really want to undertake this research, and that you are aware already of the significance of what you hope to do.
- Do you have what it takes to undertake independent study? Do you communicate a sense that you have already started your study programme because you are curious and can't wait to get on with it?
- Can you write reasonably well? You must present a clean proposal in error-free language. Your readers will not warm to you if they sense that your scripts will need a lot of editorial work.

These are some of the aspects involved in planning your project. Now let's move on to designing.

Designing your research project

Remember that your research is about creating knowledge, so your proposal will outline how you intend to do this. The knowledge is about how you have improved your practice, and that you understand your practice better. Your proposal explains how you intend to create the knowledge, test its validity, and use it. Also remember that your proposal will be judged in relation to its level of accreditation. In Chapters 6, 7 and 8 you can see what is expected at different levels in terms of depth of theoretical analysis and quality of knowledge claim, so your proposal needs to reflect these expectations.

Designing a project involves asking practical 'what?, which?, who?, when?, where?, how? and why?' questions. You do not need to use these questions in any particular order, but it should be clear that they have informed your thinking. This will give a sense of coherence and flow to your proposal and communicate your understanding that you are doing research, not just professional activities.

Probably the easiest way to design an action research project is to think of your set of action reflection questions. It is important to write a proposal that reflects your unique style and way of doing things, but this set of questions gives you a hook on which to hang your thinking about how you intend to conduct your project, and may be adapted to your own purposes and contexts.

- **What is my concern?** This question enables you to identify your research issue and formulate a research question.
- **Why am I concerned?** Spell out the contexts of your research and the values that inspire it. Outline your key conceptual frameworks, and say which literatures you will engage with. Talk about the values base of your research and explain whether or not you are realising those values in your practice.
- **How do I show the situation as it is and as it unfolds?** Talk about how you intend to monitor your practice and gather data. Explain how you intend to generate evidence from the data, and what standards you will use to judge the quality of your practice and your research.
- **What can I do about it? What will I do about it?** Outline your options for action, and choose one.
- **How do I check that any conclusions I come to are reasonably fair and accurate?** Explain how you are going to test the validity of your emergent claims.
- **How do I modify my ideas and practices in light of my evaluation?** Say how you intend to continue working, perhaps in a new direction.
- **How do I communicate the significance of my research?** Explain what the significance of your research is for your own education, for the education of others, and for the education of social and cultural formations.

If you wish, you can use this set of questions to frame your whole proposal. Just make sure you also address the issues we deal with in the next section.

The next step is to combine the two aspects of planning (logistical issues) and designing (methodological issues) into a document that becomes your research proposal. Here is how you can do it. Examples appear on pp. 99 and 101.

HOW DO YOU WRITE A PROPOSAL?

Different institutions have different requirements. Some want a proposal of 400–500 words; some want 1,500 words. Check the guidelines in the official handbooks to see what is required. Below are two examples of a proposal written for different institutional requirements.

Here is some advice on organising your ideas. Stylistically it is helpful to place each section under its own heading, to guide your reader around your text. We adopt the same technique here. You do not have to organise your proposal in the same sequence of ideas presented here, but you should aim to address them all somewhere.

Who am I?

Introduce yourself. Say where you work, how long you have been working there, and what your position is. Do not tell your life story; tell your reader enough so that they get a sense of your professional contexts. Tell them anything special about your workplace: if you work as a health care professional, or if you have special responsibility for the smooth running of a chain store.

Why do I want to do this research?

Identify an area of interest. Say that you want to improve your workplace practice, and you realise this involves carrying out an in-depth investigation, to evaluate what the practice is like at the moment and how you need to improve it. You are also looking for expert support to help you to do this. You may also wish to contribute to policy making.

Begin to formulate your research question, using the idea, 'How do I improve what I am doing?' Your question may become more refined over the period of your research. 'How do I improve my practice?' could become 'How do I learn how to be a better listener?' It is the permeating theme that guides your research. Your question, 'How do I do this?', at the beginning of your research eventually transforms into your claim, 'I have done this', at the end. Tell your reader that you understand this and will work towards generating a claim to knowledge that is grounded in your research question.

What do I hope to find out from this research?

Say what your study is about. Say that you hope to find ways to improve your practice, and that your understanding of what you do will constitute your original claim to knowledge. You know that doing research is about generating knowledge, and you feel the knowledge you create will contribute to knowledge of your field. Map out the scope of your project in terms of what you see as the possible findings and why you think these will be important. From reading this section, your reader will get a sense of whether the project is manageable within the timescale and resources you have available.

To do	Start date	Do by:
Plan project	January 16th	January 30th
Identify research participants	January 24th	February 15th
Produce ethics statement	January 24th	February 15th
Gather data	March 1st	July 20th
Analyse data	July 1st	August 24th
Generate evidence	August 30th	September 20th And so on …

Figure 5.1   Project timings

When and where will I do the research?

Draw up a timescale. Most projects for workplace and masters degrees are small-scale, lasting from three weeks to three months. Many books speak about a '100-hour project'. It is often helpful to draw up a chart to show what will be done when: see Figure 5.1.

Say where you will conduct your research. Most people conduct their research in their workplaces, but may also use other contexts, such as a library for when you do desk research or consult archives. You may also need to go outside the workplace, perhaps if you wish to survey people's attitudes towards an aspect of practice – for example, how are involuntary migrants treated? Remember to get permission from any persons responsible for the workplace and its good order (see 'Ethics', p. 95).

Who will you involve in your research?

Although the focus of your research will be you as you improve your practice, which means first improving your understanding of your practice, you will inevitably involve other people in the following capacities (see also p. 61).

Observers and friends of your project

Identify the people who will observe you as you conduct your research, or gather data on your behalf.

Participants

Identify the people you will work with as research participants. Say that you will ask them perhaps to keep a reflective journal, which they will let you see as part of your data gathering, or give you feedback through interviews and focus groups about whether you are influencing the quality of their learning.

Critical friends and validation groups

Identify your critical friends who you will consult on an ongoing basis, and a validation group who will meet on a more formal basis to listen to your progress and summative reports. Explain what kind of schedule of meetings you will draw up.

How will I conduct the research?

Say that you intend to pursue a systematic enquiry into improving your practice, which you will then make public through your report. You will disseminate your findings widely, to contribute to new thinking and practices.

Say which methodology you intend to use, and why. Say why you intend to use this methodology, what is special about it, and why no other methodology would be appropriate. Perhaps you will choose a mixed-methods methodology, in which case you need to explain which methods you will use. (Remember that 'method' refers to a technique such as a tape-recording, or triangulation; 'methodology' refers to the processes of generating theoretical understandings through research.)

How will I gather data and generate evidence?

Outline your data gathering methods, which may include either quantitative or qualitative methods or both. Explain that you need to select appropriate methods and will check the availability of necessary technology. This is especially important if you intend to use multimedia. You may also need the help of a specialised technical adviser. Will you have access?

Say what you intend to monitor and gather data about. In the case of enquiring into how you are improving your practice, especially in relation to how you are exercising your educational influence in your own and other people's thinking, you need to monitor your own changing thinking, and how it is informing your changing practice with other people. This means you will also have to monitor their thinking, and how it is informing their practice. This can be complex, because you cannot directly monitor people's thinking, so you have to ask them to do it themselves, and make their data available to you. This in turn raises issues of ethics (see below).

Say how you intend to generate evidence from the data. This involves identifying standards by which the quality of the practice and research will be judged. Because you are doing an academic course, it will also involve explaining how you will fulfil the academic criteria. Explain how you will use your research to find ways of living more fully in the direction of your values.

How will you test the validity of your claims to knowledge?

As you generate evidence in relation to your research question, you strengthen your position towards making a claim to knowledge, to say that you now know something that you did not know before. The strongest claims are original ones, that you know something that no one knew before. You need to show that these are not only your opinion, but are grounded in an evidence base that you have presented to the critical scrutiny of your critical friends and validation groups. Say how you will keep a record of these meetings, and all validation matters. Identify your standards of judgement, in terms of academic criteria, and in relation to how your values become the living standards by which you make judgements about the quality of your practice and your research.

How will you modify your ideas and practice in light of your evaluation?

Say that you will continue your research, because the end of this action-reflection cycle will become the beginning of a new one. Explain what you have learned through doing the research, and how this will inform new learning. Perhaps you may do things differently, because some elements were not so successful; if this is the case, say how you will do them better. You could indicate how you see the need for continual professional learning, and how you may contribute to this, perhaps through convening new research interest groups.

How will you explain the significance of your research?

Say how you think your research may be significant. This may be in terms of informing new practices and new policies. You also hope to contribute to new forms of theory, by placing your living theory of practice into the public domain. Say how you will disseminate your findings through publications, conference presentations, radio and TV appearances, and exercise your educational influence in the workplace for systemic transformation. You may join networks and professional associations in your field, to influence their thinking, and speak with local government groupings who may learn from you.

Ethics

Make clear to your reader that you will observe ethical conduct at all times. Say what this will involve, such as ensuring anonymity where appropriate, and respect for the other by making available tape-recorded transcripts to their originators. Say that you intend to submit your proposal to your institutional ethics committee and other stakeholders in the workplace, and secure their permission before proceeding. You will make progress reports available to them on a regular basis, if they wish, and invite their critical comment. Explain that you will draw up an ethics statement for distribution to all participants, and place a copy of this statement as an appendix to your proposal. This section is most important, because if you do not spell out how you will take ethical care, permission to do your research may not be granted. Also, do not expect an examiner to assess your report unless ethics statements are included as appendices.

Engaging with the literatures

You must engage with the literatures to some extent. The more advanced your programme of studies, the greater your engagement. Say which literatures you will access, and who some of your key authors will be. This means outlining your conceptual frameworks. Also say why you have chosen these literatures: you need, for example, to be familiar with methodological issues, to address reasons for wishing to use a self-study action research methodology, and substantive issues, to do with your subject matters.

A note about multimedia proposals

The use of digital technology, especially in the production of video narratives, is extending and transforming the forms of representation that educational researchers use (Eisner 1997). These show, much better than words on a page, how to communicate the dynamic nature of living values as the expression of cosmic energy. Vasilyuk says:

> Conceptions involving energy are very current in psychology, but they have been very poorly worked out from the methodological standpoint. ... Equally unclear are the conceptual links between energy and motivation, energy and meaning, although it is obvious that there are certain links: we know how 'energetically' a person can act when positively motivated, we know that the meaningfulness of a project lends additional strength to the people engaged in it, but we have very little idea of how to link up into one whole the physiological theory of activation, the psychology of motivation, and the ideas of energy which have been elaborated mainly in the field of physics. (Vasilyuk 1991: 63–4)

In your multimedia proposal you explain how you make these links as your original contribution, because you bring your unique constellation of values with energy into the academy for legitimation, as your explanation for your educational influences in learning.

HOW IS THE PROPOSAL JUDGED?

Your proposal serves several purposes, so it will be judged in terms of whether it is fit for purpose for different people. These include:

1. yourself
2. your readers and assessors.

How is your proposal useful for yourself?

Your proposal acts throughout as your map to doing your research, in the same way as the route map you draw up before your walking tour. It is important therefore to spend time working on your proposal, especially on formulating your research question, and to be clear about what you hope to achieve from the research. Perhaps the most important thing is to clarify your values, as the grounds for your research, and how these values will transform into your conceptual frameworks, and your criteria and standards of judgement.

Also remember that your proposal is dynamic. The details of your proposal may change. This is acceptable in action research, and to be expected, because the proposal written today is for today's contexts, but those contexts will change, so the research focus will change too. Your thinking and your research question may be refined as your analyses deepen and as you extend your cognitive range through reflection, discussion and reading. Sometimes people discard their first proposal because they see it is not viable when problematics emerge, and begin again.

Your proposal is dynamic also in how the words transform into action. It is rather like an organisation's policy statement. Although it is written as a static text on a piece of paper or a computer screen, the meaning of the proposal or the policy statement lies in the intention of the person who wrote it, and the enactment of these intentions becomes purposeful action. In Arendt's (1958) terms, it is your first step to taking your place in the world – for you, the academic world – and your statement of intent to take communicative and educational action. Husserl (1931) says that intent is at the heart of social action, and once something is intentional in the mind, it triggers the actor's capacity to take action in the social world. Said (1997) says that intent carries its entire methodology within itself; you can imagine the future in every beginning. This has implications for Habermas's (2001) ideas about the public sphere, that all persons need to have access and speak their truth through processes of communicative action (see Chapter 10). Your research proposal is your entry to the academic public sphere; your proposal communicates that you are capable of theorising your work and wish to have the work recognised as research-based practice. You are also claiming that you are a professional who does not simply react, but acts from a specific set of theoretical bases. Your proposal is therefore both about how you are going to improve your professionalism, and also how you will improve your capacity to theorise what you are doing, and test the validity of your living theory in the public domain for its possible adoption or adaptation by others.

Your proposal is, in many ways, your passport to a new place. However, like all passports it has to be approved and stamped by a passport office. In your case, the passport office contains the readers and assessors who will approve your proposal.

How is your proposal useful for your readers and assessors?

Your readers and assessors will judge your proposal in terms of their expectations, which are grounded in their values. These therefore come to act as their living standards of judgement. They judge your proposal in terms of certain questions about your capabilities:

a. Is the researcher able to undertake a systematic enquiry at an appropriate level?
b. Is the researcher able to undertake independent study?
c. Is the researcher able to write a good report?

These questions imply that you are capable of the following.

Is the researcher able to undertake a systematic enquiry at an appropriate level?

Your reader wants to see whether you understand what is involved in doing action research. In relation to action, they want to see whether you understand that action is not just about doing things in the workplace, but is intentional and purposeful, that you can articulate your reasons and purposes. In relation to research, they want to see that you appreciate the steps involved, that research involves making claims to knowledge and testing the validity of those claims. They need to see that you can articulate the importance of your work in relation to its originality, rigour and significance. They expect your proposal to spell these aspects out. They also expect to see that you understand what is involved at your level of accreditation, especially in relation to making claims and testing their validity. For example, an undergraduate report would contain a claim to improved practice, whereas a doctoral report would also contain a claim to original knowledge. These differences are explained in the next three chapters.

Is the researcher able to undertake independent study?

When you register for an award-bearing course, there is an expectation that you will be able to undertake independent study. Although your supervisor will be on hand throughout for advice and support, you have to do your own learning. You would be expected to be pro-active in finding sources of data, new ideas in the literatures, and negotiating with critical friends and research participants. Your proposal would communicate your hunger to do your study, and your eagerness to get on with it. You would probably say in your proposal that you have already begun your informal enquiry, and now wish to formalise it through institutional structures.

A reader will welcome a proposal that is optimistic, thoughtful and focused. Especially they welcome proposals that communicate the researcher's understanding that they need to learn, and are willing to put time and energy into creating knowledge. They will not welcome a proposal that communicates a lack of self-confidence or self-discipline, and assumes that this can all be over by the weekend. A proposal is a scholarly document that shows how the researcher grounds their enquiry in their knowledge of the literatures, and indicates that they know where they need to go to read more. Your proposal is your statement of intent, both about how you intend to conduct yourself over the next while in producing a high quality report, and also about your capacity to do it. It is your statement that you can finish what you hope to begin.

Is the researcher able to write a good report?

The quality of the text of your proposal indicates to your reader what the quality of your final report will be like. Think about the issues raised in Chapter 4, about what is regarded as good quality writing, and how to achieve it. This means addressing issues of technique in writing, as well as ensuring the communicability of your text in terms of its comprehensibility, authenticity, truthfulness and appropriateness (p. 70). Especially, it means not only demonstrating these criteria, but also articulating to your reader that you know that you are doing so. This is a higher-order capacity that the best proposals demonstrate. The researcher states explicitly that they know what they are doing in their writing; they do it, and let the reader know that that they know they are doing it, which is a kind of meta-analysis and demonstrates the capacity for reflexive and dialectical critique. You would therefore say things like, 'In this section I explain how I engage with issues of validity…', and then go on and do it; or 'I have shown how I have reflected on my thinking and have transformed it in light of my reading…'.

EXAMPLES OF PROPOSALS

Here are two examples to get you going. Both deal with the same subject matter, and both are pitched at masters or doctoral levels.

Example 5.1: A generic proposal

Title
How do I improve my management capacity to develop communities of educational enquiry?

Background
In 1998, Wenger developed the idea of communities of learning, as a means of enhancing sustainable workplace practices. The idea was extended by Whitehead (1999) as the development of cultures of enquiry through the creation of living educational theories, drawn from the descriptions and explanations which individual learners produce for their own educational development. Recent debates in the educational research literatures (Furlong and Oancea 2005; Whitty 2005) have focused on the problematics of the legitimation and representation of educational research and educational action research (Feldman 2003). Of particular interest are issues regarding the nature of the standards of judgement to be applied to test the validity of, and to give academic legitimacy to, an individual's claim to know their own educational development (Whitehead 2004). However, there are as yet few self-studies by university practitioner-researchers into the nature of their educational and learning relationships and into appropriate standards of judgement in professional education (Russell and Korthagen 1995), or the means to foster inclusional and dialogical practices that will contribute to the development of sustainable communities of educational enquiry (Hartog 2004).

Purpose
By undertaking a self-study of my professional practices as a university-based practitioner-researcher I intend to find ways of understanding my practice as an educational manager as I supervise the professional learning of peer supervisors. A key feature of my enquiry will be to explain how I make judgements about the quality of my practice and my research by showing how my educational values come to act as my living standards of judgement, and contribute to the legitimacy of my claim to know my own educational development, as I research the question, 'How do I improve my management capacity to develop communities of educational enquiry?'

Scope
I will investigate my professional practices as a university-based manager organising and teaching a course for peers, who are acting as schools-based tutors of novice teachers, with a focus on issues of access and social justice. I will work with six academic staff, tutoring a group of eight novice teachers during the 2009/2010 session, as they seek to encourage novice teachers to develop self-efficacy (Wood et al. 2007). My enquiries will focus on an understanding of the nature and development of educational relationships between myself and my peers, as they research their practices with novice teachers.

These processes will be explored and explicated through a negotiated programme of meetings as participants discuss their lived experiences of articulating the nature and formation of their educational relationships.

Methodology

I will adopt a methodology of self-study action research (McNiff and Whitehead 2006), which involves enquiring into and explaining the processes of improving practice, with an emphasis on contributing to improving the social context in which the practice is located. This involves systematic action-reflection cycles of expressing concerns, producing action plans, acting and gathering data, and evaluating the effectiveness of changing practice. My accounts of my practices, and my educational and learning relationships, will be subjected to the critical scrutiny of a validation group, following the procedures recommended by Whitehead and McNiff (2006). From my systematically collated database I will generate evidence to show the nature of my educational relationships in my own and others' learning.

Issues of ethics

I will seek the approval of the university ethics committee for my proposal, in relation to the proposed conduct of my research. I will ensure the protection and wellbeing of myself and my research participants, as set out by Robson (2002), and I will include all records regarding ethical conduct in my data archive and appendices.

Timings

My research programme will proceed from spring 2008 to autumn 2012. I will organise my activities as follows.

2008–2009: Desk research to investigate current thinking around peer supervision. Identification of research issue and question, engagement with issues of values, imagination of solution. Round 1 of data gathering. Interviews and focus groups with all participants to establish base line data. Maintenance of reflective journal. Reading about substantive and methodological issues. Regular meetings with supervisor and critical friends. Progress report 1. Informal validation meeting.

2009–2010: Continued desk research. Round 2 of data gathering as I implement proposed solutions. Focus on transforming data into evidence. Articulation of standards of judgement. Continuation of reflective journal, encourage participants to maintain reflective journals. Regular meetings with supervisor. Progress report 2. First formal validation meeting. Continued reading.

2010–2011: Evaluation of implemented solution. Generation of evidence from all data. Maintenance of reflective journal. Progress report 3, and plan for thesis. Regular meetings with supervisor. Second formal validation meeting. Continued reading.

2011–2012: Writing up of thesis. Regular meetings with supervisor. Third formal validation meeting. Submission of thesis and viva.

Bibliography

Include your bibliography. The references for this proposal can be found in the main references section of this book.

Indicative bibliography

You could also include an indicative bibliography, which is a short list of books and papers that you intend to read, and that will inform your study.

Example 5.2: A proposal written for the University of Limerick

The University of Limerick publishes the following guidelines:

> If you have a 'germ' of an idea, the first stage is to discuss with your supervisor or an appropriate member of staff whether or not it is worth pursuing. ... The research proposal is intended as a basis for further discussion of your thesis topic before you start your work. The aim of this preliminary activity is to ensure that you enter your first year as a research student with a clear sense of topic area and purpose.
>
> The research proposal of approximately 1,500 words should include:
>
> - A description of the topic (with suggested title), indicating the general aims of the research and how these differ from previous published work in the field
> - An explanation of the main concepts and theories relevant to the research and the proposed methods of investigation
> - An indication of any practical applications that the research might have
> - A research plan, indicting the main tasks and timescales
> - Your reasons for wishing to undertake the research at the University of Limerick
> - A short bibliography, citing the main works of reference
>
> (University of Limerick 2006: 7)

Here is a proposal written to these guidelines, appropriate for a masters or PhD. Note: some of the literatures cited are fictitious; these are marked by a star (*).

> University of Limerick
> Proposed (Masters) (PhD) programme of studies
> Janet McEniffe*
> How do I improve my management capacity to develop
> communities of educational enquiry?

Introduction

This proposal is for a Masters (PhD) programme of studies, in which I conduct a self-study action enquiry into my practices as a third level manager as I seek to develop communities of educational enquiry. Through the research I aim to generate my living theory of practice (Whitehead 1989), comprising the descriptions, explanations and analyses that I offer as I explain how I hold myself accountable for what I do. A key feature of my enquiry will be to articulate the living nature of my values as they transform into the critical standards by which I judge the validity of my original claims that I understand my practice and know how to improve it.

Aims of the research

The research I will undertake is part of my ongoing enquiry into how I can encourage third-level academic staff to develop the kind of mentoring practices that will encourage schools-based teachers to investigate their practices as they seek to exercise their educational influences in their pupils' learning. Since 2005 I have been conducting informal study seminars with academic staff around these issues, as they support the schools-based enquiries of teachers. Based at the University of Limerick, my research is an extension of my masters programme (McEniffe 2004*), which involved an analysis of my educational relationships with students in a second level school as my then place of work. That research developed and clarified my understanding of how I can develop dialogical communities of practice (Bakhtin 1981) to nurture learning. I also wish to investigate how I can encourage the development of schools–universities partnerships (Rust and Freidhus 2001) that will enable university and schools-based practitioners to engage in a dialogue of equals, as they investigate how they are influencing one another's thinking and practice. I wish to formalise these initiatives as a coherent programme of studies that will enable me to theorise my work in order to establish its academic legitimacy. The originality of my research will lie in its contribution to current debates about validity and legitimacy in educational knowledge (Feldman 2003; Habermas 1975), and how the knowledge claims of practitioners in dialogical communities may contribute to public debates about processes of social and cultural transformation.

My contexts

I have been working at the University of Limerick since 2003 as an educational manager, with responsibility for mentoring staff who work with schools-based communities of teacher-researchers, all of whom are seeking to improve the quality of their educational practices through educational research. Current policy documents (DES 2007*) recommend new forms of professional education to be developed and delivered by third level practitioners, to enable schools-based staff to undertake their action enquiries into their practices as they develop innovative forms of curriculum. Mindful that curriculum development involves teacher professional education (Hargreaves 1999), I ground the reasons for my enquiry in this new policy focus on developing communities of educational enquiry. In so doing, I am aware that I will be contributing to a reconceptualisation of educational theory, from its dominant propositional form to a new living form as I encourage those whose studies I support to address the question, 'How do I improve my practice?' Through my focus on community-building, I hope to show the processes through which this question may transform into the new question, 'How do we improve our practices?'

Conceptual frameworks

I draw on the work of key authors to guide my study and to act as my conceptual frameworks. Overarching frameworks draw on: the work of Whitehead (1989) and Whitehead and McNiff (2006), about the living nature of educational enquiry; the work of McNiff (2007) about the generative transformational nature of educational relationships; and the work of Biesta (2006) on educational responsibility. These broad frameworks embed secondary frameworks, which are themselves in a dynamic transformational relationship in the generation of living educational theories. These contain ideas about the following:

- The immanent and genetically-endowed capacity for human growth, drawing on the generative transformational work of Chomsky (1986).
- The interrelationship of all things, drawing on the transformational evolutionary work of Bateson (1979), and the ideas of Buber (1970), Fromm (1978) and Tillich (1973), as well as on the environmental philosophy of Zimmerman et al. (2001).
- The inevitable capacity for human influence, drawing on the ideas of Foucault (1980) and Said (1994b).
- The capacity of humans for making choices about the exercise of their influence, drawing on the work of Berlin (1969).
- How the production of living educational theories can influence the education of social formations (Whitehead, 2004) for sustainable global wellbeing.
- The transformation of communities of practice (Wenger 1998) into communities of educational enquiry (Whitehead 1999) through dialogical interaction (Bakhtin 1981).

Methodology

Using an action-reflection approach to investigate how I can improve my work, I address and research the following questions, where '~' indicates the potential transformation of 'I' to 'we':

- What is my~our concern?
- Why am I~are we concerned?
- How do I~we gather data to show the situation as it is and as it unfolds?
- What can I~we do about it (what options are available)? What will I~we do about it (what action is planned)?
- How do I~we ensure that any conclusions I~we come to are reasonably fair and accurate?
- How do I~we account for my~our educational influences in learning?
- How do I~we modify my~our ideas and practices in the light of the evaluation?

I focus especially on explicating how I generate evidence from my data to strengthen the evidence base of my emergent knowledge claims, whose validity I test against my values as these emerge as my living standards of judgement.

Ethical considerations

A key element of my methodology will be to ensure that I will observe good ethical practice throughout. I will ensure that my proposals are approved by the University research ethics committees, prior to undertaking my research, and I will take care to protect the wellbeing of my research participants at all times. I will distribute ethics statements and secure permission from all stakeholders before including them in my research, and I will place copies of all letters of permission in my data archive and appendices. I will make progress and summative reports available to all stakeholders on request.

The potential significance of my research

As well as demonstrating the originality of my contribution to knowledge of my field, and the methodological rigour of my research, I indicate its potential significance, in relation to the learning of others and myself.

My own learning will be enhanced in terms of my growing capacity to reflect critically on and deconstruct my thinking, as I develop awareness of the normative assumptions of my *habitus* (Bourdieu 1990). I will seek to influence the learning of students and peers as I encourage them also to become aware of how they are persuaded to believe messages communicated through the culture about the creation of their identities (Foucault 1980). I will also seek to influence the learning of the social and cultural formations of which I am a part, in order to contribute to new ways of thinking and working.

My research plan
The anticipated schedule for my research is as follows.

2009–2010: Desk research to investigate current thinking around peer and group mentoring. Identification of research issue and question, engagement with issues of values, imagination of solution. Round 1 of data gathering. Interviews and focus groups with all participants to establish baseline data. Maintenance of reflective journal. Reading about substantive and methodological issues. Regular meetings with supervisor, study group and critical friends. Progress report 1. Informal validation meeting.

2010–2011: Continued desk research. Round 2 of data gathering as I implement proposed solutions. Focus on transforming data into evidence. Articulation of standards of judgement. Continuation of reflective journal, encourage participants to maintain reflective journals. Regular meetings with supervisor, study group and critical friends. Progress report 2. First formal validation meeting. Continued reading.

2011–2012: Evaluation of implemented solution. Generation of evidence from all data. Maintenance of reflective journal. Progress report 3, and plan for thesis. Regular meetings with supervisor, study group and critical friends. Second formal validation meeting. Continued reading.

2012–2013: Writing up of thesis. Regular meetings with supervisor, study group and critical friends. Submission of thesis and viva.

Reasons for wishing to undertake the research at the University of Limerick
I wish to undertake my research at the University of Limerick for a range of reasons. I already work here, and will regard my practice as my research field. The growing reputation of UL as a progressive educational institution is attractive, and the open-mindedness of its faculty is of importance as I embark on a programme of studies within a new scholarship form of enquiry. The University of Limerick has a strong reputation in the field of action research and new scholarship forms of enquiry. I wish my work to contribute to the growing knowledge base (see http://www.jeanmcniff.com/reports.html) that aims to improve the quality of educational experience for all through educational research.

Bibliography
The bibliography for this proposal is included in the main references list for the book.

Indicative bibliography
You could also include an indicative bibliography, which is a short list of books and papers that you intend to read, and that will inform your study.

SUMMARY

This chapter has offered advice about how to write a research proposal for a higher degree programme of studies. It has outlined what goes into a proposal and how a proposal will be judged. Two examples of proposals give ideas about how you can write a proposal that reflects your unique situation and your own creative ideas.

CHECKLIST OF REFLECTIVE QUESTIONS ?

Here is a checklist of reflective questions that will help you to focus on the essentials of writing a research proposal.

Have I produced a proposal that will guide the development of my project?

- Does it show that I have planned and designed my project thoughtfully, bearing logistical factors in mind?
- Does it show my capacity for catering for possible new developments?

Will my proposal enable readers and assessors to see that I will gather valid data in addressing research questions?

- Does it show how I hope to make specific claims to knowledge about how I have tried to improve my practice?
- Do I show my capacity for methodological rigour, by introducing issues of testing the validity of those claims, in relation to identified criteria and standards of judgement?

Does my proposal indicate my capacity for independent study?

- Does it show my capacity to achieve nominated academic criteria and produce scholarly writing?
- Is the proposal itself written in a scholarly manner, and does it obey all academic conventions, including ethical permissions?
- Do I show that I have read reasonably widely and to the point, and intend to read further?

If I intend to use multimedia, have I indicated how I will do so, and in what capacity I will use my visual narratives?

- Do the narratives demonstrate methodological rigour combined with creativity?
- Do I explain the potential originality, rigour and significance of these narratives?

Is the proposal written in a comprehensible and clear manner, showing that I intend to demonstrate my authenticity, sincerity, and the truthfulness of my claims to knowledge?

If you have done all these things, you have probably produced a proposal that will get through a research committee, and also impress them with the quality of the research you intend to undertake.

We now move to Chapter 6, which is about what goes into an undergraduate report.

Writing Reports for Initial Accreditation

This chapter is about writing reports at undergraduate level for first-time researchers studying on initial and foundation degrees, and on workplace-based programmes, many of which receive in-house or external certification. Both kinds of programme and their reports are virtually the same, so throughout the book we refer to them as undergraduate reports. A wide range of programmes is available, interest is growing, and employers are insisting on workforces gaining some kind of on-the-job training, with an evidence base such as professional portfolios. Reports therefore need to demonstrate quality by describing the actions taken to improve practice, and giving explanations for why and how this was achieved.

The chapter contains the following sections:

1. What are the criteria for an undergraduate action research report?
2. How do you achieve these criteria?
3. How is your work judged?
4. An example of an undergraduate report.
5. Summary.
6. Checklist of reflective questions.

WHAT ARE THE CRITERIA FOR AN UNDERGRADUATE ACTION RESEARCH REPORT?

The focus of action research at undergraduate level/in the workplace is to improve workplace-based learning in order to improve practice. The report communicates the processes involved by giving descriptions and explanations for the action undertaken. National and international qualifications frameworks, such as the Bologna Qualifications Framework, say that reports should demonstrate knowledge and understanding that builds on secondary education, and also demonstrate problem-solving capacities and learning skills for professional contexts.

In an undergraduate action research report you do the following.

• You make a claim to knowledge that contributes to knowledge of your field, such as engineering or health science; you explain the steps you took to test the validity of the knowledge claim.

- You demonstrate your capacity to undertake original research in an appropriate manner.
- You show that you understand your context: you know your organisation, and can give reasons for how and why it works.
- You describe and explain how you have improved your practice; if not, you explain why not.
- You engage with appropriate literatures.
- You write your report in an appropriate form.

Your report is a vehicle for your claim that you have learned something new through studying your practice, and for demonstrating the validity of your claim; you explain how you have tested your claim against your evidence, in relation to identified standards of judgement, and asked for the critical feedback of others. The emphasis is on action in the workplace, which now takes the form of research. You show reasonable engagement with the literature; the bibliography for a 5,000-word assignment would contain about 20 books, articles or other references. You explain the need for, and demonstrate, some (though not in-depth) reflexive or dialectical critique.

Your reader expects to see awareness of the following in your report:

1. content
2. form
3. communication.

Content of your report

Your report should show the following:

- A claim to knowledge, and demonstration of its validity.
- It is a story of educational action. You say what you have done (descriptions), and how and why you have done it (explanations); you reflect on the action research and your own learning. The focus is on improving practice through the realisation of values in action.
- Your 'I' is at the centre of the enquiry. Your research question takes the form, 'How do I improve what I am doing?'
- You understand your context: local micro-politics, wider cultural, social, historical and economic issues.
- You explain how you have improved your learning and action, and why it was successful, or not.
- You appreciate how current learning can contribute to new learning and actions.
- You complete at least one action reflection cycle; if not, you give reasons.
- You articulate the potential significance of your action research for the personal, social and economic wellbeing of yourself, your workplace community, and possibly also the wider community.
- You engage with appropriate literatures.

Form of the report

Your report takes the following form:

- It is well structured, and describes the action research steps taken. This demonstrates methodological rigour.

- It takes a narrative form. Your descriptions and explanations for action constitute your living theory of practice. You tell your reader: 'I have generated my living theory of practice, which is grounded in my values'.
- Your 'I' is the main actor, while including other 'I's' as research participants, observers and friends. This shows the live action of educational influence, and explains how it happens.
- The form of your story is cyclical. The following questions act as a framework; these questions can also stand as section headings for your report:

  o What was my concern? What was the research issue? What was the research question?
  o Why was I concerned? What values do I hold, and were they being realised in practice, or not? Why? Why not?
  o How do I show the situation as it was and as it improved? How do I gather data and generate evidence on an ongoing basis?
  o What action did I take? What kind of action?
  o How did I check that any conclusions I came to were reasonably fair and accurate? How did I get critical feedback on my provisional claims to knowledge?
  o What changes in my learning made me change my thinking and practice?
  o How did the end of one action reflection-cycle turn into the beginning of a new one?

- You strengthen the validity of your claims through engaging with critical feedback, and with the subject and methodology literatures.

Communicating the ideas

Good communication involves the following:

- Your form of representation (written or multimedia) explains the originality, rigour and significance of your work. You give reasons for choosing this kind of report. It can be a learning portfolio to show the formative and summative processes involved in learning. You can include video evidence in a written report.
- The form of text communicates the dynamic processes of exercising educational influence, the transformational nature of the enquiry, and its potential significance for future thinking and practices.
- You reflect critically on what you have written and how you have written it. You say what doing the research and writing the report has meant for you.
- Your report uses signposts and summaries to focus the reader's attention. You write in appropriate language. You avoid jargon and ambiguous terms.
- You use scholarly language and engage with the literature.

So, how do you achieve these criteria?

HOW DO YOU ACHIEVE THESE CRITERIA?

You can achieve these criteria by following the steps outlined on p. 90, and below. This enables you to tell the story of what you did and why you did it.

If you want your report to be really good, go further and analyse your descriptions and explanations. This means doing the following.

First, think aloud as you work through the action-reflection steps, and tell your reader what you are doing as you do it. Pick out points that are worth discussing, and problematise taken-for-granted issues. For example:

- I decided to take action. I understand the need for purposeful action in contexts of social change.
- I asked my critical friend to explain further. I needed to understand properly what they were getting at.
- I asked the manager why I could not use the photocopier. I am aware that controlling the use of resources can be a form of organisational power.

Second, speak to your reader. This sounds obvious, yet is often not well done in academic writing. Your reader needs to know why you are doing what you are doing. They do not just pick it up. Write for a reader, and walk with them through your text. Guide their reading by saying things like this:

- I now move to my next point about …
- Let me explain further the importance of this point …
- In summary, the key points are …

Here are some ideas about how you can do this. We present the section headings of a basic report (we do this in the next two chapters too), and give pointers about issues within each section, and how to explain them. These are only some ideas; there are many more. The more original ideas you have, and the clearer your explanations, the greater the chances of an excellent mark.

Section headings: analysing and explaining interesting issues in each section

Your first heading is usually your Introduction.

Introduction

Your Introduction gives your reader an overview of your report, and sets out the main findings. The report is a research account, so say what it was about, for example, learning to take educational action in your workplace. Give a brief analysis of your learning, for example: 'Through doing this research I understand more clearly the importance of collective learning for organisational development.' Say that the report is about yourself and your learning, so it is written in the first person. Your 'I' is the centre of the enquiry.

Sometimes people miss out these issues. They launch straight into the story, without explaining that this is a story, or what it is about, and its significance. Readers need an explanatory frame such as: 'My story explains how I am making an original claim to knowledge. This enquiry has significance for my workplace because I am showing how an individual's learning can influence processes of whole-organisational improvement.'

Share your thinking with your reader, especially about problematic issues. For example:

- I am writing this account to show how I engaged with the micro-politics of my organisation in order to nurture democratic practices. This meant first trying to influence the way people thought about themselves.
- Few people agreed with my giving responsibility to trainees, yet I was convinced that this was the only way to encourage full participation in the workplace. My report tells the story of the risks I took, and some of the learning that emerged through the process.

What is my concern? What issues do I want to investigate? What do I want to find out?

In this section you say what you wish to investigate, and you formulate your research question.

Asking the question 'What is my concern?' is the first step in your action enquiry. You are indicating that:

- You intend to take action for improvement.
- You are trying to understand processes of improvement.

Here are some further ideas about taking action for improvement.

Intending to take action for improvement

By asking, 'What is my concern?' you are saying you are not prepared to keep things as they are. You wish to improve them. This means understanding processes of 'improvement', as well as the idea of intent.

'Improvement' is a problematic concept. Sometimes texts speak about 'improving the situation', which can be misleading, because a 'situation' is not an object, like a bicycle. A situation is constituted of people interacting with one another. People cannot be 'improved' or 'changed' (they can be physically, but not for sustainable improvement). People change and improve themselves. Your job as an educator is to try to influence them to change themselves, in an educational way, i.e. encourage them to question normative assumptions and to take responsibility for their own thinking. By asking, 'What is my concern?' you are expressing your wish to become an agent, not a bystander, and showing your awareness of the relationship between intent and action.

Achieving the aim is seldom straightforward, however, because things do not usually move in a linear way. Traditional research works towards closure, one episode after another, assuming there are answers for everything. Real life is seldom like this. Human living is about people's struggles to create their own identities according to what they believe in. Action research resists closure, grounded in a commitment to new beginnings, where each new beginning contains its future possibilities. Realising beginnings is a generative transformational process, inspired by the energy of life itself.

The question, 'What is my concern?' signals a new beginning, and any answer will contain a new problematic, so the cycle starts again. There are no endings, only new beginnings.

Understanding processes of improvement

Improvement is too often understood as moving towards a perfect end state; the end state is seen as achievable, and the desire to do so as commendable. This is not the case for most people. We are curious; we want to know more, do more, and see whether the grass really is greener on the other side. We want to create our own ideas and lives. This involves turning 'now' into an imagined future 'now' and working systematically towards it. This brings new responsibilities. The present 'now' will not get better unless we take action. This is in our power. The responsibility of action researchers is to explain how and why they took action to transform the present into a better future.

Why am I concerned?

You now give reasons for your concern, and ask 'Why am I concerned?'

The question explains that you understand the situation in relation to the values you hold about what makes life worthwhile. Some people value love, warm relationships, productive work, kindness and compassion. Other people value cruelty, greed, self-importance and position power. Whatever we value becomes our values. It may be worth pausing here and thinking about what you value. When you write about this, you will speak about the values that give meaning to your personal and professional life.

In your report you could discuss how you nurture your own and other people's wellbeing. You could argue that caring relationships are important. The methodology for achieving them is critically reflective dialogue, where people come to know in their own way. Values that promote critical thinking for new learning are educational, other-oriented, so you could argue that any practices oriented towards people's wellbeing are grounded in educational values.

In this section, discuss whether you are living your values in your practice. People often experience themselves as living contradictions, when their values are denied in their practice (Whitehead 1989). They try to find ways to resolve the dissonance, by experimenting with new forms of action. These often involve engaging with issues of power and privilege that close down opportunities for some people while promoting the interests of others. Action research is always educational, and always political.

A main focus of workplace-based learning is to develop democratic and egalitarian practices, to encourage people to get involved in the organisation of the workplace, and enjoy their work. Therefore, as a manager, you would promote democratic practices; you would encourage others to take responsibility for their own self-care and learning.

To show how you are realising your values, you offer explanations, which turns everyday action into research action. You can say that you are taking research-based action.

Formulating a research question

At this point you need to formulate a research question. Action research questions often take the form 'How do I improve what I am doing?' By asking 'How do I ...?' you accept the responsibility for personal action. By asking about improvement, you accept responsibility for your personal practice. This is a form of accountability that turns practice into praxis, morally committed action undertaken with human wellbeing in mind.

How do I show the situation as it is and as it develops?

In this section you aim to show the situation as it is and as it develops. This involves monitoring the action, gathering data, and generating evidence from the data. These are at the heart of your research, and need rigorous attention. It also involves ensuring that you are acting ethically, by inviting participants to become involved, and issuing ethics statements and letters requesting permission to do the research (see p. 89).

To appreciate the need for data gathering, go back to basics and think about how the aim of all research is to generate new knowledge. Your research aim is to make a claim that you have generated new knowledge. Now think about how the aim of the action in action research is to improve practice through improving learning; the aim of the research is to explain how and why this has been done. This means improving how we think to inform how we act. Your claim is that you have learned (come to know) about your practice, which enables you to contribute to knowledge of your field.

However, if you are prepared to make a claim such as 'I have found new ways of improving my practice', you have to back up the claim with evidence, otherwise the claim is empty. Data refers to all the information you gather about a situation, whereas evidence is those pieces of data that relate directly to the research question and ultimately the claim; so your first step is to gather data, using a range of techniques, to show the situation as it is and as it unfolds. You can then sort, categorise and select pieces from your data to stand as evidence. This whole issue is key. If you do not engage with matters of data and evidence, your research could be rendered invalid.

Let's say you claim that you have enabled employees to speak for themselves. Your evidence would show employees speaking for themselves. However, it can be tricky to find evidence to show the validity of claims like these, because you cannot get concrete evidence of their thinking. The nearest you can get is their statements about their thinking. You would look through your data to find statements such as, 'I am seeing this problem in new ways since attending your seminar', or 'I understand better now since our conversation.'

Also, you cannot say that this is a matter of cause and effect. You have not 'caused' them to think like this. You have tried to exercise your influence in their thinking. This is not a case of transmitting what is in your head directly into your colleagues' heads, because they will mediate whatever you say through their capacity for original thinking. They will decide whether to accept what you say, provided, of course, that you do not manipulate them through coercion or devices of hidden control. You need to be honest with yourself, and not cover up a hidden agenda of control by saying you are acting in their interests. When your validation group looks at your research, they will judge whether you have been authentic in your dealings.

Your evidence is in those pieces of data that relate to your research question and knowledge claim. The question, 'How do I encourage others to think for themselves?' should contain a latent claim, 'I have encouraged others to think for themselves'. Your data will contain evidence that shows this. You select your evidence from data that show people thinking for themselves. These also stand as realisations of your values, so your values form the basis of how you make judgements; your values come to act as your standards of judgement. They have been generated through dynamic transformational processes, so the standards themselves are dynamic, capable of developing further into new practices and refined values systems.

You monitor your actions throughout your enquiry, and the actions of others. Better, you invite them to monitor themselves. You gather data to keep a record and track changes. This gives you a data trail that leads from research question to knowledge claim.

What did I do? What kind of action did I take?

In this section you say what you did about the situation, what kind of action you took, and what happened.

Remember that there are different kinds of action (see p. 11): everyday action, where you do mundane things; social action, in relation to the interests of others; and educational action, enabling others to create their own knowledge. Social and educational action are strategic, with political intent.

These different kinds of action are similar to those imagined by Hannah Arendt (1958), who speaks about labour, work and action. Labour involves everyday tasks, such as filling in forms and doing the end-of-day finances. Much administrative work is labour, though it can also be work. Work, for Arendt, lies in the production of durable artefacts, such as books, works of art and manufactured products, which are important for developing the culture. Action, which is the highest form of engagement, is political action, which signals people's intent to take control of and transform their lives for the better. It is accomplished by people talking with one another (acting discursively). Habermas (1976) calls this communicative action; it is the main form of action in action research, directed towards human wellbeing and sustainability.

Make clear in your report which kind of action you have taken, and offer reasons and purposes for doing so. Evaluate whether you are acting in the other's best interests, or your own, and whether you are communicating your intent honestly, or playing a game for which only you know the rules.

Risk in action

Richard Winter (1989) speaks about risk as central to action research. Committing to the present as the basis of an unknown future involves commitment to uncertainty and instability. Committing to a form of thinking (logic) that embraces the unknown is riskier than committing to one that sees the future as predicted, which is safe but premised on a false belief. The future cannot be known or predicted. The idea itself is a high-risk strategy, because we force our lives into the shape of an imagined future. Belief in a predictable future is the greatest risk of all to human sustainability.

How do I ensure that any conclusions I come to are reasonably fair and accurate?

In this section you explain the procedures you went through to ensure the validity of your claim to knowledge by putting it to the test of critical feedback. Demonstrating validity is the point on which most reports pass or fail. If a report does not address issues of validity, it may not pass.

Demonstrating the validity of your claim is not a single event but a process that goes back to your question, 'What is my concern?' Asking the question means you are willing to do something about an unsatisfactory situation. You show how the values that inspire your practice are being denied, perhaps because of oppositional forces that are grounded in values different from yours. This is the starting point for demonstrating the validity of the knowledge claim. You gather data and produce evidence to show your values in action, or perhaps being denied. The validity of the claim is in the quality of the evidence. The evidence you generate relates directly to the question and the claim. You show the creation of your evidence base, and how successfully (or not) you realise your values. Being honest about the existence of any disconfirming data and evidence is vital, to show you can act on critical feedback. The production of a robust evidence base continues through your research, and contains the voices of all your participants.

You then engage in validation processes (p. 134), where you submit your claim and your evidence base to the scrutiny of your critical friends and validation groups. You ask them to pay close attention to the quality of your evidence. You keep a record of the validation processes themselves, as part of your evidence base. When you write up the report, your reader expects to see a record of what happened at the validation meeting.

The use of multimedia can be especially powerful here. You can show the processes involved in the production of evidence, agreeing about its quality. The video-clip at http://www.youtube.com/watch?v=12tY-v7QiFg&feature= related shows a validation process in action from Chris Jones's (2008) enquiry 'How do I improve my practice as an inclusion officer working in a Children's Service?'

How do I modify my ideas and practice in light of my evaluation?

In this section you say how you have changed your practice for the better, in light of your reflection. You tell your reader how learning from your project is influencing new thinking and action. You have re-assessed your relationships in your workplace; you have initiated new practices during meetings. The end of this cycle of action-reflection is the beginning of a new one.

Comment on the significance of what you have learned and done, and how your research may have implications for future practices. Perhaps it has the potential to influence new policy debates, or contribute to the education of your organisation or professional association. Be bold in saying that what you have done is meaningful for other people.

We now turn to issues of assessing the quality of your report through judging the validity of your claim to knowledge.

HOW IS YOUR WORK JUDGED?

This section deals with issues of judging the validity of a claim to knowledge. This involves thinking about:

1. Criteria and standards of judgement.
2. A first validity check: living values in practice.
3. A second validity check: engaging with criteria of social validity.

Criteria and standards of judgement

Your report is judged in relation to several issues. The first is to do with whether you have fulfilled the academic criteria. These will include:

- Have you made a claim to knowledge of your field, and demonstrated its validity?
- Have you demonstrated your capacity to undertake an original piece of research in an appropriate manner?
- Have you shown that you understand contextual issues?
- Have you shown improvement in practice, and explained the processes of how it was achieved? If you have not shown improvement, have you explained why it did not happen?
- Have you engaged with the literatures?
- Have you written your report in an appropriate form?

You can also ask your assessors to judge the quality of your report and practice in terms of your own living standards of judgement. In judging the quality of your report you could say:

- I show that I have produced a coherent and comprehensible report.
- My report aims to speak to my reader's experience.

In judging the quality of your practice you could say:

- I show how I have realised my democratic values through the development of processes of collaborative enquiry.
- I claim that I have developed communities of practice which are grounded in my commitments to participative working.

In judging the quality of your research you could say:

- I show how I have conducted an action enquiry in a rigorous way.
- I explain how I have demonstrated the validity of my knowledge claims.

You also need to do two validity checks (see also p. 26). The first relates to how far you are living your values in your practice. The second relates to how far you demonstrate Habermas's criteria of social validity (comprehensibility, authenticity, truthfulness, appropriateness). The following explains further.

A first validity check: how far do you live your values in your practice?

Your claim is that you have contributed to improvement in your workplace. You have learned how to do things better, and have helped other people to do the same.

The improvements you speak about are to do with workplace-based learning, and influencing sustainable practices. These include democratic participation, consideration for the other, clear communication, nurturing of personal capacity and power. This can be demonstrated through: provision of staff rooms or quiet spaces; participation in professional learning programmes; and access to information such as the formation of newsletters and databases.

A second validity check: how far have you engaged with Habermas's criteria of social validity?

To fulfil Habermas's (1976) criteria of social validity (comprehensibility, authenticity, truthfulness, appropriateness), you talk about the following:

You can show that your practice is comprehensible

- You show how you act in a rational way, without prejudice, and with care and consideration for all.
- You give reasons and justifications for your actions.
- You explain that these are grounded in your values, and say what these are.

You can show that your practice is authentic

- You show how you have fulfilled your values over time.
- You show how you have reflected critically on what you have done.
- You show that you have acted sincerely and in the other's best interest. You show awareness of ethical issues and the need to safeguard participants' wellbeing.

You can show that your practice is truthful

- You include an evidence base. This is strengthened through rigorous gathering, analysis and interpretation of your data.
- You test the validity of the evidence against the critical feedback of others, in relation to your articulated standards of judgement.
- You show how you have subjected your accounts to the scrutiny of validation groups, and have made records of these meetings public.

You can show that your practice is appropriate to its context

- You show your understanding of contextual issues.
- You show your understanding of some of the cultural, historical, economic and political forces that have created the current situation.
- You show your commitment to transforming your existing situation into a better one.

Here is an example of a workplace-based/undergraduate report that shows all these processes in action. The example represents a progress report from the induction phase of a workplace programme, and the topic and style have been chosen as a reminder that you can do action research in any walk of life, including 'ordinary' aspects, and that it can be written in creative ways. The main thing is to produce a report that demonstrates originality, rigour and significance. You can find further examples of workplace based reports in our other books, such as: *Action Research for Teachers* (McNiff and Whitehead 2005); *All You Need to Know about Action Research* (McNiff and Whitehead 2006); and *Action Research: Living Theory* (Whitehead and McNiff 2006).

AN EXAMPLE OF AN UNDERGRADUATE REPORT

Example 6.1: A workplace-based action research report

Introduction

I work as a semi-professional golfing coach. This means that young men and women – mostly men – come to me for extra tuition, sometimes to learn the game from scratch, and sometimes to attend to some aspect of their game that has gone astray. This report is the story of one such young man, and my own story.

Jonah Biggs had been a brilliant player when he was a boy, but over his teenage years he had become self-conscious of his game, and self-consciousness is one of the biggest obstructions in playing a good game. Now, a highly competitive twenty-something business executive, he was looking to find his game again, for those important golf-course business meetings, I guess, so he came to me, in the hopes that I would find it for him. This I could not do, and I told him so, but he would have none of it, and just kept saying, 'Find my game. I want to get back to where I used to be'.

So I decided that we had to do this in a more systematic way, and, because I was now retiring, and so had enrolled for my first degree (something I had always wanted to do and which was possible now that I was getting some free time), I decided to use this situation as the field of study for my action enquiry module. A first task was to identify what my area of study would be, and here it was – how I could help Jonah Biggs find his game. So let me write this down, as an organised report.

What was my concern?

My concern was that Jonah wanted me to find his game for him, but I knew, from my long years as a golfer, that no one can find your game for you. You have to find it for yourself. You don't hit the ball, so much as feel it; you work with the field and the flag, just you and the club and the ball. There was no telling this to Jonah, though, although I tried to. He would just respond, 'You know what I have to do. You have years of experience. Tell me where I'm going wrong and what I have to do to put it right'.

I thought about this a lot, and after a lot of thinking I concluded that I needed to find a new way of helping Jonah to see himself differently, maybe not as a competitor, more as a player. So my question became, 'How do I help Jonah to find his own game?'

Why was I concerned?

Jonah was on the wrong track, as far as I could see, because he was seeing golf as an opportunity for furthering his ambition rather than a form of fulfilling personal experience. More, he wanted me to fix him and I could not do this. I know that each person has their own game in life. From my beginners' reading lists, I knew from Hannah

Arendt (1958) that the life of each person is their special contribution to the world, and from Paul Tillich (1973) that you have to engage fully with life if you are to understand your own experience. I knew from Michael Polanyi (1958) that you have to commit to your personal knowledge to live a productive life, which meant not relying too much on technical and procedural knowledge (Ryle 1949), which is precisely what Jonah was doing. He had grown to see golf as a matter of technique and had lost touch with his own feelings with the game. Golf is more than technique, as George Hibbard (2008) explains:

> In a word, there is a core concept, a motion, an action, a 'thing you do' at the very heart of swinging a club that must come FIRST in your approach to the game, without which following directions about grip, stance, posture, alignment, etc. is empty and sterile – and which provides the meaning behind those details. (http://www.perfectimpact.com/index.shtml, emphasis in original)

Jonah was not staying true to his own game, as far as I could see, and I felt that resolving the dilemma would involve finding a way of getting him back with his feelings, to find his spiritual connectedness with himself and his game.

How could I show the situation as it was and as it unfolded?

In his new position as rising business executive, Jonah had all the latest gadgetry – hand-held computer that he took with him around the course, mobile videophone – you name it, he had it. I found the technology distracting. It got between Jonah and the ball, and between Jonah and me. It interfered with the values of commitment that are needed for the game. So I told him so. 'Jonah', I said (and I wrote this down in my notes to keep a record back in the office in the club house), 'Jonah, I can't think straight when you talk with other people when we walk, or when you are concerned with the videophone rather than addressing the ball. Why don't you leave it all behind for a change – just to help me concentrate'. I had to keep saying this before he agreed, but he finally did; and at last it was just me, Jonah and the ball out there on the fairway. You could feel the difference immediately. You could focus on the clean air, the way the grass moved with the moving sun, the glinting light off the water. You could connect with the earth, and with yourself. Jonah seemed to start thinking about the feel of the club in his hand rather than the feel of the phone, and I believe he started to connect again with himself through his club. He said so on a few occasions. He said, 'I think I'm beginning to connect somewhere, but I'm not sure how.'

This connectedness was not consistent though. Jonah is after all an ambitious young man, and although he left his technology behind to please me, I knew he was fretting. So I decided that I had to compromise too, but in a way that would be in Jonah's best interests. So I said to him, 'Look, why don't we get one of the club caddies to bring along your camcorder and video your swing. Then you can watch yourself and see where you can improve'. He was delighted of course, so this is what we did. We got one of the caddies to come with us and video Jonah's swing, so that Jonah could later watch himself, with me, and critically analyse where he could improve his technique. We assured the caddy that we were not videoing him – just Jonah, and I even wrote down on a piece of clubhouse paper that I would keep the caddy out of the frame, just for the record (you can see my original note in Appendix 1 to this report). The return to technology seemed to work. It then became a matter of focusing on the technology intermittently within an overall strategy of learning how to focus on the ball. This of course meant that Jonah focused on himself and his connectedness with the ball and the field.

How do I check that any conclusions I come to are reasonably fair and accurate?

Jonah was of course delighted with his videotapes and took every opportunity to show them to his friends. He would take his camcorder, with its instant replay facility, and show the videos to anyone in the locker room who happened to be nearby. 'Look,' he would say excitedly, 'look at this one. See how I have improved my swing – don't you agree? Look at how my grip has changed there, and how I am standing differently on the tee'. Then a conversation would ensue, about how he was doing, and how he could change this bit, or that, and he would faithfully record the differences the next time round and continue to pester his friends for their critical feedback. And because Jonah is a likeable young chap, they indulged him, and he was pleased.

How do I explain my educational influences in learning?

I did not do what Jonah initially wanted me to do, which was to find his game, because he had his game already within himself. But I did help him to find it. As far as I could see, he had got lost in the trees for a while and needed a bit of guidance about how to find his way back onto the fairway. I walked the course with Jonah, chatting about this and that while he began to re-focus, noting all the while how he was learning to re-connect and beginning to see that technology has a place, even on a golf course, but it needs to be used with discipline. Jonah did a lot of growing that season, and I guess I grew with him, as I deepened my understandings of how important it is to help people to find their own way in golf, and in life.

How do I modify my practice and ideas in light of my evaluation?

I will be retiring soon, but will continue to play. Golf is the greatest game on earth within this larger game called life. I will continue to work with young golfers, but now informally, perhaps in my study group, and I will use my knowledge of the game to help me with my own studies, foreign territory that it is for me. I now have to focus on my learning, but I already know the greatest lesson of all, which is to stay true to my own knowledge. So I will find out what these great authors like Foucault and Butler have to say, and learn a bit from them. But I bet I could teach them a thing or two about golf.

(This example was inspired by watching *The Legend of Bagger Vance*, directed by Robert Redford and starring Will Smith, Matt Damon and Charlize Theron. If you haven't seen it, you have a treat in store.)

SUMMARY

This chapter has set out what goes into an undergraduate report and what it looks like. Undergraduate reports are similar in content and form to workplace-based reports. They show processes of improvement of learning in action. The chapter has set out the criteria for an undergraduate report, and explained how these can be achieved and how the report will be judged. An example is given to show the processes in action of improving learning for improving practice.

We now move on to considering what a masters dissertation looks like and how you write one.

7   *Writing a Masters Dissertation*

This chapter is about writing a masters dissertation. Masters (M level) work is becoming increasingly common, given the current intensified emphasis both in higher education and in the accreditation of workplace-based learning. Professions such as teaching are required to be all-masters professions (if this is not already the case, it soon will be); postgraduate certificate modular programmes must have a minimum number of M level modules; and most professions mandate some kind of continuing professional development for their members.

This chapter outlines the expectations of M level work, how these can be achieved, and how reports are judged. The ideas are organised as follows:

1. What are the criteria for an action research masters dissertation?
2. How do you achieve these criteria?
3. How is your work judged?
4. Summary.
5. Checklist of reflective questions.

WHAT ARE THE CRITERIA FOR AN ACTION RESEARCH MASTERS DISSERTATION?

An action research masters dissertation builds on work already undertaken at undergraduate level, so this includes the ideas in Chapter 5, with important additions. The expectation is still to make a claim to knowledge, but now with the additional criterion that the work demonstrates critical engagement.

Most higher education institutions stipulate the following criteria:

- The work makes a claim to knowledge.
- The work demonstrates critical engagement. Sometimes this is referred to as 'critical engagement with ideas in the literature', and sometimes not, which has implications for how the work is judged, as explained below.

Note: the claim to knowledge at M level need not be an original claim, whereas it must be at doctoral level. Masters dissertations that make original claims to knowledge, and articulate their potential significance, would receive additional credit.

Although many accrediting institutions stipulate critical engagement with the literatures, critical engagement comes in other forms too. It is, generally speaking, awareness of the need to problematise issues. At masters level it is not enough, as at undergraduate level, only to make claims and to test their methodological validity. Claims now have to be tested against other people's ideas, such as validation groups (as done at undergraduate level), and also the ideas of people in the literature, and analyses of contemporary debates, which gives conceptual frameworks for your study. You have to:

1. Demonstrate the methodological rigour of your research, as at undergraduate level.
2. Show that you have read widely and can engage critically with debates in the literature within your chosen field.
3. Develop your own conceptual frameworks, drawing on those literatures.

Critical engagement serves to strengthen the validity of a knowledge claim. The process gets more rigorous as the standards and levels get higher.

Because the emphasis is now on critical engagement and conceptual analysis, examiners would read your dissertation with these expectations:

- Do the writings make critical use of literature, professional experience and, where appropriate, knowledge from other sources, to inform the focus and methodology of the study or enquiry?
- Do the writings make appropriate critical use of the literature and, where appropriate, knowledge from other sources, in the development of the study or enquiry and its conclusions?
- Do the writings demonstrate an ability to identify and categorise issues, and to undertake an educational study or enquiry in an appropriately critical, original and balanced fashion?
- Do the writings demonstrate an ability to analyse, interpret and critique findings and arguments and, where appropriate, to apply these in a reflective manner to the improvement of educational practices?

(adapted from criteria for masters modules at the University of Bath)

Here is what you need to do to achieve these criteria.

HOW DO YOU ACHIEVE THESE CRITERIA?

At every stage of your enquiry you need to demonstrate critical engagement with your own thinking, which takes the form of:

1. reflexive critique, and possibly
2. dialectical critique
3. engaging with the thinking of others in the literatures.

Here is what these terms mean.

Reflexive critique

Reflexive critique means being aware of your thinking, how it manifests in your speech and actions (your discourses), and how it changes over time. Sometimes people speak unreflectively. They talk about a 'manned spacecraft' (sexist language), or 'these people' ('othering' language). Using appropriate forms of language is essential, because what we say can betray unspoken oppressive tendencies. Derrida (1997) says that we need to decentre ourselves in promoting participative discourses; Butler (1999) warns against assuming there is a 'norm' against which everyone is measured. Every person is unique, and cannot be compared with an imaginary norm. We need to take care not to slip into unreflective discourses.

Dialectical critique

Dialectical critique means being aware of the historical, political and cultural forces that have led to your present situation, including the way you think. Many people think in stable categories; for example that 'society' is an homogenised group of individual people. This is seldom the case. Inglis (2008), taking Ireland as an example, shows how a society can be understood as global flows of ideas, beliefs and knowledge that shape individuals' lives. These ideas are relevant for your action research because you position yourself as an acting agent who can influence the form and direction of local and global flows by expressing the values that give meaning to your life. This involves the dialectical critique of destabilising previously stable categories such as 'society', 'people', and even 'I'.

Engaging with the literatures

Show that you have read other people's ideas about your topic, and taken these into consideration.

The literatures you read enable you to develop the conceptual frameworks for your study. A conceptual framework is where you identify a concept or idea as a permeating theme. Your conceptual frameworks are grounded in your values. If gender inequality is an issue you decide to investigate, gender becomes an conceptual framework; similarly, issues about globalisation, the marginalisation of minority groups, or social justice. You can have several interlinked conceptual frameworks for your study, and you should explain the relationship between them. Read as widely as possible around these concepts. You do not need to write a chapter called 'Literature review', though you may if you wish, and some issues deserve a chapter of their own; for example, Máirín Glenn (2006) and Ray O'Neill (2008) write about different conceptions of technology. You are expected to show how you have drawn on the literatures to inform your thinking, incorporated the ideas of other thinkers within your own, and say whether and why you agree with them or not. You are also expected to say how your report will contribute to the literature.

Engaging with the literatures means engaging. Do not drop names: 'This point has been made elsewhere (Black 1993; Brown 1996; Greene 2000; White 2004) ...' and then scurry on to the next list of names (see Bassey 1999, cited on p. 60, about the need for thorough engagement). An experienced examiner will see whether you have read the works or picked them up elsewhere. Show your critical engagement by bringing the ideas into your debates. Say for example:

> I explain how I made social wellbeing a topic of interest in my organisation. Drawing on the work of Sen (1999) and Young (2000) I show how I helped employees develop their capacity for self-determination, and take control of their own self-development.

The idea of critical engagement is your capacity to engage critically with your own thinking, and ground your ideas in the literature, to incorporate others' ideas and see whether your ideas can hold their own.

Here are some suggestions about how you can demonstrate critical engagement at each stage of your action enquiry. Each section heading gives advice and examples from real-life masters dissertations and also doctoral theses where the researcher has developed ideas from their masters degree.

Section headings: demonstrating reflexive and dialectical critique and engaging with the literatures

Your first section heading is your Introduction.

Introduction

Here you outline your main themes and explain how you are generating your living theory of practice. Explain what you mean by your 'living theory of practice': this demonstrates reflexive critique through engaging with issues of theory generation. Show that you understand how living theory is different from propositional theory.

Your main themes are to do with epistemology and methodology, which involve values and logics, as well as your subject literatures. For example, if you are a business manager studying for an MBA, your literatures will be about management, leadership and organisational learning. You would choose texts such as: Senge (1990), about learning organisations; Wenger (1998), about communities of practice; and Wheatley (1994), about organisations as self-organising systems.

Link these subject areas with literatures about epistemology, research design and methodology: Schön (1983, 1995), about developing new institutional epistemologies; Polanyi (1958), about individuals' capacity for personal knowing; and Kuhn (1962), about revolutions in scientific enquiry. The main points in your Introduction are to make clear what your claim to knowledge is, how you arrived at it, and how you feel justified in making it; and how you locate your studies in epistemological and methodological debates within your subject areas.

You need not read every book on your subject. Sometimes, in traditional literature reviews, authors produce booklists, who wrote what and when. Your job is to show your engagement with relevant literatures, so choose about ten key texts to carry you through your studies, and another ten subsidiary texts. Engage thoroughly with these. You will not be penalised if you do not read more (it is different at doctoral level, where you are expected to read widely and eclectically). At masters level aim to show that you can engage with some key ideas thoughtfully and critically, and incorporate them within your own living theory of practice.

Here is an extract from the Introduction to Erica Holley's (1997) thesis 'How Do I as a Teacher-researcher Contribute to the Development of a Living Educational Theory through an Exploration of my Values in my Professional Practice?'. The whole thesis is at http://www.actionresearch.net/erica.shtml

> My thesis is a description and explanation of my life as a teacher/researcher in a comprehensive school in Swindon from 1990 to 1996. In writing it I have fulfilled a personal commitment to celebrate and explain my developing educational values, practices and knowledge. In submitting it for accreditation and legitimation to the Academy I am attempting to fulfil my professional commitment to the development of research-based professionalism in education.
>
> Those processes of thinking, acting and making sense of my work, the narration of those processes and the changes that have taken place in my actions and understanding show how knowledge can assume a living form because it is always being reformulated and reworked. In my writing I have kept these words by James Britton in mind:
>
> 'It is the continual reformulation of what we know in the light of what we perceive that matters: and the hardening of what we know into a formula that we apply ready made instead of reformulating – that is the danger. Thus, our most powerful ideas are relatively general, relatively unformulated starting points from which we constantly reformulate' (Britton, J. 1982). (Holley 1997)

We now move to the first step in your action enquiry.

What is my concern?

This first step involves saying what you wish to study. You identify your research issue, and formulate a research question of the kind, 'How do I improve my practice?' You explain how your question is grounded in your values, which you wish to realise in your practice. The focus of this section is to explain what the issue is and why it is worth investigating. This demonstrates reflexive critique because you show that you understand why you have decided to investigate the issue.

Regardless of your subject area, engage in a discussion of your values and your ontological perspectives. Bullough and Pinnegar say that, 'The consideration of one's own ontology, of one's being in and toward the world, should be a central feature of any discussion of the value of self-study research' (2004: 319). The literature about values is enormous, and informs other philosophical areas: how we understand the good (Grayling 2003), justice (Rawls 1971), and personal identity (Foucault 1990). Your study begins and is grounded in your values.

Your main values may be things like democracy, entitlement, care and concern for the other's wellbeing, justice in the workplace, and environmental health and wellbeing. Your research shows how you turn these abstract values into living practices. Explain that you will use these values as your living standards of judgement (Whitehead 2004) to test the validity of your claim to knowledge.

A useful starting point is Whitehead's (1989) idea of experiencing yourself as a living contradiction when your values are denied in your practice. You aim to find ways of lessening the ontological dissonance, so that your values are more fully realised. Like Polanyi (1958), you have decided to understand the world from your own point of view and make your claim responsibly and with universal intent.

Living values

Most of the literatures about values adopt a propositional stance, making statements about values, and analyse them as concepts. Rawls (1971) speaks about justice, and Midgley (1981) integrates rationality and spirituality. Machiavelli (1992) speaks about power and privilege; Worsthorne (2004) explains why democracy needs aristocracy. Each person has their own view of what a good society looks like, and each view is informed by values.

Writing about values in a propositional form keeps values as conceptual abstractions. Raz (2003) speaks conceptually about realising values in practice, so his rhetoric is denied by his actions. There is a deep contradiction in many propositional texts between their form of theory and the living practices narrated.

Aim to show how you live your values in your practice. When speaking about justice, give descriptions of what you have done: how you practise in a just way; explanations of why you wanted to live justly; and purposes, that justice is the basis of a good society. Show the integration of rhetoric and practice by showing how your explanations (your living theories of practice) are grounded within the practice. In the best action research masters accounts, the author comments reflexively on how their practice embodies their values and constitutes their living theories; these living theories inform new forms of practice and theory.

Here is an excerpt from the masters dissertation of Je Kan Adler-Collins to show the focus on values and power relations. You can access the whole dissertation from http://www.jackwhitehead.com/jekanma.pdf

In this dissertation I will engage with many issues which are fundamentally important to me as a teacher, and will underpin my research and practice, as I reflect on and hold in tension the question asked by Whitehead (1989), *How do I improve my practice?* These tensions are both internal and external, the internal being my engagement with my learning and values, the external being my engagement with the academy, the medical profession, their validation and ideas of knowledge.

As I evolve this dissertation in the form of my educative journey through a taught Masters programme in education over a time span of five years, I place the journey both of my self and the reader against the backdrop of radical changes and tensions that are present in education today. These changes are challenges represented by the advent of new forms of representing knowledge such as the Internet, DVD, Digital technology, CDs etc ...

Many of these tensions are external in nature but there is a very real internal tension within Academia as it struggles to engage and adapt, or not, as the case may be. The politics and power issues of education cannot be ignored by the modern day researcher as they have a direct bearing on the practitioner. All are touched by these issues and I believe that our participation in these issues and debates has never been more important as the very shape of education and knowledge is changing. (Adler-Collins 2000: 9–10)

The next step in your action enquiry deals with the reasons for your concerns, also linked with your values.

Why am I concerned?

Give reasons for your concerns. Perhaps your values of care for the environment are being denied in your workplace because of a lack of recycling policy (see Zimmerman et al. 2001 for issues about environmental care), or employees' voices are not heard because of a lack of democratic structures (see Habermas 2001 on the inclusion of the other in your workplace), or perhaps there is a lack of awareness of the need for inclusion of people from other countries (see Rutter 2006 on the treatment of refugee children in the UK).

Outline the contexts of your research. These would include the following.

Your personal context

If the issue is bullying in the workplace, draw on your own experience of being bullied (see Church 2004). If it is marginalisation of the other, explain the injustice of marginalising practices (see Cahill 2007). In the Introduction to her thesis, Caitríona McDonagh says:

I am a teacher and a researcher, and this thesis is my explanation for how I have generated my own living educational theory of learning to teach for social justice. I make this claim on two counts. First I can show how I have enabled children with specific learning disability (dyslexia), who were previously marginalised, to celebrate their value and come to see that they have a contribution to make in the public domain. 'Specific learning disability' (dyslexia) is a term used to categorise some children who have difficulties learning the 'three Rs' – reading, writing and arithmetic. (McDonagh 2007: 1)

Your locational context

Tell your reader where you are located, and where you work. Máirín Glenn works in a remote rural school, so she deliberately set up interactive projects for her children using ICT. She says:

> For many years, in my professional life as a primary school teacher, my work practices have incorporated the creation of learning opportunities, in the form of collaborative projects with other teachers and people outside the classroom, which usually include aspects of information and communication technology (see http://www.iol.ie/~bmullets for examples of some of these projects). (Glenn 2006)

Daisy Walsh contextualises her enquiry 'How do I improve my leadership as a team leader in Vocational Education in Further Education?' like this:

> This dissertation is concerned with showing how I, as a Programme Area Team Leader, for Vocational 'A' level, GNVQ and GCSE ICT, at a Further Education College in the United Kingdom, have focussed on my commitment as an educator and team leader in an action enquiry. (Walsh 2004)

Your policy context

What are the policies around your subject area? Seamus Lillis explains how he reconceptualised community development, from being about a consultant giving advice to communities, to how they should develop themselves. He contributes to policy debates about which form of knowledge grounds community development. He writes:

> The study reconceptualises the nature of rural community development by shifting perceptions of development as an externalised focus of study – which may be theorised about by detached 'outside' experts – to focusing on the insights from participants' experiences. These experiential insights facilitate a process where practitioners, other stakeholders and I can generate our own theories of how rural community development is advanced. (Lillis 2001)

Theoretical contexts

Engage with theoretical contexts. Mary Hartog (2004) explains how she supported the validation and legitimating of practitioners' knowledge within an institutional context of propositional knowledge. Hymer (2007) and Huxtable (2008) explain how current theory around gifted and talented education is premised on a theory that only some children are gifted and talented, which denies the idea that all children are gifted and talented in their own way.

Other contexts may be especially relevant. Shobbrook (1997) and Mead (2001), as police officers, engage with the literatures of policing; Charles (2007) and Majake (2008a) engage with intellectual and personal transformation within a context of previous colonisation; Punia (2004) reconceptualizes his practices as an educational provider; Adler-Collins (2007) develops a healing curriculum within a nursing setting. Each uses literatures to contextualise their subject matters, linking these with epistemological issues around whose knowledge is valid and who should be seen as a knower.

Hartog explains her influences as a higher education tutor. She writes:

> In this chapter I aim to provide a review and critique of *Women's Ways of Knowing: The Development of Self, Voice and Mind* (Belenky *et al.*, 1986). The ideas that this book have given rise to are especially relevant to this thesis. I first read this book within a few years of its initial publication. Its ideas had resonance for me and gave me the tools to describe my own learning history. Furthermore, I believe it shaped my emergent 'living theory' of what developmental education required, in turn, influencing the design of the [programme I teach], in respect of an approach to learning based on a community of learners. During my inquiry, I have read this book many times, developing with each reading a deeper understanding of the text, helping me clarify over time how I could improve my practice. (Hartog, 2004: 102)

We now move to the next step in your action enquiry, which is to do with monitoring practice, gathering data and generating evidence.

How do I show the situation as it is and as it develops?

This section involves explaining your methodology, especially around data gathering and evidence generation, and justifying your choice of methodology. You now explain how your report becomes a narrative enquiry (Clandinin 2007) and your story becomes your living educational theory (McNiff 2007).

Paint a picture of the situation you are in and as it is. Tell stories and vignettes from your practice. This is especially relevant to action enquiry, where data collection is the source of generating evidence to establish the validity of your knowledge claim. You show your capacity for rigorous research by gathering data that refer to your research question and research claims.

Data gathering and evidence generation can be problematic because there is often no direct link between the claim to knowledge and the evidence. The validity of the claim, 'I have toothache', cannot be tested against any empirical evidence, yet the claim is valid for the person with toothache. Ideas about objectivity now get destabilised, new ideas emerge, and the rigour of educational research takes on new meanings. Dadds and Hart (2001) explain how they supported teachers' innovative accounts that, while respecting the need for rigorous methodologies, also took risks, so that risk itself became the methodology, while incorporating traditional research methods. All the members of the group agreed that, at some point, they decided to break with conventional ways of reporting:

> Susan Hart had begun to wonder if, for the purposes of practitioners' own enquiries, formal knowledge of research methodology could, in some cases, be deskilling rather than enabling. … [She] had begun to feel uncomfortable about her own contribution to research

methods' courses; to wonder if it would be more helpful to strengthen practitioners' own creative and critical thinking powers and to affirm these as legitimate and for some purposes sufficient resources for research (Hart 1995). (Dadds and Hart 2001: 7)

It is now widely acknowledged that evidence in action research is not always the cut and dried body of empirical data that tends to be sought in traditional forms of research (see Law 2004; Mellor 1998).

This is where newer multimedia forms of representation can be valuable.

Multimedia forms of representation

While demonstrating methodological rigour, multimedia representations offer new perspectives about linking evidence with claims to knowledge. Videotapes of practice can show the living reality of claims to knowledge. If a researcher says, 'I have enabled people to enhance their self esteem', a videotape can show the living reality of the person speaking for themselves, and feeling good about it. Embodied evidence can be more adequately tested using multimedia forms of representation rather than simple linguistic statements.

For example, Farren and Whitehead have explained the processes involved in communicating educational influences in learning with visual narratives:

In this presentation, we intend to show, through the use of digital video, our understanding of ontological values of a web of betweenness and pedagogy of the unique (Farren, 2005) as they are lived in practice with students, in this case, practitioner-researchers on award bearing programmes. We both work with a sense of research-based professionalism in which we are seeking to improve our educational practice with our students in action research enquiries of the kind, 'How do I improve what I am doing?' The visual narratives, in the form of digital video clips, of our educational practice, include our engagement with practitioner-researchers as we seek to understand our educational influences in their learning so that we can influence the education of social formations [Whitehead 2004]. This relates to the idea of social formations as defined by Bourdieu (1990) and points to the way people organise their interactions according to a set of regulatory values that can take the form of rules. In studying our own educational practice, with the help of digital video, we hope to influence the education of social formations so that others will begin to question their underlying values, assumptions and epistemologies that inform their practice. The purpose of this paper is to communicate to a wider audience and network with other higher education educators through visual narratives of our work in higher education. There is a lack of research in how educators in higher education are influencing the education of their students. This area of research is one which we develop through this paper. (Farren and Whitehead 2006: 220)

Ethical considerations

A key aspect of demonstrating critical engagement is to show awareness of ethical considerations, which involves care for the wellbeing of the other. This means that you have to extend basic courtesies to all participants, such as inviting them to be involved, promising confidentiality as appropriate, and ensuring them of your good faith at all times. You would include letters requesting and granting permission in your appendices, and you would indicate throughout that you had acted properly and professionally. In your report you would write a section outlining how you ensured ethical conduct, and you would demonstrate throughout how you did so.

We now turn to issues of taking action to address the identified concerns.

What can I do? What will I do?

You have now decided to take action, so say which kind of action you took. You can draw on literatures to do with taking social action, such as social theory, social choice theory, rational actor theory and critical activity theory. Do not be intimidated by the titles. Think about how you can incorporate these into your writing. Here is a brief summary of what they involve.

- **Social theory**: This is a large body of work ranging across many disciplines, including sociology, history, geography, literature and economics. It provides the theoretical frameworks through which social structures and phenomena may be analysed and explained.
- **Social choice theory**: This is also a wide-ranging body of work, which draws on the literatures of social, economic and political theory, and focuses on how individuals and groups make choices about their future lives while recognising that they are in a social context with established rules and norms.
- **Rational actor theory**: Also known as rational choice theory, rational actor theory is a broad framework used to analyse and explain social, political and economic behaviour, assuming that individuals and collectives make informed choices within their social contexts.
- **Critical activity theory**: Critical activity (or action) theory provides theoretical frameworks for how people can take critical action within their own contexts.

You can add to these categories: critical feminist theory, symbolic interactionism, environmental theory, theories of justice and entitlement. Select those that appeal directly to you and your topic. Sometimes action researchers go outside conventional scholarly literatures and draw on cultural studies, chaos and complexity theory, spirituality, personal consciousness, folklore and fairy tales. Do whatever is right for you. Spiro (2008), for example, draws on her experiences as a writer of fiction and poetry. Aim to produce a report that shows your originality as you make sense of your own experience, while including the insights of other key thinkers. Many universities now provide access to e-journals and journals such as *Educational Action Research*, *Action Research* and *Reflective Practice*. The e-journal *Action Research Expeditions* also offers multimedia accounts as well as more conventional action research studies. Always try to include some contemporary references as well as key texts from the past to emphasise where possible the significance and topicality of your research enquiry.

The following extract from Beatrice Egües de Grandi's masters dissertation shows how ideas from key texts from the past are used to emphasise the significance of the enquiry, rather than from recent texts.

> Educational technology's focus on the learning of the use of skills in my area, those of the historian, has moved the narrow understanding of knowledge away from the mere body of facts to that of problem solving, to find by extrapolation, different solutions to new problems (Dewey, 1916 in Kelly, 1989). Historical knowledge highlights the role of man [*sic*] as the artificer of society. As such, knowledge must necessarily evolve and its incorporation by the students is done through a process of using it to create surrogate experiences of real events.
>
> Jerome Bruner's scaffolding has been refined (Pithers and Soden, 2000: 244) by the introduction of the Socratic method of questions and answers to consider other arguments with the goal of developing openmindedness. Presenting questions of 'how' and 'why' aiming at diversification, I intend to ease the learner's zone of proximal development by taking on the role of tutor to the student's role of apprentice (Vigotsky, 1978 in Pithers and Soden, 2000: 245). This student-centered/learning oriented mode (Kember, 1997 in Pithers and Soden, 2000: 247) places the teacher beside the student to think together by means of discussion and dialogue (Bailin et al., 1999: 289) (Grandi 2004: 22)

The next step in your action enquiry deals with demonstrating the validity of your knowledge claim.

How do I show that any conclusions I come to are reasonably fair and accurate?

You now focus on demonstrating the validity of your claims to knowledge, and testing them against critical feedback. This is one of the most problematic areas in the literature, because different writers have different ideas about what validity means, and what it takes to establish validity.

Some traditional writers say that the validity of a claim can be established when the research demonstrates replicability and transferability of findings. Slavin (2002) says that quality research may be tested through repeat trials that show how findings can be applied to other contexts. However, action research is not about applying other people's theories to your practice but about generating your own living theory of practice from within the practice. It is then a matter of subjecting knowledge claims to the scrutiny of other people, to see whether they stand the test of stringent critique.

As explained earlier on p. 26 there are two kinds of validity for knowledge claims: personal validity and social validity. However, these ideas can become problematic when related to the literatures, as follows.

Personal validity

Think again about your values. They are the grounds for the research. The denial of your values is often the incentive to start your research programme. The truthfulness of your claims can be established by checking how closely you are living in relation to your values, as demonstrated by your evidence base. You need to feel passionate about these values, to commit to your own knowledge (Polanyi 1958). If your claim 'feels' right, it probably is – but you may be mistaken, which is why you need to subject the claim to procedures of social validity (see below).

The literatures you draw on about the values you feel passionate about are the ones that form your conceptual frameworks. Polanyi (1958), Fromm (1978), Buber (1970) and Senge (1990) speak about ontological values. Feyerabend (1975) and MacIntyre (1981) speak about epistemological values. Said (1991) and Chomsky (1991) focus on socio-political values. Arendt (1958) and Kristeva (1986) speak about values around human worth. Sen (1999) speaks around human capability for social and economic development. The point is to locate your claims within your values base, so you cite authors who write about those values.

Social validity

The key author here is Habermas (1976). He explains how agreement about a knowledge claim can be reached through rational debate leading to inter-subjective agreement. People agree certain ground rules for their thinking and actions. Habermas maintains that the four criteria of comprehensibility, authenticity, sincerity and appropriateness are the key principles by which consensus may be achieved (see p. 116).

Habermas's work is globally influential, yet has come in for critique (for example Crossley and Roberts 2004). A problematic area is whether it is desirable to reach substantive consensus, i.e. that everyone agrees on subject matters. Consensus is often impossible in conversations about contested rights claims. Different governments lay claim to the same territory; separated parents lay claim to children and family goods. There are no 'rights' and 'wrongs', more a case of competing rights. Action researchers always see human relationships as fluid and problematic. However, while we may not agree about substantive issues, we do need to agree about procedural issues if we are to reach a point where we can talk reasonably.

Example 7.1

One of the clearest illustrations of the influences of a validation group in strengthening the validity of a research report and in assisting the researcher to improve practice has been given by Martin Forrest (1983) in his MEd Dissertation on the teacher as researcher. In his dissertation Forrest examines his own effectiveness as an in-service tutor in helping primary school teachers to improve the quality of pupils' learning about the use of historical artefacts. In the first validation meeting Forrest asked the group to include responses to the questions:

1. How can we know that an improvement has taken place in the school classroom? What criteria do we use to judge whether an innovation has led to an improvement in the quality of learning?

2. In the context of my work as an inset tutor, how effective am I in my role as a dis-
    seminator and supporter of innovation? What evidence is there to support my claim
    to be helping teachers to improve the quality of their children's learning?

Following his presentation of his first report Forrest was asked to strengthen the data
in relation to his claim that he was being effective in helping the teachers to improve
their pupils' learning. The validation group needed to see more compelling evidence
that Forrest had helped teachers to improve the quality of their children's learning.
Several months later Forrest returned to the validation group with evidence, that
included video-tapes, showing that a teacher did not believe that her pupils were
capable of certain kinds of thinking. Having been shown a video of a class of similar
aged children actually doing what she didn't believe to be possible with her pupils,
the teacher tried out ideas and artefacts that Forrest supplied, and found that her
pupils were capable of forms of thinking that she initially had not thought to be possible. The evidence provided by Forrest convinced the validation group that he had
sufficient evidence to justify his claims. (For Forrest's account of the validation group
see http://www.jackwhitehead.com/jack/cycle3.pdf)

The next step in your action enquiry is to show how your learning is helping
to improve your practice, and the significance of this relationship.

How do I modify my ideas and actions in light of my evaluation?

You now speak about how you are changing ideas and practices in light of your
evaluations. Outline what new directions your practices and ideas will take in
light of your evaluation. Especially explain what the significance of your research
is for your own continuing education, for others' education, and for the education of the social formation in which you are located, such as engineering or
health sciences. Show how you have given new meaning to your life through
your enquiry. Say that you are able to comment critically on the relationships
between theory and practice, and are generating your living theory of practice,
to inform new kinds of theory and practice. Draw on critical transformational
theories of social change (Foucault 2001), and critical transformational theories
of the epistemological change in which personal and social change is rooted
(Rayner 2008, Whitehead 2008c).

   You may also outline the potential implications of your research, and how
it can contribute to new policy debates in your field and make important contributions to the literatures.

   For example, Whitehead has contributed to the literatures on the nature of
educational knowledge through his work on living educational theory. In a
recent paper (Whitehead 2008b), he explains the implications of his research
for policies on representation in international refereed journals and for an
incusional epistemology.

   The third epistemology I use is that of inclusionality. This is grounded in a relationally
   dynamic awareness of space and boundaries as connective, reflexive and co-creative

(Rayner, 2004: 1). I want to be clear that what I am meaning by increasing inclusionality in educational research is bringing the living logic of inclusionality with its living standards of judgment into the academy.

For me, inclusionality in educational research is distinguished by flows of life-affirming energy and a gaze of recognition of the other. These are omitted from representations of educational phenomena on pages of written text, such as I am producing here. These are the usual forms of representation in the established and renowned international refereed journals of education. The radical suggestion I am making here is that the usual forms of representation in such journals are masking or omitting the life-affirming energy that distinguishes what should count as educational knowledge, educational theory and educational research. I am stressing a difference between education research and educational research. I see education research as research being conducted in educational settings by researchers in the philosophy, sociology, psychology, history, economics, leadership and management of education. I see educational research as research that is focused on information gathering and educational theory generation and testing for explaining educational influences in learning. (Whitehead, J. 2008b: 16–17)

This now brings us to how your work is judged.

HOW IS YOUR WORK JUDGED?

There is no 'one way' of making judgements about the validity of research reports, especially within new scholarship forms, which include action research. Yet it is vital that the community of scholars, including your assessors, should see that your research is methodologically and epistemologically rigorous, to maintain its credibility and integrity. This means developing new forms of criteria and new standards of judgement by which the quality of the research may be judged and agreed. We are suggesting a shift from criterion-based assessment to standards-based assessment (Spiro 2008), bearing in mind that the terms 'criteria' and 'standards' are themselves frequently confused and are open to (mis)interpretation.

Criteria-based and standards-based assessment

A criterion is an indicator or marker by which a thing may be judged or decided. Criteria are set in advance and are specific to the thing in question. On p. 30 we said that hotels would be judged in terms of certain criteria – cleanliness, service, degree of comfort. You would decide to buy a coat in terms of certain criteria – e.g. fit, colour and cost.

Within the identified criteria, you would think of levels and standards. The criteria for a three-star and a five-star hotel would be the same, but their quality would be judged by different standards: the degree of cleanliness, the quality of the service. You would judge the coat in terms of whether it fitted perfectly or moderately, whether the colour was just right or near enough. The standards you bring to your judgements are based in your values; they are value-judgements. You judge the quality of the thing in terms of how commensurable it is with your values. You choose the hotel that most adequately meets your values of cleanliness and comfort; you purchase the coat that fits best or meets your colour requirements. Standards are part of evaluation procedures; you evaluate the quality of something, and this is done in hindsight, from the experience of the thing in question.

The same principles apply to making judgements about the quality of your research report. Reports are judged at all levels by more or less the same criteria (claim to knowledge, demonstrating the validity of the claim, and so on), which are set in advance. The work is judged (evaluated) in relation to how adequately the criteria are met, and in relation to the reader's standards and value-judgements of what counts in quality practice, research and writing.

This raises issues about new approaches to assessing academic work. In earlier times, there was little room for manoeuvre, because reports were judged mainly in terms of stated academic criteria. These criteria tended to be objectivist, couched in behaviourist terms. The work was judged good quality if the writer showed that they could carry out a piece of research according to standardised procedures – writing literature reviews, demonstrating methodological rigour, testing findings according to established (usually statistical) procedures. The validity of the work was demonstrated in terms of whether the findings could be generalised to and replicated in other like situations. The standards were linked to these criteria. The standards tended to be behaviouristic, and were grounded in conformity with traditional forms.

Action research focuses on values-based assessment. As well as addressing established criteria, new scholarship forms of enquiry also emphasise that practices are grounded in emancipatory and inclusional values, to be assessed in terms of whether those values are realised as emancipatory and inclusional practices. These values are different from those underpinning traditional forms of research to do with conformity and closure. The standards of judgement for action enquiries are about the realisation of humanitarian values, openness to dynamic transformational forms of logic, practice, research and writing.

You need to show awareness of these issues. At masters level it is sufficient to demonstrate awareness, while at doctoral level you need to engage critically with analyses of the issues. In your masters dissertation your reader would expect you to:

- Explain that you are judging the quality of your work according to your identified standards of judgement, and how far you can show the realisation of your values, in relation to: (1) the quality of your workplace-based practice; (2) the quality of your research; and (3) the quality of your text.
- Identify and articulate the standards you have used to judge the quality of these aspects, for example:

- o 'A main standard of practice is my duty of care to others; my dissertation shows how I live my value of a duty of care to others.'
- o 'A main standard of research is my capacity for demonstrating methodological rigour; my dissertation shows how I have addressed issues of methodological rigour.'
- o 'A main standard of writing is my ability to reflect critically on what I have written.'

The works cited in this chapter show how this can be done.

- Invite your reader to engage with you, and explain how your values emerge through your practice as living standards, which enable you and your reader to appreciate how you can make judgements on its quality.

These ideas are developed further in Chapter 8.

SUMMARY

This chapter has set out what goes into a masters dissertation, and how success can be achieved. A distinctive feature of masters level work is the demonstration of critical engagement, especially in terms of reflexive critique, dialectical critique, and critical engagement with the literatures. Drawing on successfully completed masters dissertations and doctoral theses the chapter gives advice about how these aspects may be woven into every step in an action enquiry, and how a dissertation will be judged in relation to these criteria.

CHECKLIST OF REFLECTIVE QUESTIONS ?

Here is a checklist of reflective questions.

Have I fulfilled all the nominated assessment criteria for my dissertation?

- Have I explained how I attempted to improve my practice in my workplace?
- Have I produced a strong evidence base to show how I ground my knowledge claims?
- Have I tested the validity of these knowledge claims in relation to identified standards of judgement? Do I show how I go through rigorous validation procedures?

Do I demonstrate critical engagement in terms of reflexive critique and dialectical critique?

- Do I problematise my thinking, and explain how I have come to question my own normative assumptions, and those of others? Do I explain the processes involved?
- Do I show understanding of how external and internal forces bear on my thinking, and that I take these into consideration in making my knowledge claims?
- Do I demonstrate ethical practice throughout?

(Cont'd)

Have I engaged with the literatures in a critical manner?

- Do I show how I incorporate debates in the literature into my own understanding, and am able to contribute to these debates?
- Do I communicate my awareness of the significance of doing so?

If you have demonstrated all these aspects in your dissertation, you can be reasonably sure that you have produced a dissertation that your examiners will enjoy and learn from.

We now move to similar issues, in relation to doctoral level work.

8 Writing a Doctoral Thesis

A doctoral thesis is as high as it gets in terms of academic accreditation. Writing one therefore takes a lot of hard work, reading and time. You must be hungry for a doctorate to study for one, and in love with your topic, because it is going to take over your life for a while. It is worthwhile, however, because everyone knows that 'Dr' in front of your name is the sign that you have earned it.

Achieving your doctorate means that you have to fulfil every criterion mentioned in this book, in relation to: (1) your practice in your workplace; (2) the quality of research reported; and (3) the form of writing of your text. The quality of the thesis must also be as good as it gets. There is little leniency for errors or omissions. The standard is high, and must not be compromised.

This chapter explains how you can achieve the quality expected at doctoral level. The ideas are organised as follows:

1. What are the criteria for a doctoral thesis?
2. How do you achieve the criteria?
3. How is the work judged?
4. Summary.
5. Checklist of reflective questions.

WHAT ARE THE CRITERIA FOR A DOCTORAL THESIS?

The criteria for a doctoral thesis are much the same for a PhD, EdD, DProf or DBA. A doctorate is a doctorate, whatever its label.

Although there may be individual differences, most universities expect that the work fulfils all the criteria set out on p. 27.

At doctoral level, readers are looking specifically for:

- Originality (of claim and contribution to knowledge).
- Critical engagement: with your own learning (reflexive critique); with contextual issues (dialectical critique); and with appropriate literatures.
- A text of outstanding technical excellence and scholarship that contains material worthy of peer-reviewed publication (this criterion is explored in further in Chapters 9 and 10).

So, as well as demonstrating critical engagement, as at masters level, a key issue is now demonstrating originality. Let's consider what this involves.

First, let's look again at the differences between undergraduate, masters and doctoral levels, to see how the levels of theoretical analysis develop.

Differences between undergraduate, masters and doctoral levels

Undergraduate level

At undergraduate level you focus on what you did to improve things in your workplace. You offer descriptions of what you did, explanations for why you did it, and what you hoped to achieve. You claim that you have improved your practice, say how its quality should be judged, and how you have achieved it. If your practice did not improve you say why. You explain why you chose action research and what was involved. You comment on the significance of your learning for new ideas and practices.

- To illustrate, take the analogy of working in a helicopter factory. You try to improve any unsatisfactory elements, in order to build good helicopters. You write a report to say what you did and how and why you did it.

Masters level

At masters level you offer a more in-depth analysis and explanation for why you did or did not achieve the quality of practice you wanted. You focus on theorising (explaining) your practice: this involved interrogating your ideas and values. You explain how you have tested your thinking against the ideas of real people and those in the literature. Your dissertation offers a critical explanation for what you are doing in your workplace. You explain your conceptual frameworks, and comment on the significance and possible implications of your action research for the learning of yourself and others.

- In your helicopter factory, you analyse what you are doing in terms of your own theory of building helicopters. This may involve learning how to work better with others. You engage with the literatures of helicopter building and organisational practices, to deepen your understanding.

Doctoral level

At doctoral level you incorporate all the elements of undergraduate and masters levels within your refined capacity to make judgements about them. You comment critically on the process of coming to this knowledge. You make your original claim to knowledge and explain in what way it is original and what its significance might be for your own education, for the education of others, and for the education of social and cultural formations. Your thesis demonstrates your capacity for meta-reflection, an analysis and explanation for your critical capacity.

- You get into the helicopter and fly over the factory, offering critical theoretical analyses of what you have done, the significance of your research, and its potential to inform other helicopter factories and workplace practices in general.

Ideas about originality and critical engagement

Now let's return to ideas about originality and critical engagement.

Originality

Originality is a defining feature of doctoral work, and can take a range of forms. Drawing on Phillips and Pugh (2000), Murray sets out a range of definitions, including:

- You say something no one has said before. …
- You synthesize things that have not been put together before. …
- You look at topics that people in your discipline have not looked at.
- You test existing knowledge in an original way. …
- You continue an original piece of work.

(Murray 2002: 52)

The idea is that something is being done for the first time. In action research, the 'something' is this:

- You know how and why you have improved your practice.
- In doing so, you have generated your living theory of practice.

Critical engagement

Action research emerged from earlier theoretical traditions, including critical theory. The aim of critical theory was to critique normative assumptions, including your own, to improve thinking and action within a particular situation.

A first step in an action enquiry is therefore to problematise anything that is taken for granted, within discourses, practices and ideas. You challenge normative assumptions in your creatively original way, beginning with your own normative assumptions. Here is how you can do so.

HOW DO YOU ACHIEVE THE CRITERIA?

To achieve the criteria you show the originality of your living theory of practice by explaining what was involved in generating it, and its significance for knowledge of your field. You say how your capacity for critical engagement led to this original contribution to knowledge.

Here are some ideas. Again we look at the steps in an action enquiry, and explain how you can demonstrate originality and critical engagement within each step.

Section headings: demonstrating originality of mind and critical judgement

Title and abstract

This is where you state specifically that your thesis demonstrates originality, criticality, rigour and significance.

The first things your reader encounters are your title and abstract. Both should communicate the essence of the research. Your abstract is a summary of the key features of your thesis, including your claims to knowledge. The claims made in the abstract should be fulfilled in the thesis. The abstract should make clear what the original contribution to knowledge is, and the context in which the research was carried out. Leave writing the abstract till last, to make sure that you cover everything you have written about. Most abstracts are 250–400 words, so this means focusing on what people really need to know.

Introduction

In your Introduction say that you are making an original contribution to knowledge of your field through investigating and improving your practice. Define your field, such as horticulture or retail, and say what your original contribution is and why it is important.

Your original contribution is your claim to know your practice. You know what you are doing in your work (epistemological issues), and how you have come to know this (methodological issues). You know what you do (practical issues), and your reasons and purposes (ontological and socio-political issues). You know how you have tried to live your values in your practice. You know why you practise as you do; this is your epistemology of practice. You have created this knowledge, which makes it original by definition. Explain the significance of this knowledge for your field. Comment on your capacity for reflective explanation and theoretical analysis, a kind of meta-cognition, where you analyse your capacity to analyse, and explain your capacity to explain.

This ability to stand outside and comment on the quality of your research, and your text, is essential, and demonstrates your capacity for reflexive critique (awareness of the transformation of your thinking) and dialectical critique (awareness of the influences acting on you). Also comment on your capacity for agency in influencing other people's thinking.

Explain how you organise your text so that it stands as your living educational theory (McNiff 2007), and the importance of adopting a narrative form. Outline your methodology, and explain how it is communicated through the form of the text. Make sure that your introduction is directly related to your abstract. Look at the examples below to see how researchers set out the ideas in their abstracts. These are expanded in their introductions.

Jane Spiro (2008) writes in her abstract:

How I have Arrived at a Notion of Knowledge Transformation, through understanding the Story of Myself as Creative Writer, Creative Educator, Creative Manager, and Educational Researcher

Abstract

My aim in this thesis is to tell the story/stories of how I arrived at a living theory of creativity which I shall call 'knowledge transformation'. I explore this theory through 'story' as a methodology that connects both the creative writer and action researcher, and raises questions about self, reflective process and voice that are central to my enquiry. In telling these stories, I ask the question: what does it mean to be creative, as a writer, an educator and a manager? Is the nature of creativity transferable across each of these roles? How has this knowledge improved my practice as an educator? My examination leads to a theory of learning called 'knowledge transformation', which suggests that deep learning leads to change of both the learner and what is learnt.

My premise is that 'knowledge transformation' involves the capacity to respond to challenge, self and other, and is central to the notion of creativity. I consider how far this capacity can be transferable, teachable and measurable in educational contexts, arriving at a notion of 'scaffolded creativity' which is demonstrated through practice in the higher academy.

My journey towards and with this theory draws on my experience of four personae, the creative writer in and outside the academy, and the educator, team leader, and researcher within it; and explores the strategies and issues raised by bringing these roles and intelligences together. This theory of 'knowledge transformation' represents an aspirational contribution to our understanding of what it means to be 'creative' . It explores how educational objectives can lead to deep learning and positive change. It also explores how values can be clarified in the course of their emergence and formed into living standards of judgment.

Marian Naidoo (2006) writes:

I Am Because We Are (a Never Ending Story). The Emergence of a Living Theory of Inclusional and Responsive Practice

Abstract

I believe that this original account of my emerging practice demonstrates how I have been able to turn my ontological commitment to a passion for compassion into a living epistemological standard of judgement by which my inclusional and responsive practice may be held accountable.

I am a story teller and the focus of this narrative is on my learning and the development of my living educational theory as I have engaged with others in a creative and critical practice over a sustained period of time. This narrative self-study demonstrates how I have encouraged people to work creatively and critically in order to improve the way we relate and communicate in a multi-professional and multi-agency healthcare setting in order to improve both the quality of care provided and the well being of the system.

In telling the story of the unique development of my inclusional and responsive practice I will show how I have been influenced by the work of theatre practitioners such as

Augusto Boal, educational theorists such as Paulo Freire and drawn on, incorporated and developed ideas from complexity theory and living theory action research. I will also describe how my engagement with the thinking of others has enabled my own practice to develop and from that to develop a living, inclusional and responsive theory of my practice. Through this research and the writing of this thesis, I now also understand that my ontological commitment to a passion for compassion has its roots in significant events in my past.

We now move to the first step in your action enquiry.

What is my concern?

In this section you identify your area of concern, and formulate a research question. Identifying the area for research is not always straightforward, and more than problem solving, as some literatures say, though this can be the case. The problem may be poor organisational relationships, or lack of access to goods and entitlements, and can give rise to research questions such as, 'How can I enable people to develop good relationships?' or 'What do I need to do to ensure access and opportunities?'

While it can be about problem solving, a doctoral programme is more about problematising, interrogating assumptions and making the familiar strange. The question, 'How can I enable people to develop good relationships?' involves deeper questions, such as 'How do I understand the "good" in "good relationships"?'; and 'What do I need to do to ensure equitable access and opportunities?' could generate, 'Why should all participants have equal access? Why do they not have equal access?' This means analysing your own preconceptions, as well as other people's. Change begins with changing yourself.

You also need to confront problematics such as these:

- What is it possible to achieve and what not?
- Is it possible to find a solution to an identified problem? Will the new situation be sustainable?
- What may be the possible benefits and losses?

What is it possible to achieve and what not?

Knowing what it is possible to achieve involves political wisdom. Sometimes people identify an impossible issue such as, 'How do I change the violence in my neighbourhood?' or 'How do we change organisational management practices?' These issues are probably outside your range. You can, however, influence people at local level, and long-term sustainable change has been effected through the power of one determined individual who succeeded in spite of overwhelming odds (Adler-Collins 2007; Whitehead 1993, 2008a). Systemic transformation means first changing yourself, as part of the system you are in.

Is it possible to find a solution to an identified problem? Will the new situation be sustainable?

This involves problematising the idea of 'problem'. Many people believe that problems can and should be solved, which is not necessarily so. Sometimes problems are irresolvable, and sometimes you have to walk away. Learning to cope can offer creative spaces to find new ways of acting. Imposed solutions are seldom sustainable, because sustainable solutions come from the people involved.

What may be the possible benefits and losses for your context?

Sometimes a 'solution' may generate new problems. Enabling people to challenge means that they may challenge you. They may also get silenced if their voices are not welcomed. Exercising critique can be risky, yet it is the foundation of sustainable societies. Said says:

> I take criticism so seriously that, even in the very midst of a battle in which one is unmistakably on one side against another, there should be criticism, because there must be critical consciousness if these are to be issues, problems, values, even lives to be fought for. (Said 1991: 28)

In this section you formulate your research question, which can also be problematic.

Formulating your research question: The problematics of 'I'

Action research places the 'I' at the centre of the enquiry, and research questions take the form, 'How do I improve …?' This can raise new problematics, such as:

> You are working collaboratively with others, but you are the actor-agent in the research. What is the relationship between 'I' and 'we'?

Remember that 'I' am part of a social situation in which 'we' work collaboratively. 'I' can become 'we' when 'we' share the same value commitments. Although the 'I' focuses on one's own learning in company with other 'I's', each 'I' focuses on one's own learning, and shows how they could be influencing the learning of the other 'I's'. Each person holds themselves accountable for how they are with the others.

> Action research aims to influence processes of social change, so does focusing on the individual 'I' mean that society is seen as a group of individuals? (see Noffke 1997)

When a group of 'I's' share the same values, they work as a 'we' to realise them. They move from the personal to the social and the political. Each 'I' explains how they transform themselves into a 'we', while retaining a sense of personal agency.

What is the relationship between the 'I' who does the research and the 'I' who is part of the social situation?

Your researcher 'I' offers their account of their actor 'I', as they exercise their educational influence, with others who are doing the same. The experience can be transformational, where the 'I's' transform themselves into a collective 'we' (see Chapter 9).

Bernie Sullivan's (2006) abstract addresses these kinds of issues.

A Living Theory of a Practice of Social Justice: Realising the Right of Traveller Children to Educational Equality

Abstract

This thesis is an articulation of my living theory of social justice that evolved through undertaking research in the area of educational provision for Traveller children. It demonstrates how my embodied values of social justice and equality compelled me to engage in social and educational practices that refused to privilege some children at the expense of minority or marginalised groups. I explain how I transformed these values into the living critical standards of judgement by which I wish my work to be evaluated. Through using a self-study approach, within an action research methodology, I was able to reflect on my practice, with a view to learning how to improve it. This process contributed to an enhancement of my personal and professional development, and enabled me to theorise my practice as a form of emancipatory education. My emergent living theory of practice, therefore, incorporates a theory of social justice that reflects an ethos of equality of respect for all. It goes beyond traditional propositional theories of justice in that it has evolved from the lived reality of social practices in an educational institution. I explain how I arrived at an understanding that a practice of inclusion is more appropriate for a living theory of justice than one of assimilation, which often seeks to deny difference, or integration, which frequently attempts to eliminate difference. A practice of inclusion that is grounded in an intercultural ethos may take account of individual differences and transcend normative institutional hegemonic structures and discourses that are grounded in a logic of domination. Through developing my living theory of social justice as equality of respect for all, and as the recognition and acceptance of diversity, I became aware of the possibility that a process of inclusion could have a greater probability of success in achieving sustainable social evolution if it originated from the marginalised space. In this context, my research could have significance for other marginalised groups, as well as for the Traveller children in whose interests the research was undertaken.

So, you have set out your research issues. The next step of your action enquiry gives reasons for these concerns.

Why am I concerned?

The reasons for an action enquiry are to realise your values in your practices (Whitehead 1989). This idea can be problematic, in terms of the following:

- Why values?
- Which values?
- Whose values?

Why values?

Discussions about values often transform into discussions about action. As noted, there are different kinds of action. Some actions are unintentional, as when we trip over or blink. Others involve purpose and intent. Intentional action is underpinned by values, which can transform into practices that give meaning to our lives. The question arises, what kind of intent – to control, emancipate or persuade?

At the beginning of your enquiry, clarify which values you hope to realise. It can take time for the values to emerge through practice. Take the stance that you judge the quality of your practice in relation to the realisation of your values, so the values emerge as the living standards by which you make judgements about the quality of your actions.

Which values?

Values are what we believe in. We value whatever gives us pleasure, such as love. If something does not give us pleasure, such as cruelty, we do not value it, though we recognise these things as other people's values. So when speaking of our values, we speak about the practices we are involved in, which give meaning to our lives, and how we engage in those practices as a way of bringing our values into the social world.

This view raises problematics. First, there is the question of turning abstract ideas such as 'kindness' and 'love' into real-life living practices (see p. 9). Values are grounded in discursive practices (talking about values); the challenge is to turn these into social practices (living the values), so that talk becomes political action, and to explain the processes involved.

Whose values?

Any social situation involves different people who hold different values, which raises questions about whose values should be accepted. Some people insist that their values are better than other people's. This can lead to contradictions, for example, when the abstract value of justice is promoted within a lived reality of injustice. People who are good at the rhetoric of values do not necessarily show how they live the values they speak about – a question of espousing values (Schön 1995) without living them fully.

In your thesis, explain how you engaged with these issues. State your values and how you negotiated them with other people. Say whether your values changed through the course of the enquiry, perhaps from control to emancipation. Say how and why you took action, perhaps to enable others to realise their values of self-determination and self-development.

James Finnegan (2000) explains how his thesis communicates these processes.

How Do I Create my own Educational Theory in my Educative Relations as an Action Researcher and as a Teacher?

Abstract

My enquiry is based on four qualitative studies [1994–1997] in a boys' secondary school in the Republic of Ireland. I adopt a living educational theory approach to action research in my study.

In creating my own educational theory, I demonstrate how I have become a more reflective educational action researcher in developing and defining an original set of standards of judgement for judging my action research and teaching practices. These include my methodological, educational, and social standards of judgement.

In helping to facilitate an expression of student voices in my teaching, as I seek to improve their learning, I enable my sixth form students and myself to engage in more democratic actions and more egalitarian power relations in the classroom, primarily through the elicitation/creation, greater enactment, and evaluation of teaching/learning communicative activities. In this, How can I help you to improve your learning? is a question worth asking my sixth form students.

My work also shows that I have become a more reflective practitioner as I dialogue with the writings of other educators whilst seeking to relate my values concerning democratic action and social justice to my classroom teaching.

Having given reasons for your concerns, your next step talks about gathering data and generating evidence, to show the situation as it is and as it develops.

How do I show the situation as it is and as it develops?

This step involves monitoring practice, gathering data and generating evidence in which to ground your claim to know your practice. These areas are notoriously problematic. Many books are available that deal with technical issues about choice of data and how to gather them. We focus on some different issues:

- Which data are relevant?
- How do you ensure that you represent people fairly?
- How do you generate evidence from the data?

Which data are relevant?

When they begin their enquiries, researchers often gather too much data. This is no bad thing initially, but as the enquiry progresses, start to home in on only those data that are relevant to the research question (but do not discard your other data too soon, because new issues may arise for which your old data may be useful). If your question is 'How do I improve my management practices?' the data would show how your practices changed over the course of the enquiry.

Remember that your enquiry is about improving your practice, not other people's. This again raises the issue of who can improve what. One person cannot say that they 'improved' another, because people improve themselves. You may have arranged conditions to enable them to improve themselves, but you cannot say you improved them. You also cannot say that you improved the social situation, because the social situation consists of people, including yourself, who all want (hopefully) to improve their practice. You can, and should, focus on how you improved yourself. This requires keeping records and gathering data of your own processes of learning and action, and how you may be influencing other people's learning and action. You would ask your research participants to give you critical feedback on how they are responding to you. The data are in the nature of their responses.

How do you ensure that you represent people fairly?

You must work with people in an honourable manner. Your research must be ethical, which involves matters of confidentiality where appropriate, negotiating access and ensuring that you do no harm. This involves more than issuing ethical statements and securing permissions, and is to do with how you portray yourself and others.

Many critical literary theorists, such as Said (1991) explain how people are often represented in the media, including literature, in ways that reinforce stereotypes, and the reader is expected to internalise the author's assumptions. Many authors deliberately use language to reproduce the culture in this way, and some challenge such practices. Kipling (1901) had racist ideas, whereas Kristeva (1986) challenges sexist assumptions. Butler (1999) explains how it becomes a cultural expectation to accept cultural expectations, the double whammy of uncritical acceptance, and not questioning the lack of criticality.

Your capacity for critical engagement informs your choice of data. How do you represent yourself? Do you gather only those data that reinforce the rightness of your own position and say things such as, 'All participants agreed that this was right.' An experienced examiner would ask, 'How do I know that everyone agreed? Where is the evidence?' Better quality reports show the processes involved, including episodes of dissent. They ensure that voices are not filtered through the sanitising lens of the researcher's wish to portray themselves in a good light.

Good quality reports therefore explain how and why the research findings may be contested. Examiners warm to an author who explains that doing the research was problematic, how they interrogated their thinking and the difficulties involved. Examiners get suspicious when the story is presented as unproblematic with a happy ending. Action research stories have interesting, not happy, endings that show the possibilities for new actions. Interesting rather than happy any day.

How do you generate evidence from the data?

Representing the situation truthfully and authentically raises issues about generating evidence. Remember that evidence is in those pieces of data that directly show the processes involved in transforming a research question into a knowledge claim.

You therefore look for those pieces of evidence that show the nature of your practices as you commit yourself to your own and others' learning. Your evidence is grounded in your values. Say what your values are, especially your value of openness to enquiry through dialogue. Your evidence shows the realisation of these values in practice (or their denial), and how the values emerge through the practice as the means by which you assess progress (your living standards of judgement).

The following abstracts contain issues of evidence generation and representations of self and the other.

Moira Laidlaw (1996) writes:

How Can I Create my Own Living Educational Theory as I Offer You an Account of My Educational Development?

Abstract

I intend my thesis to be a contribution to both educational research methodology and educational knowledge. In this thesis I have tried to show what it means to me, a teacher-researcher, to bring, amongst others, an aesthetic standard of judgement to bear on my educative relationships with Undergraduate, Postgraduate, Higher Degree education students and classroom pupils in the action enquiry: 'How do I help my students and pupils to improve the quality of their learning?' By showing how my own fictional narratives can be used to express ontological understandings in a claim to educational knowledge, and by using insights from Coleridge's 'The Ancient Mariner' to illuminate my own educational values, I intend to make a contribution to action research methodology. By describing and explaining my own educational development in the creation of my own 'living educational theory', I intend to make a contribution to educational knowledge.

Kevin Eames (1995) writes:

How Do I, as a Teacher and an Educational Action-Researcher, Describe and Explain the Nature of My Professional Knowledge? Action Research, Dialectics and an Epistemology of Practically-Based Professional Knowledge for Education.

Abstract

This thesis is an attempt to make an original contribution to educational knowledge through a study of my own professional and educational development in action-research enquiries of the kind, 'How do I improve what I am doing?' The study includes analyses of my educative relationships in a classroom, educative conversations and correspondences with other teachers and academics. It also integrates the ideas of others from the wider field of knowledge and from dialectical communities of professional educators based at Bath University, Wootton Bassett School and elsewhere. The analyses I make of the resulting challenges to my thinking and practice show how educators in schools can work together, embodying a form of professional knowledge which draws on Thomism and other manifestations of dialectical rationality.

Contributions to educational knowledge are made in relation to educational action research and professional knowledge. The first is concerned with the nature of professional knowledge in education, and how action research can constitute the form of professional knowledge which I see as lacking at present. The second contribution is concerned with how we represent an individual's claim to know their own educational development. These contributions contain an analysis in terms of a dialectical epistemology of professional knowledge, which includes contradiction, negation, transformation and moral responsibility within a dialogical community.

Now let's look at how you took action.

What can I do? What will I do?

Here you explain how you took action to address the emerging situation, which involves the problematics of taking politically oriented action; for example, some people may not wish to change, and will resist you.

It can be argued that processes of social and cultural evolution begin in the mind. Changing surface-level practices therefore means first changing the deep-level thinking that informs those practices, which is easier said than done. As noted earlier, Bourdieu (1990) points out that we are born into a *habitus*, the social, political, economic and cultural system, underpinned by an epistemological system, which we usually accept unproblematically so that we act normatively (see Chapter 9). Foucault (1980) also explains how we internalise rules so that we learn to supervise and regulate ourselves.

The ownership of your learning and knowledge is at stake. According to Habermas (1975), humans cannot *not* learn in processes of social evolution. This raises the question, 'What do we choose to learn?' When you take action, what kind of learning do you encourage, and how do you do this?

Much learning can be termed mis-educational: it does not generate emancipatory or inclusive knowledge, because people listen to others who tell them to act normatively and learn to silence themselves. Nurturing educational knowledge is about supporting people to think freely and creatively. Doing this means being stringently honest through critical self-analysis, to ensure that you really are encouraging people to be the persons they wish to be and not clones of yourself.

These issues are addressed in the following example.

Jacqueline Delong (2002) writes:

How Can I Improve my Practice as a Superintendent of Schools and Create My Own Living Educational Theory?

Abstract

One of the basic tenets of my philosophy is that the development of a culture for improving learning rests upon supporting the knowledge-creating capacity in each individual in the system. Thus, I start with my own. This thesis sets out a claim to know my own learning in my educational inquiry, 'How can I improve my practice as a superintendent of schools?'

Out of this philosophy emerges my belief that the professional development of each teacher rests in their own knowledge-creating capacities as they examine their own practice in helping their students to improve their learning. In creating my own educational theory and supporting teachers in creating theirs, we engage with and use insights from the theories of others in the process of improving student learning.

The originality of the contribution of this thesis to the academic and professional knowledge-base of education is in the systematic way I transform my embodied educational values into educational standards of practice and judgement in the creation of my living educational theory. In the thesis I demonstrate how these values and standards can be used critically both to test the validity of my knowledge-claims and to be a powerful motivator in my living educational inquiry.

The values and standards are defined in terms of valuing the other in my professional practice, building a culture of inquiry, reflection and scholarship and creating knowledge.

This brings us to questions about demonstrating the validity of knowledge claims.

How do I ensure that any conclusions I come to are reasonably fair and accurate?

If you claim that your learning and actions are morally good, and that your story demonstrates rigorously conducted procedures, you need to engage in the kind of validation processes outlined on p. 134, which involve your responses to public critique. However, before people can agree about the validity of other people's work they need to agree their own standards of judgement about what they hold as 'good'. This raises questions:

- What counts as good in social practices?
- What counts as good in research practices?
- What counts as good in assessment practices?

What counts as good in social practices?

Good social practices can be understood as those that realise the ontological and social values of the people involved, which incorporates, considering what 'good social values' means. The ground gets muddy, because different people hold different values.

We authors, Jack and Jean, ground our ideas about 'the good' in relation to what we see in the natural order and its sustaining energy. The key characteristic of the natural order is its capacity for self re-creation. Life goes on, unless disrupted or destroyed. The purpose of life is more life. The energy that sustains living evolutionary processes is inclusional because it works for all, and relational because everything is embraced within the flow of its force-field. We like Feynman's idea that scientific enquiry is 'the pursuit of understanding of some subject or some thing based on the principle that what happens in nature is true and is the judge of the validity of any theory about it' (Feynman 2001: 240).

From this, we understand how inclusional social practices may be nurtured. Given that social practices can also be understood as force-fields in flow, underpinned by values, the question becomes, 'What kinds of values and practices will sustain life for all? How should people be towards one another?' It follows that the values and practices in question are inclusional and relational, and enable all to enjoy life as people of equal worth, entitled to make their contributions to social living.

This is well communicated in the thesis of Madeline Church (2004) who writes:

Creating an Uncompromised Place to Belong: Why Do I Find Myself in Networks?

Abstract

My inquiry sits within the reflective paradigm. I start from an understanding that knowing myself better will enhance my capacity for good action in the world. Through questioning myself and writing myself on to the page, I trace how I resist community formations, while simultaneously wanting to be in community with others. This paradox has its roots in my multiple experiences of being bullied, and finds transformation in my stubborn refusal to retreat into disconnection.

I notice the way bullying is part of my fabric. I trace my resistance to these experiences in my embodied experience of connecting to others, through a form of shape-changing. I see how question-forming is both an expression of my own bullying tendencies, and an intention to overcome them. Through my connection to others and my curiosity, I form a networked community in which I can work in the world as a network coordinator, action-researcher, activist and evaluator.

I show how my approach to this work is rooted in the values of compassion, love, and fairness, and inspired by art. I hold myself to account in relation to these values, as living standards by which I judge myself and my action in the world. This finds expression in research that helps us to design more appropriate criteria for the evaluation of international social change networks. Through this process I inquire with others into the nature of networks, and their potential for supporting us in lightly-held communities which liberate us to be dynamic, diverse and creative individuals working together for common purpose. I tentatively conclude that networks have the potential to increase my and our capacity for love.

Through this research I am developing new ways of knowing about what we are doing as reflective practitioners, and by what standards we can invite others to judge our work. I am, through my practice, making space for us to flourish, as individuals and communities. In this way I use the energy released by my response to bullying in the service of transformation.

What counts as good in research practices?

Research practices are usually recognised as 'good', i.e. 'good quality', when they demonstrate the researcher's capacity to undertake a systematic enquiry and make it public (Stenhouse 1983) with educational intent, and to generate new knowledge and theory. Your claim to have done this must be shown as valid (truthful and verifiable). You explain how your claim is the outcome of rigorous research processes: from the articulation of your research intent to testing your provisional claims against the critical feedback of others; and you are now putting your claim, in the form of your thesis, into the public domain.

This can be problematic for some researchers who wish to experiment with creative forms of representation, such as multimedia work, while still showing the methodological rigour of their research, especially when their accounts tell different forms of story, and include different voices.

These ideas inform the thesis of Je Kan Adler-Collins (2007), who writes:

Developing an Inclusional Pedagogy of the Unique: How Do I Clarify, Live and Explain my Educational Influences in my Learning as I Pedagogise my Healing Nurse Curriculum in a Japanese University?

Abstract

The social context of this thesis is embedded in the processes and reflections experienced during the development, implementation and evaluation of a healing nurse curriculum, using action research enquiry on my teaching practice, in a Japanese rural university in the years 2003–2007. These processes include the evolution of my ontology and the creation of an inclusional pedagogy of the unique with transitional certainty as a living epistemological standard of judgment. An energy-flowing, living standard of inclusionality as a space creator for engaged listening and informed learning is offered as an original contribution to knowledge.

Two major strands of enquiry are interwoven and inseparable in this thesis. The first is my life-long self study of my own learning and the values and practices that embrace all the different facets of my life, including being a nurse, educator, and Buddhist priest. The second extends the first, putting them firmly in the context of a specific time frame, weaving a textual narrative that passes between the different aspects of my multiple selves, building a picture for my readers that is grounded in my actual praxis. This narrative gives insights to the growth of my educational knowledge as I research the unique position I hold of being the only white, male nurse, foreign educator in a culture that is so completely different from that of my birth and early education. Finally, I use the analysis of the voices of my students' experience of my teaching and curriculum to mirror back to me my own values as they were seen through the eyes of others in their emergence in praxis. Such usage brought about fundamental ontological changes in me and my practices as a teacher.

In the last chapter we quoted from the masters dissertation of Adler-Collins. In this Chapter we are quoting from his doctoral thesis. Action researchers who generate their living theories often sustain their enquiries in their life-long learning, like Adler-Collins and ourselves.

What counts as good in assessment practices?

This is probably the most problematic area of all, because assessment practices can be seen as good when all parties reach intersubjective agreement about the validity of the claims being made and about the quality of the research. This can be problematic because criteria and standards of judgement need to be negotiated. The research has to fulfil predetermined 'objective' criteria and standards, while the practice may be better judged by values-based 'subjective' criteria and standards, which the researcher may wish to articulate themselves.

Then the examiners need to interrogate their own expectations, and whether the thesis has fulfilled them.

The next step of your action enquiry deals with how your learning enables you to improve your practices.

How do I modify my ideas and practices in light of my evaluation?

Say how you intend to develop your practice and research in light of the learning from your evaluation. Perhaps you could have done things better, or recognise that you were too ambitious or did not see opportunities. Also celebrate what you have done, state its potential significance for the learning of yourself and others, and set out some of the implications. Explain how you have overcome some of the problematics through determination and spiritual resilience. Show how you have influenced the learning of other people, so that they learn how to transform their lives; you have exercised your agency for cultural and social transformation. Say how you intend to disseminate your work via a range of media and platforms. Remember that there are no happy endings in action research, only constant new beginnings.

So, now that you have written your doctoral thesis, how will it be judged?

HOW IS THE WORK JUDGED?

A doctoral thesis is usually examined by an external examiner from another university, and an internal examiner from the home university. Neither examiner should have had substantial previous contact with the candidate. Both examiners compare notes about your thesis prior to the *viva voce* examination, which is an additional aspect of most doctoral examinations.

A *viva voce* examination is an oral examination, during which you defend your thesis. You stand up for what you have written and justify why you have written it. Most vivas last between one and two hours, and take the form of a critical conversation. The examiners ask questions about your action (substantive issues about ideas and practices) and your research (epistemological and methodological issues). The aim is not to catch you out with trick questions, but to ask you searching questions that give you an opportunity to show what you can do. Often they ask you questions that enable you to show that you have addressed the university criteria.

Here are some commonly asked questions, which refer to the criteria, and the kinds of points you should include in your responses. The responses are idealised, and you should always respond in your own creative way, but these ideas show the kind of answers examiners are looking for.

Question: 'Tell us about your thesis.' This is a frequent 'settling down' question. The examiner also wants to see whether you understand the requirement to make an original claim to knowledge, and that you can articulate the significance of your original contribution to your field.

Your answer could include the following:

- 'My thesis contains my original claim to knowledge.' Explain what you mean by this. Say why you positioned yourself as the author of your own narrative, and why you chose a narrative form.
- 'My claim is that I have generated my living theory of practice' or 'my living theory of educational leadership' or whatever aspect of practice your thesis deals with. Explain how living theory is different from traditional propositional theory. Say what your job is, and what your practice involved. Briefly outline what you did during your action research. Explain how you have improved your practice (or not), so that you are confident in testing the validity of your claim in the public domain.
- 'My claim is that I have developed a living epistemology of practice.' You know what you are doing and you know how and why you are doing it. You could say this instead of, or in addition to, the above. If you give this answer, you need to be confident about issues of epistemology, because your examiners will pursue this line of thinking.
- 'The originality of my contribution is that I am influencing learning (my own, other people's, the learning of social and cultural formations). My research enables me to contribute to new practices and new thinking.' Explain how and why your research is influencing new practices and thinking at workplace or policy level.
- 'I undertook my research in my workplace, and I appreciate how I have negotiated existing cultures and normative practices.' Say what these were. Explain how you negotiated the processes of your research, through your developing awareness of normative political, socio-economic and cultural assumptions.
- 'I show how I have generated evidence against which I test the validity of my knowledge claims. I test their validity in relation to identified standards of judgement. I can explain how my values come to act as my living standards of judgement.' You must show that you understand the importance of testing the validity of knowledge claims. Say what your living standards of judgement are, e.g. 'I show how I have realised the value of social justice as a living practice.'
- 'I intend to pursue my research in the following ways … .' Explain that the end of this programme is the beginning of a new one.
- Link everything you say to the literature wherever possible. Cite names and dates.

Question: 'What has doing your research meant for you?' Your examiner wants to see what you have learned, and how this will inform new learning and practices. They want to see if you demonstrate critical engagement with your own thinking.

Your answer could include the following:

- 'I have learned to become critical. I have developed the capacity for reflexive critique (Winter 1989) by deconstructing my previous assumptions, and the capacity for dialectical critique by deconstructing other people's assumptions.' Explain what you mean by this, and how you have changed your thinking.
- 'I have a deeper understanding of processes of social and cultural transformation.' Say what you have learned through learning how to become critical.

- 'I have learned that I have the capacity for sustained study, and I value my capacity for knowledge creation.' Explain how long your study took, what it involved, and how you delight now in the knowledge you have created.
- Link everything you say to the literature wherever possible. Cite names and dates.

Question: 'What are the main findings of your research?' The examiner wants to see what you have found out through doing the research, and if you can comment on its originality, rigour, and significance for knowledge creation.

Your answer could include the following:

- 'My main findings are that I have contributed to new thinking and new practices.' Say what these are, for example that you have introduced new forms of communication, or have encouraged people to become more critical of what they are doing.
- 'I have learned to exercise my educational influence in my own and others' learning, so that our workplace is a more open society (Popper 1945).' Explain what you mean by 'educational influence' and how you have achieved this.
- 'I am aware of the significance of action research for improving practice through knowledge creation.' Explain how you have improved practice through knowledge creation.
- 'I can show how systematic enquiry can lead to improved practice through knowledge creation.' Explain how you know what you have done. This is key – you say what you have done, and you also say that you know what you have done, and how and why you have done it.
- Link everything you say to the literature wherever possible. Cite names and dates.

Question: 'Please speak about the experience of writing the thesis.' The examiner wants to hear if you are aware of what writing a PhD thesis involves, and whether it is all your original work. They want to hear that you are aware that you have the capacity for independent study and 'writing knowledge'.

Your answer could include the following:

- 'I developed a regular writing schedule.' Explain your awareness of the need for independent enquiry in doctoral studies and for maintaining a research focus in your practice.
- 'I tried to demonstrate ironic validity throughout.' Say what you mean by ironic validity and why this is important.
- 'As I wrote, I tried to show, through the form of the text, how I was generating my personal theory from within my narrative of practice.' Outline the form that your narrative took, and say why you used this form.
- 'I consulted the literatures at all stages, incorporating the ideas of key theorists within my living theory of practice.' Outline who your key authors were and what you found attractive about what they had to say. Be prepared to engage in a discussion of their ideas. Your examiners know these things!
- 'It took me some time to develop the conceptual frameworks for my study.' Explain what conceptual frameworks are, and how you developed yours.
- Link everything you say to the literature wherever possible. Cite names and dates.

Question: 'How will you disseminate your work? How will you develop it?' The examiner wants to see if you appreciate that you have to publish the work in a range of ways, and if you still have a hunger for intellectual engagement.

Your answer could include the following:

- 'I have learned the importance of speaking my truth. I will continue to do so through making my work public.' Say how you intend to continue challenging normative assumptions through writing for publication, and presenting your work in public places such as conferences.
- 'I have learned the importance of writing, and of multimedia forms of representation. I intend to produce video narratives of my ongoing research into my practice, and make them public through web-based publishing.' Say that you intend to contribute to new e-journals and develop documentaries and other visual forms.
- 'I intend to move my research into a new phase where I investigate the following issues …' Say what you intend to do now, and how you will do it.

These are only some questions you could be asked, but they give a flavour of the kind of answers that will earn you a doctorate.

SUMMARY

This chapter has set out what writing a doctoral thesis involves. It has revisited ideas about critical engagement, and emphasised the need for originality of thought and innovative contributions to the literature. Advice is given on how to demonstrate originality and critical engagement at each step of an action enquiry, and on how the quality of a thesis will be judged. Suggestions are made about the kind of questions examiners will pose during a *viva voce*, what the examiners are looking for, and the kind of responses to give that will show your understanding of what is involved in doing a doctorate.

CHECKLIST OF REFLECTIVE QUESTIONS

Here is a set of questions that may act as a checklist for your doctoral work.

Do I show that I understand what is required at doctoral level?

- Do I demonstrate originality in my research?
- Do I make clear how I understand the originality and significance of my research, how it is original, and for whom it is significant?

Do I take care in how I represent myself and others?

- Do I show my capacity to engage critically with my own normative assumptions, as well as those of other people?
- Have I grounded my claims in a strong evidence base, to show these transformational practices in action?
- Have I articulated which standards of judgement I wish to use in assessing the quality of my practice, research and thesis?

Am I prepared for my viva, by rehearsing the kind of answers I will give to possible questions?

- Can I speak with disciplined passion about what my research means for me, and could mean for others, including my examiners?
- Am I satisfied that I can defend every aspect of my thesis, while also recognising that I still have much to learn and may, after all, be mistaken?

If you can do all these things, you will demonstrate that you deserve a doctorate, and that you have earned your title. Congratulations!

We now turn to Part III, and consider some of the implications of what you have done.

PART III

WHY SHOULD YOUR REPORT BE WRITTEN?

This part deals with the question, 'Why should you write an action research report?' It contains Chapters 9 and 10.

Chapter 9 asks, 'What is the significance of your report?' It outlines some key areas of significance, in terms of your original contribution to the field and your capacity to engage critically with creating knowledge for improving practice.

Chapter 10 asks, 'What are the implications of your research and your research report?' It outlines some important implications of what you have written, and of the fact that you have now positioned yourself as an authorised writer.

Both chapters give ideas about how your report has implications for the field of educational enquiry, and can influence the development of sustainable social orders.

The Significance of Your Research Report

So now you have written it. This report that has taken weeks or even months of your time, countless books and conversations, and a vast amount of thinking. Has it been worthwhile?

Yes. Here is why.

Your report is your means of placing your action research, and your knowledge claims, in the public domain. You are saying that you know that you are making an original contribution to your field, and you know the importance of that contribution. The key question for this chapter therefore becomes, 'In what ways is your contribution significant?'

However, it is one thing making your knowledge public; it is another getting it taken seriously, and this is largely down to you. First you need to produce a quality report that people will read; second, you have to explain why your knowledge claims should be legitimated as significant, for whom, and why legitimacy is important. You cannot expect other people to celebrate your work as an original and important contribution unless you do so first.

The word 'significance' implies 'meaning'. Your contribution is meaningful in many ways and for many people – for yourself, the wider community, and for the future (posterity) – and these are linked: the personal transforms into the social, which then transforms into the political, for sustainable forms of human interaction. This transformational process is imbued with your spiritual energy, and with cosmic energy.

Your contribution is significant for *what* you say, *how* you say it, and *that* you say it. Now that you are making the validity of your work public, you are also making a case for why those claims should be legitimated, in these terms; and this is also how the chapter is organised.

1. The significance of *what* you say.
2. The significance of *how* you say it.
3. The significance of the fact *that* you say it.
4. Summary.
5. Checklist of reflective questions.

Furthermore, *what* you say, *how* you say it, and *that* you say it are meaningful for new learning: for yourself, for others, and for posterity; so each section contains ideas about the significance of your capacity to speak at these different levels of transformation.

THE SIGNIFICANCE OF WHAT YOU SAY

In his book *Fearless Speech* (2001), Foucault speaks about *parrhesia*, a Greek word meaning 'free speech'. Free speech implies speaking frankly and truthfully. This is a necessary practice, but it can be dangerous because sometimes people do not want to hear the truth, which often amounts to criticism, so they try to silence the speaker. Speaking freely is therefore linked with issues of power, and, given that most people with position power are also those with privilege, it is linked with financial and social capital. Foucault's stated intent was 'not to deal with the problem of truth, but with the problem of the truth-teller, or of truth-telling as an activity: … the importance of telling the truth, knowing who is able to tell the truth, and knowing why we should tell the truth' (2001: iii). Foucault's main concerns were how the individual is able to create their own identity through reflecting critically on what they and others are doing.

These themes appear in the work of other key authors, such as Said (1991) and Chomsky (2002). They also speak of the dangers of lack of critique to public well-being, including the closing down of the capacity to think for oneself and understanding how people's thinking can be manipulated. Developing the capacity for critique means interrogating discourses for hidden strategies of control.

Doing action research involves this: learning how to understand what is going on in social situations and why, and how to challenge normative practices and contribute to improving the social order.

Here are some ideas about the significance of your contribution in different spheres.

The significance of what you say for your own education

You have given your reasons and purposes for doing your action research. These link with your underpinning ontological and spiritual values, and transform into social and political practices. You look back at your life and claim it as worthwhile. Reflecting on these issues, and drawing on some of Marx's unpublished notes written in 1844, Bernstein (1971) says we are twice affirmed through our productive lives: first, when we 'produce' or create our own lives, and second, when we contribute, through our own, to the life of another.

You can claim your life as worthwhile in relation to your ontology of being, your relationship with yourself. You understand yourself as a person whose existence and capacity to speak are your contribution on earth (Arendt 1958).

Only you occupy your place on earth, so you need to occupy it well (O'Neill 2008). You are able and willing to engage with your sense of being (Tillich 1973). You value those things that give your life meaning, while rejecting mis-educational (Chomsky 2000) influences that aim to persuade you not to commit to being more than you are.

In identifying her research concern, Rita Moustakim, a senior lecturer concerned about issues of immigration and 'asylum seekers', writes:

> Driven by the desire to improve my learning and confronted with injustice directed at others, I felt I had to take purposeful action to effect change for the greater good of society. I can relate to Blackburn (2001), who uses the term 'deontological notions', stemming from the Greek word *deontos*, which means duty. I consider the struggle for social justice to be a duty which cannot be denied. I desired to be active and engaged in making a difference for good, in particular in relation to supporting involuntary migrants who I considered to be a group marginalised by society. … In order to clarify why I was concerned and how my values came to act as my living standards of practice and judgement, I shall first explain my reasons for being.

> I believe we all have an innate purpose in life. I do not feel it is by chance that any one of us is here or remains here for a given length of time. I consider that my reason for being, in part, is to speak on behalf of others who for whatever reason are unable to speak for themselves. I also consider it my duty to support all people, as I am a citizen of a wider world and not just in relation to my current and immediate situation. I can relate to the work of Freire (1973) who suggests there is an indivisible solidarity between humans and their world, and that they are not just in the world, but with it. We cannot live or work in isolation; each one of us has needs and difficulties and, however insignificant they may appear in relation to another's, at the time for us, they may be all encompassing. I feel compelled to support other people not for self-serving purposes but as a purposeful action which is part of a wider reason for being. (Moustakim 2008: 7–8)

You show how you engage with issues of epistemology. Foucault (2001) says that, because we have the capacity to tell the truth, we also have an obligation to tell it. You can do this because you have learned to deconstruct your own and others' thinking.

Julie Pearson, a senior lecturer in Physical Education, writes about her processes of becoming critical:

> I have realised through my research that I have been schooled in certain ways of thinking and have reproduced the practices I have come to view as the 'norm' and for which I have been rewarded [as a professional educator]. … I understand now that my traditional form of pedagogy not only raised the value of the 'norm' (Derrida 1981), but also devalued me as a professional educator and as a facilitator of change. I was failing myself alongside those I was supporting (past, present and future). Now, however, since beginning to become more critical of my epistemological stance, and of my practice, I no longer view myself as more knowledgeable than those I teach, or as a member of a 'specialised class' (Chomsky 2000). I now position myself alongside the students I teach, becoming part of the teaching and learning process. I have moved from a knowledge-getting process (Bruner 1966: 72) towards knowledge creation, allowing for the interaction and creative encounters between

people (Elliott 1998) in order to progress and improve. In a constructively critical manner, I have begun to challenge the process of learning by challenging my own practice (Schön 1995). (Pearson 2008: 2, 4)

You are telling your research story from your commitment to criticality, demonstrating its authenticity, rigour and scholarship. You have worked perhaps within cultures of oppression, yet did not give in, through your commitment to life (Frankl 1959; Todorov 1999). Foucault was obsessed with death (Miller 1993); you are obsessed with life.

The significance of your contribution for the education of others in your contexts

Drawing on the renewable energy of the universe, you bring your learning to your relationships with others. You exercise your educational influence in their learning out of your own generosity of spirit, because you understand that the world is sustained through the capacity of all to contribute freely and to ask for nothing in return. Your contribution is to share your knowledge so that others can learn from it and develop it. This is not interfering or 'intervening', but helping them appreciate their capacities for original critical thinking and political action. It is not about 'doing projects', but rather a lifelong commitment to working with communities who have come together, willing to share their common goals, on an equal footing, and rooted in their self-knowledge as free people of equal worth.

Sometimes making one's contribution to others' learning can be painful. King, Mandela and Gandhi were silenced for advocating justice. This has not stopped their global influence. Chomsky and Said have been vilified for critiquing policies that aim to control the public mind (Chomsky 2002; Said 1994a). This has not stopped their voices being heard. Through your capacity for knowledge creation, you are enabling people to think for themselves.

You are showing how it is possible to enable people's self-determination for self-development (Young 2000). This can have implications for how the public sphere can be re-thought, and new understandings about economics developed, which could be a major contribution from your research. Dominant understandings are that the public sphere works as a system of market exchange, where what is exchanged is consumer and social goods (Heilbroner and Thurow 1998). Gift cultures work like this, the idea that if A gives B a present, B must reciprocate with a better gift. Gift cultures perpetuate the superiority of some over others, where the capacity to pay entitles one to entry into the society. Legitimacy is achieved by virtue of what you can offer. Currently, Britain's policy on immigration is to accept those who have market capacities, such as key skills, or sufficient money to support themselves. This kind of integration works in terms of legalistic regulation (see Habermas's (2001) *The Inclusion of the Other*). People are included because of external rules and regulations, but this is not a sustainable form of inclusion. Sustainable forms come from free people thinking and speaking freely. What matters is not a capacity to pay but a capacity to be.

You are therefore contributing to sustainable forms of living, through freedom for all; and this carries conditions. Sustainability as freedom can happen only when people agree to it. John Hume, former leader of the SDLP in Northern Ireland, famously commented that decommissioning begins in the mind, not with the laying-down of arms. Social freedom begins in the individual mind, and grows through relationships of influence. This has implications for a new form of public sphere: social goods are in people's learning, and exchange mechanisms are in the sharing of critical stories, an economy of shared understandings, grounded in a commitment to freedom (Sen 1999). The unit of currency is a willingness to show how people hold themselves accountable for what they do. Freedom for all is built in to the regulation of society, a shift from a legalistic view to a relational view, where the structures of society take the form of permeable boundaries that enable all to enter one another's dynamically evolving spaces through the sharing of their personal knowledge for public transformation.

Alex Sinclair, a senior lecturer in Science, writes about the significance of his research:

> The significance of my research can also be thought of in terms of developing new forms of theory and how I am generating my own living theory of practice. In this way I am contributing to the debates surrounding the nature of education and pedagogies and what constitutes knowledge. By encouraging my students to learn independently I am asking them to make their learning explicit. In turn they will be developing their own living theories around their practice and hopefully developing a critical approach towards reflection and critical thinking. In this way it may break the cycle of socialising teachers as unthinking implementers of normative theories who may be able to pass on these necessary skills to the children they subsequently teach. I hope that it has been possible for my students to have learnt with me as I gain a better understanding of how I can best develop my practice and that I am working towards an epistemology of symbiotic practice. (Sinclair 2008: 17)

The significance of your contribution for the education of cultural and social formations

A social or cultural formation refers to groups of people who share a common social or cultural heritage. These groups do not simply come into existence, as if their heritage was the way things have always been. Cultures, including their knowledge systems, emerge, and are frequently different from one another. The knowledge systems of industrialised societies work in terms of 'this' or 'that', a traditional Aristotelian logic that excludes contradiction, whereas in the intellectual traditions of indigenous societies, things tend to be seen as in relation, connected through an underpinning philosophy of relatedness (see Brown 2004 on African philosophy and Reagan 2005 on non-western educational traditions).

Cultures emerge through people interacting with one another through speech and action. The problem is, as Habermas (1976) explains, these knowledge systems often detach themselves from the people who created them, and become reified, things in themselves, so people lose touch with their own systems. They say, 'That's the way things are because that's the way things are', forgetting that this is the way people have made them. They also forget that what is made can be improved. Nothing is static, least of all culture. Look at a photo of yourself taken 20 years ago, and see how culture changes. You also have a hand in cultural change. By following dominant thinking you contribute to reproducing the existing culture; by changing your thinking, you can contribute to new, improved cultures.

New ways of thinking and acting have entered the cultural formation of educational research, for example, through action research. You are contributing to cultural transformation through enabling all voices to be heard in your organisation. You are showing what it means to develop culture as 'a concept that includes a refining and elevating element, each society's reservoir of the best that has been known and thought' (Said 1994: xiii). You have become a cultural entrepreneur; you have cultural capital because you have what counts in cultural affairs.

This is where you can have real educational influence. You have something of worth to contribute. You have encouraged new cultures of inclusion (Cahill 2007; Sullivan 2006), through developing practices that include the other as the grounds for social action. Inclusion begins in the mind, when people deconstruct their own thinking around what counts as 'me' and 'the other'.

Mark Cordery, a senior lecturer in IT in education, writes:

> Prior to becoming a teacher I was a research scientist engaged in medical and veterinary microbiological research. My initial training saw me working within a scientific research paradigm using a positivist empirical approach to planning, collecting and presenting data and developing theory. The precision of this approach and its well defined use of numerical data and statistical analysis worked very well with the bacteria, viruses and blood samples with which my research was concerned. The precise nature of this research paradigm positioned the researcher outside the research forum as an impersonal observer. When I moved into the field of education I found, and indeed I used, many of these research methods applied to the classroom situation. In my own professional development as a primary school teacher I was encouraged to 'cross the threshold', a process for which I was required to submit bland statistics to 'demonstrate the progress' of the children in my class and to prove my worth as an educator.
>
> Through my studies I have begun to realise the need to embrace a more emancipatory, empowering research methodology, which goes beyond generating theory through propositions which determine relationships between variables and begins to seek answers to the question 'How do I improve the process of education here?' (Whitehead 1989) and thus makes me a living participant in my own research as I strive to generate my own living theory of practice. (Cordery 2008: 8–9)

You show how you have deconstructed your thinking. Mr Incredible (of *The Incredibles*) says, 'When everyone is super, no one will be.' You have decentred yourself, so you no longer see 'here' as the centre, because there is no 'here'; 'here' is someone else's 'there', so 'here' and 'there' become meaningless. You have destablised your thinking, and fixed categories; you have destablised the very idea of 'category'. 'Identity' is not a fixed category; it is a living, creative process.

THE SIGNIFICANCE OF HOW YOU SAY IT

You have chosen to tell your story in your unique way and from your decision 'that I must understand the world from my own point of view, as a person claiming originality and exercising his [or her] personal judgement responsibly with universal intent' (Polanyi 1958: 327). This has considerable implications for yourself, others, and your social formation.

The significance of how you tell your story for your own education

Through telling your story in your own way you communicate how you have given meaning to your life. You show how you have moved from experiencing yourself as a living contradiction, to realising your potentials for educational influence. Through your written and visual narratives you show the processes you have engaged in, as you struggled to create your own identity.

You are communicating how you are reconceptualising educational theory as within the practice, and not only as words on a page. You are showing the validity of your knowledge claims through the living practice. You give an account of yourself; you can show that 'there is a relation between the rational discourse, the *logos*, you are able to use, and the way that you live' (Foucault 2001: 97). You can show 'the relationship between one's way of life and knowledge of the truth. ...', the 'idea that a person is nothing else but his [*sic*] relation to the truth, and that this relation to truth takes shape or is given form in his own life ' (2001: 117). Feynman noted (2001: 240, see p. 152) that 'what happens in nature is true and is the judge of the validity of any theory about it'. You are showing, through the way you live and present your story that your way is the judge of the validity of your own living theory.

The significance of how you tell your story for the education of others

Now that you have told your story, you are encouraging others to do the same, so that their stories can be legitimated in the public domain. Your story contributes to the public knowledge base (Chapter 10), through contributing to new epistemologies.

We have said throughout that traditional forms of research and practice are grounded in traditional logics and epistemologies – the idea that 'this' is separate from 'that', and that everything works in terms of cause and effect ('If I do this, that will happen'). It is the basis of modernist forms of thinking, where things are seen as fixed – fixed categories, roles and social structures. Gray (2002) points out that this is the basis of many social ills, because many people pay more attention to fitting others into the structures than to seeing them as people. It is also the basis of traditional institutional epistemologies, including those of modern research universities. This has serious consequences, given that the university is still one of the highest bodies for legitimating what counts as knowledge and who is seen as a knower.

You are changing this. Your action research is part of the New Scholarship (Boyer 1990), different from traditional scholarship, and grounded in new fluid and transformational epistemologies. Schön (1995) says that the new scholarship requires new epistemologies, through action research, and you are showing how this can be done. Communicating these fluid forms requires new dynamic forms of representation (Eisner 1997), and you are showing this, too.

The significance of how you tell your story for the education of social formations

Through telling your story in your own way, you are contributing to the transformation of the university. Given that the university is also one of the most powerful bodies for influencing cultural development, you are contributing to new forms of culture. The spread of the culture can be influenced through new forms of global communication such as e-journals and multimedia representations. For example, the *Ontario Action Researcher* (available at http://www.nipissingu.ca/oar/), *ARExpeditions* (available at http://arexpeditions. montana.edu/index.php), and the *Educational Journal of Living Theories (EJOLTS)* (available at http://ejolts.net/drupal/index.php) are all electronic journals that invite full participation by all contributors as part of a knowledge-creating process.

Many stories are told about the dangers of globalisation, that it is about profit over people (Chomsky 2002) and strengthens the divide between the haves and the have-nots. You are contributing to new forms of globalisation, through the free exchange of free ideas. Some studies (e.g. Perlmutter 2000) explain how the media are policed in order to control the public mind; and how the internet provides new open forms which reduce the control of thought-police (although the thought-police also patrol the internet, though perhaps with more difficulty). It is possible to create new virtual networks of communication, informed by new dynamic epistemologies that confer public legitimacy in new ways. The internet provides virtually unlimited freedom of communication; whereas previously it was possible to challenge existing forms only through subversive pamphlets and secret meetings, now it is possible to do so through the informal networks of cyberspace.

However, this kind of social freedom can be achieved only if you have intellectual freedom, and this is the hardest thing of all, as we now discuss.

THE SIGNIFICANCE OF THE FACT THAT YOU SAY IT

Perhaps the most significant aspect of making your account public is that you are able to tell your story of personal emancipation and are claiming the right to speak, because speaking frankly and truthfully to oneself and others can happen only in a context where one is permitted to do so. Often, external and internal mechanisms of control prevent this. External mechanisms can be visible – censorship, thought control, punishment for whistleblowing (Alford 2001) – while more subtle forms are invisible – e.g. propaganda (Marlin 2002) and the diversion of attention away from things that really matter through promoting a culture of entertainment and trivialisation (game shows, reality TV). It is then a question of becoming sufficiently critical to combat the influences of these external forms.

It is much more difficult, however, to combat the influence of internalised forms, because it is then a question of deconstructing the mode of thinking while using the same mode of thinking. This is at the heart of the matter, as Bourdieu (1990), Butler (1999), Said (1978) and others explain.

We commented earlier on Bourdieu's (1990) idea of the *habitus*. We are all born into an existing culture with social and epistemological norms and standards. We grow up using a particular form of thinking, without thinking about it. Bourdieu uses the analogy that a fish does not know it is in water. Most people go through life without realising that they are using a particular form of thinking, and that there are other ways.

Butler (1999) illustrates this by drawing on Kafka's (2003) *Before the Law*. The story tells how people wait before a Gate, knowing there is someone behind who will tell them what to do and how to think. Most traditional epistemological systems work like this. They reinforce their legitimacy by perpetuating the mythology that someone is behind a Gate somewhere; this 'Someone' knows the Law. People come to internalise the Law and the Gate. This is of course nonsense, because there is no law and no gate. The only gate that exists is the one we create in our own minds through believing the stories, as we create things that go bump in the night. But mental images take on their own fearful reality; the monsters under the bed become very real. Dislodging the stories can be difficult and scary, because it means actually changing the way you think, and once you have done this there is no going back. You make your eyes different (Polanyi 1958: 143).

This has consequences for your own education, for the education of others, and for the education of social formations.

The significance of the fact that you speak for your own education

Changing your eyes can be difficult, because you have to learn to see things anew, like learning to trust again after emotional trauma. We like the way Warren distinguishes the 'arrogant eye' from the 'loving eye':

> When one climbs a rock as a conqueror, one climbs with an arrogant eye. When one climbs with a loving eye, one constantly 'must look and listen and check and question.' One recognises the rock as something very different, something perhaps totally indifferent to one's own presence, and finds in that difference joyous occasion for celebration. One knows 'the boundary of the self,' where the self - the 'I', the climber – leaves off and the rock begins. There is no fusion of two into one, but a complement of two entities, *acknowledged* as separate, different, independent, yet *in relationship*; they are in relationship *if only* because the loving eye is perceiving it, responding to it, noticing it, attending to it. (Warren 2001: 331, emphasis in original)

Changing perceptions involves making conscious decisions, the first of which is to disbelieve that you can't do it and begin to believe that you can. Frankl (1959) tells of how prisoners of war refused to believe they would inevitably die in captivity. For many people, committing to life means hard work.

It can also bring awesome consequences. In olden times, people shot the messenger who brought disturbing news. Things are not so different today. If you challenge the status quo you are positioned as a radical, a lefty, a troublemaker, or mad. These concepts are social constructions, as Foucault (1979) explains. Chomsky (1996–98) says that Aristotle would have been called a dangerous radical in his day, and Socrates and Jesus were simply killed off for speaking the truth and encouraging others to do so – 'inciting' in the language of power. We should recognise the language of power for what it is.

Yet you need to keep at it, not be lulled into a sense of complacency, where you simply apply other people's knowledge to your practice and reproduce the status quo. Your job is to disturb the status quo. This means turning yourself into a public intellectual, and insisting on your intellectual engagement. This also brings consequences. Said (1994b) speaks about the differences between academics and intellectuals: traditional academics tend to focus on traditional scholarship, saying more of the same about existing practices; whereas intellectuals engage in innovative forms of enquiry, generating original knowledge of their own practices. Being an intellectual can also be lonely, because intellectuals automatically place themselves on the outside. Intellectuals are never part of an in-group, because their job is always to critique, and never get drawn into a culture of consensus.

Julie Pearson, mentioned earlier, comments on these processes:

> I now realise through my engagement with my Masters studies that I have always been capable of learning and generating new theory, but that I have been previously silenced by the systems in which I engaged and unwittingly served. I have moved from being an academic to being an intellectual (Said 1994b); rethinking assumptions and generating new critical knowledge.
>
> I believe that if given opportunities to work in environments where learning can be shared and experiences are valued, colleagues may also be motivated to improve their practices; learning through action and new informed action. By encouraging colleagues within the teaching profession to undertake their action enquiries, I hope to demonstrate the opportunities for research and change within practice. I wish to engage in research which explores and directly informs practice. I view my role as a professional educator to facilitate opportunities for people to use their own voices (Glavey 2008) and to express their experiences and understanding of primary education and help to deconstruct authoritarian voices that speak for or on behalf of others. I hope that, as I have, colleagues may transform themselves from being submissive conformists to being active change agents in their own lifeworld (Fullan 1993). The more individuals I can assist to increase their self confidence, skills or knowledge alongside my own, the better I believe the quality of educational experience will be for the people we teach. (Pearson 2008: 18–19)

As a practitioner, you need also to become a public intellectual. Granted it may be scary, but you should have courage and faith in your capacity to speak your truth. Polanyi says: 'In spite of the hazards involved, I am called upon to search for the truth and state my findings' (Polanyi 1958: 299).

He also says that we are born into a world for whose making we are not responsible, yet which determines our calling. This brings us to the next section.

The significance of the fact that you speak for the education of others

We are speaking about validity and legitimacy. There is a big difference between them, though both are interrelated. Validity means that a thing does what it says it does. 'It does what it says on the tin' means that you can expect the product to work. Your claim, 'I have improved my practice' means that a reader can expect to see improved practice and an explanation from you on how it has improved. A knowledge claim must demonstrate its validity, or believability. It then transforms into a truth claim.

Legitimacy has nothing to do with telling the truth, and everything to do with establishing how the truth may be told and who will do so: 'who is able to tell the truth, about what, with what consequences, and with what relations to power' (Foucault 2001: iii). Granting legitimacy means granting legitimacy to the validity of your truth claims, and to you, as a speaker of truth.

When you explain the validity of your knowledge (truth) claims, you are showing that your work can be believed, in relation to different aspects. You can claim the following forms of validity: these are a few examples – many more exist, and you can create others.

- Personal validity: you ground your insights in your values, and draw on writers such as Polanyi (1958).
- Ontological validity: you ground your work in insights about your relationship with yourself and draw on writers such as Tillich (1973).
- Social validity: you ground your work in insights about communication and the evolution of society and draw on writers such as Habermas (1987).
- Ironic validity: you ground your work in insights about reflecting on the influence of normative assumptions and draw on writers such as Lather (1991).
- Epistemic (epistemological) validity: you ground your work in insights about the nature of knowledge creation processes and draw on writers such as Code (1987).
- Catalytic validity: you ground your work in insights about the use and generalisability of ideas and draw on writers such as Lather (1991).
- Political validity: you ground your work in insights about legitimising knowledge claims and draw on writers such as Chomsky (2002).
- Empathetic validity: you ground your work in insights about personal and social relationships and draw on writers such as Dadds (2008).

You should be creative in the kinds of validity claims you make – but make sure that you are confident about what demonstrating validity involves, because these ideas are at the heart of scholarly work, and examiners will quickly pick up on them. Explain to your reader what forms of validity you are claiming, and why. For example, we authors, Jack and Jean, claim that this book achieves all the forms of validity above. Especially we claim that we are demonstrating catalytic validity, in the hope that our ideas will influence yours.

This is where you can have the greatest influence in the learning of others. You demonstrate the validity of your knowledge and truth claims throughout your research report: this is part of establishing the methodological rigour of the research. You demonstrate legitimacy through showing that your report is endorsed by critical readers and examiners, that you are trustworthy. If they trust you, people may be willing to try things out for themselves.

Dot Jackson, a senior lecturer in Design and Technology, writes about learning from her research:

Although this action enquiry was with a small group of students, the quantity and quality of learning has been immense. I will take my new learning into my future practice with all my cohorts and continue with new cycles of reflection-on-action. Since embarking on this research I am able to articulate that my pedagogy has transformed towards collaborative praxis across all my teaching courses, from challenging an expectation of craft and moving towards innovative designerly practice. I have made changes informed by my dynamic reflections towards my own living theory of creative practice. My learning has taken place at a range of levels and in various places from individual conversations to pedagogical reflections. I recognise new ways in which I can support the development of necessary skills and knowledge in design and technology whilst also providing a critical 'creative ecosystem' (Harrington 1990), where co-creation of knowledge can take place. I continue to work towards empowering students to challenge normative pedagogical practices, recognising their ability to create their own knowledge and to move confidently towards living their values in their practice. My new living theory of practice will be disseminated to the wider academy in papers and at educational conferences as I contribute to a new epistemology for a scholarship of educational knowledge.

My learning may gradually flow into schools through the pedagogy of my students as they take their new learning into schools. I use a river delta as a visual metaphor for my transformational learning as my enquiries develop and branch out in various directions while flowing in the general direction of new understanding and knowledge creation. (Jackson 2008: 23–4)

The way to exercise greatest influence is through writing, making ideas/knowledge public in different forms and for different audiences. This brings us to how to contribute to the education of social formations.

The significance of the fact that you speak for the education of social formations

Now that you have turned yourself into a writer, with academic legitimacy, you are in a position of potentially considerable influence. A key aspect is that you can influence new forms of thinking in your workplace and in the academy; and, given that the academy can influence social and cultural transformation, you are positioned as someone who can influence the future.

You therefore need to be clear about what you wish to say and how to say it. This depends on your values, what you stand for. It is said that unless we stand for something we will fall for anything. Be ready to say what you stand for, and what you are prepared to live (and possibly die) for.

Consider what this means, and how you are advancing the existing range of mainstream literatures, which still speak in a propositional form, about ideas such as self-critique and reflective practices, without showing what they mean in action.

Here is the greatest source of your influence. You are showing, through the content and form of your report, how you are fulfilling your obligations to the truth, and speaking with your own voice. You are also saying that other people can do this, and should do it. You are pointing out to people in your workplace what needs to be done in order to improve working conditions, and to the academy that their primary responsibility should be finding ways of promoting wisdom for human wellbeing. You are saying to your academic colleagues that they also should create themselves as public intellectuals and stand up for those who are not able to stand up for themselves.

Sally Aston, a senior lecturer of Design and Technology, writes about the significance of her research for her ongoing practice.

By undertaking this research I have identified ways I can continue to transform and improve my practice in future, as a practitioner reflecting in and on action. I believe that some [research] participants [now] have the capacity to develop a deeper level of critical consciousness. I feel that if I encourage students to make closer connections with the natural environment and the wider global community, their level of critical engagement will be raised and they will feel that they, as participating and informed citizens, can change things for the better. At this time of transition we have reached what Freire described as an 'historical epoch' which is 'characterised by a series of aspirations, concerns and values in search of fulfilment' (2005: 4). As citizens, we can participate in these epochs by creating, recreating and making decisions which will influence our future. I think it is my responsibility in my position [as a senior lecturer] to influence both future teachers and, indirectly, their pupils, to encourage participation as citizens who have the power to instigate positive change in society. ... With this in mind, I want to continue to develop my learning of ways to improve and understand my practice, as a form of praxis ... where I feel I comfortably inhabit my values. (Aston 2008: 22–3)

Through exercising your potentials for educational influence you can contribute to this process of cultural transformation. In Chapter 10 we speak about how you can do this through the development of a knowledge base, how you can make your contribution to the body of public knowledge, and so contribute to discourses about social and cultural evolution.

SUMMARY

This chapter has considered the significance of your research for yourself, the wider community, and for the future. In each of these contexts, you can show its significance for the education of yourself, of others, and of social formations. You can claim significance for what you say, how you say it, and the fact that you say it. Through doing so, you show how you give meaning to your life, and contribute to the meaning that others give to theirs.

CHECKLIST OF REFLECTIVE QUESTIONS

Here is a checklist to remind you of how you can explain the significance of your knowledge and your report.

Do I communicate the significance of what I say?

- Do I explain how I am contributing to my own education, to the education of others, and to the education of social formations, through what I have to say?
- Have I produced a strong evidence base to show the nature of my educational influences in learning, and the range of those influences?

Do I communicate the significance of how I say what I say?

- Do I explain how I am contributing to processes of the legitimation of knowledge through my form of communication?
- Have I produced a strong evidence base to show the procedures involved in exercising my educational influences in learning, and the complexities of those procedures?

Do I communicate the significance of the fact that I am able to speak for myself?

- Do I explain how I am contributing to debates about the legitimacy of all to speak for themselves through showing the potentials involved?
- Have I produced a strong evidence base to show the legitimacy of the struggles involved to get my knowledge validated and legitimated?

If you have done all these things, you can be fairly confident that your voice will be taken seriously in the research and wider communities, and that people will consider your influence in their own processes of learning.

We now move to the final chapter, which sets out ideas about creating a new public sphere through developing and sharing the kind of knowledge that is dedicated to improving practice for the benefit of oneself and others.

Some Implications of Your Research and Your Research Report

We now consider some of the implications of what this book has said, and the potentials of its messages. In this sense, we authors return the book to ourselves, by making judgements about its quality, in the same way as you make judgements about the quality of your work. The book represents a summary of our present best thinking and experience as supervisors and examiners of higher degree work. We have experience of what is required at all levels, and we know how people can achieve it. We are sharing these ideas because we believe that all people should achieve their dreams of a higher degree, and also because we see these awards as having the potential for far-reaching personal, social and cultural improvement.

The focus of this chapter therefore turns to judging the quality of our work. We have done our best in offering our ideas to you, and we judge their quality in terms of their potential, how they are affirmed by others in their lives and work. Hence it is important for us to know whether you feel the ideas are worthwhile and realisable, and how any outcomes may be judged. We are also hopeful that you will share your own living theories with us as you work and research to enhance your educational influences in your own learning and in the learning of others.

The chapter is organised in terms of these questions:

1. What are the potentials of the ideas we are communicating?
2. How can these potentials be realised?
3. How are the outcomes judged?
4. Summary.
5. Checklist of reflective questions.

WHAT ARE THE POTENTIALS OF THE IDEAS WE ARE COMMUNICATING?

We ground the ideas in this book in an appreciation of the uniqueness and indispensability of your contribution to human knowledge and learning. We explore these ideas further; and we begin by considering the concept of a public sphere, and its knowledge base, and how you can contribute to the realisation of an authentic public sphere through strengthening a form of knowledge base that is commensurable with the underpinning values of a public sphere. First let's consider:

1. What 'the public sphere' means.
2. What kind of knowledge base is appropriate.
3. How this can be achieved.

What is the public sphere?

We said in Chapter 9 that the public sphere can be understood as a form of social life where people come together, on an equal footing, to discuss what makes their lives worthwhile and how they can achieve the kind of lives and world they wish to live in. The public sphere therefore becomes a space in which rational discussion is encouraged, and where decisions are reached discursively. We see the public sphere as an intermediate space between the private sphere of the creation of ideas, and the cultural, political and economic spheres of the public authority of the State which establishes the regulative principles, already discussed in the public sphere, in legalistic terms (the Law). In many literatures, the relationships between the private sphere, the public sphere and the State distinguish particular forms of democracy.

This all looks fine on paper, but there are problematics in real life. Here are some.

- On paper it is assumed that everyone has a place and that everyone will agree about who goes where, and whether they will stay there. In reality, of course, it does not work so smoothly. Social life is in a process of continuous change, and there are tensions between the pressures that reproduce existing social formations and those that transform the social formations.
- It is assumed that people will act discursively and courteously to one another, that all opinions will be heard, and that everyone, regardless of rank or privilege, will have an equal say. It is further assumed that all people will be able to speak for themselves, and will know what to say and why they should say it. This is not the case in real life where many people are deliberately prevented from speaking for themselves, and many do not know how to do so or what kind of language will be listened to.
- It is assumed that the public sphere is a specific space, separate from other spaces, and also separate from the people who make it up; in other words, the idea of a public sphere tends to be made abstract and idealised, so the idealisation comes to be taken for granted, and the realities of the lives of individuals are ignored.

These ideas need to be deconstructed, as communicated throughout this book, and new ideas established in the literatures and everyday discourses, to say: that there are many public spheres, all interconnected; that no one is 'essentialised' and so no one is positioned in a particular way; that all people have an equal chance of speaking for themselves, and can speak the language that has been negotiated as appropriate; and that a public sphere is a real place, not somewhere only spoken about in books.

What kind of knowledge base is appropriate for the development of an authentic public sphere?

Achieving this idea of the democratisation and practical realisation of the public sphere involves considering what kind of knowledge base underpins it. Currently the kind of knowledge that underpins normative assumptions about the public sphere is propositional and abstract, ideas in the head that may have been drawn initially from real-life experience but have lost connection with this experience. It is what Lyotard (1984) calls 'grand theory' and Ngugi (1993) calls 'universal knowledge'. Both make the case that, to understand real-world interactions, 'local knowledge' (Ngugi 1993) also needs to be legitimated, knowledge that is particular to real people. Nor are these different kinds of knowledge separate, belonging to and emanating from different fields of cultural discourse, 'as if cultures within a nation and between nations have developed on parallel bars towards parallel ends that never meet, or if they meet, they do so in infinity' (Ngugi 1993: 26). In terms of this book, such local knowledge can be communicated through your report, your account of your living theory of practice, that incorporates within itself insights from the most influential of propositional thinkers, yet which has not got stuck within the structures of idealisation. By demonstrating your capacity to speak multiple languages across and between cultures, you show that you can swim in 'the sea of our connections with our common humanity' (Ngugi 1993: 29).

How can this be achieved?

This capacity can be achieved through undertaking your action enquiry, where you deliberately deconstruct the normative assumptions that you have learned from childhood. With occasional exceptions, all people are born into a culture, with its own norms, practices, values and assumptions. The actions of the people communicate the values that inform the culture of which they are a part. We said earlier that culture is popularly assumed to be 'the way we do things around here'; this applies as much to ways of thinking and what knowledge is seen as valuable as to ways of acting. Developing ideas from Chapter 1, it is possible to see how epistemological and ontological values can influence the culture; so what is known and how it comes to be known, and what is valued, inform what is done in real-life practices.

In many western and post-industrialised societies, the culture is premised on technical-rational knowledge, which factors out the values base of real people living real lives. It ignores the needs and desires of real people, the need for attachments, the quarrelsome nature of real people who seldom agree on areas of substantive interest, and the capacity for engaged and critical dialogue that prevents life from being understood as a Utopia that has lost connection with real life. While technical rational knowledge is vital for keeping planes in the air and computers working, it is not adequate to offer explanations for the lives of real people as they work out for themselves how they should live together. This needs other kinds of knowledge, the kind of knowledge you rely on for your daily practices, while drawing on technical rational knowledge for specific purposes, and which you produce as you study your practices.

Here are some ideas about how valuable this kind of knowledge can be, and how it can be created.

HOW CAN THESE POTENTIALS BE REALISED?

Let's stay with the idea of people producing and sharing their living educational theories of practice, and consider how an authentic public sphere, grounded in this idea, can be developed. In these terms, an authentic public sphere can be most effectively achieved when new cultures come into being, with new ideas about:

1. What counts as knowledge.
2. Who counts as a knower.
3. How these processes can be negotiated.

What counts as knowledge

We have said throughout that what counts as knowledge is held in place mainly by the Academy, though sources such as the media can be equally powerful. The Academy counts as one of the greatest sources of influence for how knowledge is communicated to new generations, and therefore influences the reproduction of societies through the reproduction of their cultures. As noted, technical rational knowledge is held as dominant, a form of knowledge that sees reality in terms of this or that and of causal relationships – 'If I do this, that will happen.' This view is so strong that people often do not question it. Indeed, non-questioning is part of the underpinning epistemology, where everything is seen as given and as working towards a pre-defined state of closure, when it will be demonstrated as correct. In reality, this is seldom the case. However, because the idea is so unquestioned, the idea itself becomes the reality, so people end up obeying what they think should be the reality at the cost of paying attention to what is the reality.

The kind of knowledge you have demonstrated in studying your practice and producing your account is grounded in your practical experience of life, albeit while perhaps incorporating technical rational knowledge into your thinking. Your knowledge is grounded in your lived experience of situations and relationships that are always contested and need to be negotiated through dialogue. Your reality is a dialogical one, where all people's voices are heard, all learn to speak the other's dialect, and all demonstrate a willingness to listen and attend to the other rather than expect the other to do so first. This kind of knowledge is relational.

It can also be transformational, in that, through speaking multiple dialects you communicate that you are not imposing your dialect on others, and are prepared to learn and engage in a universal language that is grounded in values to do with honouring the other and appreciating the context you are in. You hold your present knowledge lightly, open to contestation before validation; however, once validated, you regard it as worthy of entering the public domain as valuable knowledge from which others may benefit. The knowledge you bring to your context is your contribution to your own and other people's understanding of your field, in the same way that the life you live is your contribution to the planet. You are valuable, as Arendt maintains (1958), simply because you are alive, and the fact that you speak your truth is valuable because you speak it.

This kind of personal and social knowledge is as (possibly more) valuable for social evolution and sustainability as technical rational knowledge or propositional theories, which tell about ideas, but do not necessarily show the ideas in action or their influences in human living. Through demonstrating the validity of your knowledge claims in your research account, and through having them legitimated by the Academy, you are stating that your contribution may be valued as strongly as any other kind of contribution. You are a valuable researcher and creator of knowledge, in relation with other people, who are doing the same (Whitehead, 2008c).

Who counts as a knower

Before action research became popular, it was generally held that only people positioned in the Academy were capable of generating knowledge. Local knowledge was held to be of lesser importance than propositional knowledge (Schön 1995), not to be taken seriously in debates about how social relationships should be understood or what contributed to social evolution. Things have changed.

It is now widely recognised that all people are capable of creating knowledge. In the ideas expressed in this book, all people are capable of generating an infinitude of knowledge. It does not matter what you are: what matters is who you are. It does not matter where you come from, what gender or colour you are, how old or able or rich you are or what you believe in. These categorisations are social constructions, invented and sustained because they provide convenient means of slotting people into boxes and so controlling them effectively; the idea of 'category' is a social construction. What *does* matter is that you are a person, capable of generating knowledge, testing its validity, and showing how it has enabled you to improve what you are doing and contribute to other people's understandings of how they can do the same.

However, you need to recognise that, because you are engaged in a higher degree programme, with the Academy as your accrediting body, you are positioned within normative contexts where the view of higher education personnel as legitimate knowledge creators (but not practitioners) is still endemic, though things are changing. This has implications for you and the need to ensure the quality of your research and report, so that they will stand with the best of what is still held as legitimate academic knowledge. Although you are a workplace practitioner, you are now an academic by virtue of the fact that you are studying at the Academy. The Academy is a noble and worthwhile site, whose main job is to create knowledge, and, because you claim that you are creating knowledge, you need to show that the knowledge qualifies for validation when judged against the most stringent standards. As a practitioner who has deliberately engaged with academic study, there is no point in saying, 'Poor me,' and expecting your work to be accredited simply because practitioners and their knowledge have been marginalised in the past. Like many previously marginalised people, it is up to you to show that you are capable of speaking multiple dialects, if you have a mind to, and of achieving the highest levels in terms of the standards appropriate to judging the quality of work in your field. This can of course be difficult, but it is the name of the particular political game you are in, so be aware of what you need to do in these processes of the reconstruction of what counts as academic knowledge, and then do it.

How can these processes be negotiated?

The first thing to do in negotiating access is to develop a perception of yourself as a valuable person who can make their unique and vital contribution to human history in their own way. Human relationships that work on the basis of the asymmetrical distribution of power are seldom life-affirming for all involved. This view is borne out in a range of literatures: for example, the literatures of colonisation and post-colonialism, or of feminist discourses. In any relationship where one party is dominant and the other subservient, both suffer, as Memmi (1974) explained in his work on the coloniser and the colonised; both get caught up in the system of belief that some people are better than others and may exercise their authority over the other. This applies to all kinds of emotions and attitudes: too much gratitude can be as disabling as fear. Both parties become prisoners of the colonising system, the most insidious form of which appears in how we think.

As noted earlier, the most powerful form of imprisonment is imprisonment of the mind (Chomsky 2000). Many people are persuaded to think what other people tell them to, even though these ways may be in contradiction to what they value. Colonisers know this well, and often deliberately adopt strategies of persuasion to lead people to distort their thinking, such as coming to believe that it is their fault that they are subjugated. Many people come to believe that it is their responsibility to believe things told to them through the culture, even though these things are alien to their own beliefs. You can see many powerful arguments in the media about the need for death row or for imprisoning people without trial in the interests of national security. You can read many powerful stories that deliberately mislead: popular stories about the origin of concentration camps are quickly debunked from a visit to the memorial cemeteries of the women and children of the concentration camps in Cape Town and Pretoria, created by the British. The mind becomes imprisoned when we internalise the rules of imprisonment; many people become subservient because they come to believe that this is how they should be.

To achieve access to equal entitlement and full recognition, the first thing to do is to appreciate fully that your life is your contribution to human wellbeing. No one can occupy your place on earth, or live for you; no one can die for you. Your life is unique and indispensable, to be used creatively for universal evolution. You do not have a responsibility to think according to what other people tell you; your responsibility is to think for yourself, so that you can make your best contribution. Thinking and acting responsibly in terms of making your full contribution within the Academy, and through the Academy for social and cultural re-creation, involves ensuring that your research report is of the highest standard, so that it will stand on its own merits during examination procedures. You can then make the case that your work has met all the requirements of quality reporting, from the authority of your own scholarship.

This means appreciating that you have a right to speak and be heard, but that what you say needs to be informed, and spoken with discernment. It needs to be grounded in quality scholarship and thorough research, which have been demonstrated as of high quality with an appreciation of the originality, rigour and significance of your work, and put to the test of stringent assessment procedures. You exercise your wise judgement, and conduct yourself with toughness and grace. You are bound to encounter opposition, in the form of people who do not wish to include you in the discourses, and this is where you demonstrate that you can challenge even the idea of inclusion, and go beyond this, through your capacity to create your own living theory of practice (Farrell and Rosenkrantz, 2008), as we now explain.

HOW ARE THE OUTCOMES JUDGED?

The main outcome of your exercise of your capacity to speak your knowledge and have it validated and legitimated is that you initiate discourses that move beyond inclusion. The idea of inclusion and beyond inclusion communicates the generative transformational processes that we have been speaking about throughout.

The idea of inclusion is part of metaphors of structuration. In normal usage, something is included within or as part of something else, an existing structure: for example, you would be included in a team or on a list of invitations. In politics, or in theories of democratic participation, inclusion tends to be seen in legalistic terms: we speak about people being included or excluded in activities (e.g. Habermas 2001). Minority groups are usually included within majority groupings (but see Sullivan 2006 for a different perspective). The idea of inclusion makes sense when it is assumed that someone or something is invited to take part in an existing game. We authors have frequently spoken about 'inclusional epistemologies', referring to the idea that all people may think in their own way, and that personal forms of knowing need to be recognised as of equal validity as technical propositional ways of knowing.

We are extending our own thinking now to say that inclusional epistemologies need to be understood not as bounded within a given field of many epistemologies (similar to Ngugi's (1993: 39) idea of a field of flowers of different colours) so much as an emergent element of unbounded ways of thinking (Mitroff and Linstone 1993). By 'unbounded ways of thinking' we mean that knowledge itself needs to be seen as always on the move, always expanding, pushing the boundaries rather than closing them in, part of the infinite capacity for originality and self-recreation. Rayner, who shares these ideas about creative forms, speaks of 'inclusionality' and says:

> At the heart of inclusionality … is a simple shift in the way we frame reality, from absolutely fixed to relationally dynamic. This shift arises from perceiving space and boundaries as connective, reflective and co-creative, rather than severing, in their vital role of producing heterogeneous form and local identity. (2004: 1)

We also want to highlight the importance of understanding that, from a perspective of inclusionality, we are all included in the dynamics of a common living-space that flows with life-affirming energy. Lumley (2008: 3) explains the importance of recognizing 'an inspiring pool-of-consciousness that seems to include and connect all within a unifying dynamical communion … as ineluctably included participants'.

The capacity for unbounded epistemologies is grounded in a capacity always to re-think, make new connections, tap into the webs of connectedness and reconfigure them in new ways. The possibilities for the re-configuration of patterns are endless. So it is both a case of finding the patterns that connect (Bateson 1979) and of creating new connective patterns, which have never been experienced before and which themselves have the potentials for new ways of being.

This is the main way in which the outcomes of your work will be judged for their overall quality. Your report will be judged in relation to the criteria we have indicated throughout – does the work demonstrate originality, critical engagement, rigorous scholarship, appreciation of its significance, a flawless presentation … and so on. Coming back to this book, which is a report of our research, we ask, 'Do we demonstrate these qualities?' However, while your report may be judged in these terms, the quality of your work, which is different from your report, will be judged in terms of whether you demonstrate a capacity for new thinking and for exercising your educational influence in ways that communicate the endless possibilities of life itself. In terms of this book, do we authors, Jack and Jean, do this? Do we communicate to you that no one can take your place, that you have a unique and indispensable contribution to make to human and ecological evolution, that you are priceless? If we have gone some way towards communicating this to you, then this book may be judged as worthwhile.

We end by saying that we also continue to say to ourselves, to each other, and to other people, 'You can do this. You have the capacity to be more than you are, to enable others also to be more than they are. Just find ways of doing it. You will not know until you try.'

And this is what we will continue to do.

SUMMARY

This chapter has set out some of the implications of your research in terms of its potential influences for social good. It shows the relationships between your capacity for knowledge creation and the development of dialogically-constituted communities for sustainable social development. Your knowledge and your life are indispensable contributions to the universe, and may be recognised as such through your capacity to speak your truth with authority.

 ## CHECKLIST OF REFLECTIVE QUESTIONS

Here is a checklist of reflective questions that may enable you to reflect further on the significance of your contribution.

- Am I aware of what my contribution is for improving practice, and its significance for knowledge creation?
- Do I appreciate the links between my knowledge and the social order?
- How will I use my knowledge for social good?
- What strategies do I need to develop to sustain my learning?
- How do I judge the quality of my work and my life?
- Do I appreciate my potentials for infinite knowledge creation?
- What do I do next?

References

Adler-Collins, J.K. (2000) 'A Scholarship of Enquiry'. MA dissertation, University of Bath. Retrieved 5 August 2008 from http://www.jackwhitehead.com/jekanma.pdf

Adler-Collins, J.K. (2007) *Developing an Inclusional Pedagogy of the Unique: How do I Clarify, Live and Explain my Educational Influences in my Learning as I Pedagogise my Healing Nurse Curriculum in a Japanese University?* PhD thesis, University of Bath. Retrieved 20 June 2008 from http://www.actionresearch.net/jekan.shtml

Alford, C.F. (2001) *Whistleblowers: Broken Lives and Organizational Power.* Ithaca, NY, Cornell University Press.

Arendt, H. (1958) *The Human Condition.* Chicago, University of Chicago Press.

Arendt, H. (1977) *Eichmann in Jerusalem.* London, Penguin.

Aston, S. (2008) Academic Paper: Module 7, MA PVP programme, St Mary's University College, Twickenham. Available at http://www.jeanmcniff.com/stmarys/

Bailin, S., Case, R., Coombs, J. and Daniels, L. (1999) 'Common Misconceptions of Critical Thinking, *Journal of Curriculum Studies,* 31: 269–83.

Bakhtin, M. (1981) *The Dialogic Imagination: Four Essays* (ed. M. Holquist). Austin, University of Texas Press.

Barry, P. (2002) *Beginning Theory: An Introduction to Literary and Cultural Theory* (2nd edn). Manchester, Manchester University Press.

Barthes, R. (1970) *S/Z.* New York, Hill & Wang.

Barthes, R. (2000) *Mythologies.* London, Vintage.

Bassey, M. (1999) *Case Study Research in Educational Settings.* Buckingham, Open University Press.

Bateson, G. (1979) *Mind and Nature: A Necessary Unity.* New York, Dutton.

Belenky, M., Clinchy, B., Goldberger, N. and Tarule, J. (1986) *Women's Ways of Knowing: The Development of Self, Voice, and Mind.* New York, Basic Books.

Berlin, I. (1969) *Four Essays on Liberty.* London, Oxford University Press.

Bernstein, R. (1971) *Praxis and Action.* London, Duckworth. (Drawing on some of Marx's unpublished notes written in 1844.)

Biesta, G.J.J. (2006) *Beyond Learning; Democratic Education for a Human Future.* Boulder, CO, Paradigm Publishers.

Blackburn, S. (2001) *Ethics: A Very Short Introduction.* Oxford, Oxford University Press.

Bohm, D. (2006) *On Dialogue* (ed. L. Nichol). New York, Routledge.

Bourdieu, P. (1984) *Distinction: A Social Critique of the Judgement of Taste.* London, Routledge.

Bourdieu, P. (1990) *The Logic of Practice.* Cambridge, Polity.

Bruner, J.S. (1966) *Toward a Theory of Instruction.* New York: W.W. Norton & Company Inc.

Boyer, E. (1990) *Scholarship Reconsidered: Priorities of the Professoriate.* New Jersey, Carnegie Foundation for the Advancement of Teaching.

Britton, J. (1982) *Prospect and Retrospect: Selected Essays of James Britton* (ed. G. Pardl). London, Heinemann.

Brown, L. (2004) *African Philosophy: New and Traditional Perspectives.* Oxford, Oxford University Press.

Buber, M. (1970) *I and Thou*. Edinburgh, Clark.

Bullough, R. and Pinnegar, S. (2004) 'Thinking about Thinking about Self-study: An Analysis of Eight Chapters', in J.J. Loughran, M.L. Hamilton, V.K. Labosky and T. Russell (eds), *International Handbook of Teaching and Teacher-Education Practices*. Dordrecht, Kluwer.

Butler, J. (1999) *Gender Trouble*. London, Routledge.

Cahill, M. (2007) *My Living Educational Theory of Inclusional Practice*. PhD thesis, University of Limerick. Retrieved 20 June from http://www.jeanmcniff.com/margaret cahill/index.html

Callahan, R. (1962) *Education and the Cult of Efficiency*. Chicago, University of Chicago.

Charles, E. (2007) *How Can I Bring Ubuntu as a Living Standard of Judgement into the Academy? Moving Beyond Decolonisation through Societal Reidentification and Guiltless Recognition*. PhD thesis, University of Bath. Retrieved 19 June 2008 from http://www.actionresearch.net/edenphd.shtml

Chomsky, N. (1957) *Syntactic Structures*. The Hague, Mouton.

Chomsky, N. (1986) *Knowledge of Language: Its Nature, Origin and Use*. New York, Praeger.

Chomsky, N. (1991) *Media Control: The Spectacular Achievements of Propaganda*. New York, Seven Stories Press.

Chomsky, N. (interviewed by D. Barsamian) (1996–98) *The Common Good*. Tucson AZ, Odonian Press.

Chomsky, N. (2000) *Chomsky on MisEducation* (ed. D. Macedo). New York, Lanham, Rowman & Littlefield.

Chomsky, N. (2002) *Understanding Power: The Indispensable Chomsky* (eds P.R. Mitchell and J. Schoeffel). New York, The New Press.

Chopra, D. (2004) *The Book of Secrets: Unlocking the Hidden Dimensions of your Life*. New York, Random House.

Church, M. (2004) *Creating an Uncompromised Place to Belong: Why Do I find myself in networks*. PhD thesis, University of Bath. Retrieved 20 June 2008 from http://www.actionresearch.net/church.shtml

Clandinin, D.J. (ed.) (2007) *Handbook of Narrative Inquiry: Mapping a Methodology*. Thousand Oaks, CA, Sage.

Code, L. (1987) *Epistemic Responsibility*. Hanover, Brown University Press.

Cohen, L., Manion, L. and Morrison, K. (2007) *Research Methods in Education* (6th edn). Abingdon, Routledge.

Cordery, M. (2008) Academic Paper: Module 7, MA PVP programme, St Mary's University College, Twickenham. Available at http://www.jeanmcniff.com/stmarys/

Crossley, N. and Roberts, J.M. (2004) *After Habermas: New Perspectives on the Public Sphere*. Oxford, Basil Blackwell.

Dadds, M. (2008) 'Empathetic Validity', *Educational Action Research*, 16(2): 279–90.

Dadds, M. and Hart, S. (2001) *Doing Practitioner Research Differently*. London, RoutledgeFalmer.

Dainow, S. (1997) *Be Your Own Counsellor*. London, Judy Piatkus.

Delong, J. (2002) *How Can I Improve my Practice as a Superintendent of Schools and Create my Own Living Educational Theory?*. PhD thesis, University of Bath. Retrieved 20 June 2008 from http://www.actionresearch.net/delong.shtml

Derrida, J. (1981) *Dissemination*. Chicago, University of Chicago Press.

Derrida, J. (1986) 'But, beyond … (Open Letter to Anne McClintock and Rob Nixon)' (trans. Peggy Kamul), *Critical Inquiry*, 13 (Autumn): 155–70.

Derrida, J. (1997) *Of Grammatology*. Baltimore, Johns Hopkins Press.

Deutscher, P. (2005) *Derrida*. London, Granta.

Eames, K. (1995) *How Do I, as a Teacher and an Educational Action-Researcher, Describe and Explain the Nature of My Professional Knowledge?* PhD thesis, University of Bath. Retrieved 20 June 2008 from http://www.actionresearch.net/kevin.shtml

Eisner, E. (1997) 'The Promise and Perils of Alternative Forms of Representation', *Educational Researcher*, 26(6): 4–10.

Elliott, J. (1998) *The Curriculum Experiment: Meeting the Challenge of Social Change*. Buckingham, Open University Press.

Farrell, J. and Rosenkrantz, M.L. (2008) 'Cultivating Collaborative Self-study Living Theory: Laying a Foundation for Teacher Learning', in M.L. Heston, D.L. Tidwell, K.K. East and L.M. Fitzgerald (eds), *Proceedings of The Seventh International Conference on Self-Study of Teacher Education Practices on Pathways to Change in Teacher Education: Dialogue, Diversity and Self-Study*. Iowa, University of Northern Iowa. pp. 120–4.

Farren, M. (2005) *How Can I Create a Pedagogy of the Unique through a Web of Betweenness?*. PhD thesis, University of Bath. Retrieved 20 June 2008 from http://www.actionresearch.net/farren.shtml

Farren, M. and Whitehead, J. (2006) 'Educational Influences in Learning with Visual Narratives', in M. Childs, M. Cuttle and K. Riley (eds), *DIVERSE: Developing Innovative Video Resources for Students Everywhere*. Glasgow, Glasgow Caledonian University.

Feldman, A. (2003) 'Validity and Quality in Self-Study', *Educational Researcher*, 32(3): 26–8.

Feyerabend, P. (1975) *Against Method*. New York, New Left Books.

Feynman, R. (2001) *The Pleasure of Finding Things Out*. London, Penguin.

Finnegan, J. (2000) *How Do I Create my Own Educational Theory in my Educative Relations as an Action Researcher and as a Teacher?*. PhD thesis, University of Bath. Retrieved 20 June 2008 from http://www.actionresearch.net/fin.shtml

Formby, C. (2008) 'How Do I Sustain a Loving, *Receptively Responsive* Educational Relationship with my Pupils which will Motivate Them in Their Learning and Encourage Me in my Teaching?'. MAS assignment, University of Bath. Available at http://www.jackwhitehead.com/tuesdayma/formbyEE300907.htm

Forrest, M. (1983) *The Teacher As Researcher: The Use of Historical Artefacts in Primary Schools*. MEd dissertation, University of Bath.

Foucault, M. (1979) *Discipline and Punish: The Birth of the Prison*. New York, Vintage Books.

Foucault, M. (1980) *Power/Knowledge: Selected Interviews and Other Writings 1972–1977* (ed. G. Gordon). New York, Pantheon Books.

Foucault, M. (1990) *The History of Sexuality: Care of the Self*. New York, Vintage.

Foucault, M. (1994) *Critique and Power: Recasting the Foucault/Habermas Debate* (ed. M. Kelly). Cambridge, MA, MIT Press.

Foucault, M. (2001) *Fearless Speech*. Los Angeles, CA, Semiotext(e).

Frankl, V. (1959) *Man's Search for Meaning*. Boston, MA, Beacon.

Freire, P. (1973) *Pedagogy of the Oppressed*. New York, Seabury.

Freire, P. (2005) *Education for Critical Consciousness*. London, Continuum.

Fromm, E. (1978) *To Have or To Be?* London, Jonathan Cape.

Fullan, M. (1993) *Changing Froces: Probing the Depths of Educational Reform*. London, Falmer Press, International Publishing Group.

Furlong, J. and Oancea, A. (2005) *Assessing Quality in Applied and Practice-Based Educational Research: A Framework for Discussion*. Oxford, Oxford University Department of Educational Studies.

Geras, N. (1995) *Solidarity in the Conversation of Humankind*. London, Verso.

Glavey, C. (2008) *Helping Eagles Fly: A Living Theory Approach to Student and Young Adult Leadership Development*. PhD thesis, University of Glamorgan. Retrieved 9 July 2008 from www.jeanmcniff.com/theses/glavey.html

Glenn, M. (2006) *Working with Collaborative Projects: My Living Theory of a Holistic Educational Practice*. PhD thesis, University of Limerick. Retrieved 19 June 2008 from http://www.jeanmcniff.com/glennabstract.html

Grandi, B. (2004) 'An Action Research Expedition: How Can I Influence my Students in Developing Their Creativity and Critical Thinking? A Self Study'. MA dissertation. Retrieved 27 May 2008 from http://www.actionresearch.net/grandi.shtml

Gray, J. (2002) *Straw Dogs.* London, Granta.

Grayling, A.C. (2003) *What is Good?* London, Weidenfeld and Nicolson.

Habermas, J. (1975) *Legitimation Crisis.* Boston, MA, Beacon Press.

Habermas, J. (1976) *Communication and the Evolution of Society.* Boston, MA, Beacon.

Habermas, J. (1984) *The Theory of Communicative Action, Volume One: Reason and the Rationalisation of Society.* Cambridge, Polity Press.

Habermas, J. (1987) *The Theory of Communicative Action, Volume Two: The Critique of Functionalist Reason.* Oxford, Polity Press.

Habermas, J. (2001) *The Inclusion of the Other.* Cambridge, MA, MIT Press.

Hampshire, S. (2000) *Justice is Conflict.* Princeton, Princeton University Press.

Hargreaves, D. (1999) 'The Knowledge Creating School', *Journal of Education Studies,* 47(2): 225–37.

Harrington, D.M. (1990) 'The Ecology of Human Creativity: A Psychological Perspective', in M.A. Runco and R.S. Albert (eds), *Theories of Creativity.* London, Sage.

Hart, S. (1995) 'Action-in-Reflection', *Educational Action Research,* 3(2): 211–32.

Hartog, M. (2004) *A Self Study of a Higher Education Tutor: How Can I Improve my Practice?.* PhD thesis, University of Bath. Retrieved 19 June 2008 from http://www.actionresearch.net/hartog.shtml

Heilbroner, R. and Thurow, L. (1998) *Economics Explained.* New York, Simon & Schuster.

Herr, K. and Anderson, G. (2005) *The Action Research Dissertation.* New York, Sage.

Hibbard, G. (2008) Available from http://perfectimpact.com/index.shtml

Holley, E. (1997) *How Do I as a Teacher-researcher Contribute to the Development of a Living Educational Theory through an Exploration of my Values in my Professional Practice?.* MPhil thesis, University of Bath. Retrieved 20 June 2008 from http://www.actionresearch.net/erica.shtml

Husserl, E. (1931) *Ideas. A General Introduction to Pure Phenomenology.* London, Allen and Unwin.

Huxtable, M. (2008) Marie Huxtable's home pages. Retrieved 20 June 2008 from http://www.spanglefish.com/mariessite/

Hymer, B. (2007) *How Do I Understand and Communicate my Values and Beliefs in my Work as an Educator in the Field of Giftedness?.* EdD.Pscyh., University of Newcastle. Retrieved 20 June 2008 from http://www.actionresearch.net/hymer.shtml

Ilyenkov, E. (1977) *Dialectical Logic.* Moscow, Progress.

Inglis, T. (2008) *Global Ireland.* Abingdon, Routledge.

Jackson, D. (2008) Academic Paper: Module 7, MA PVP programme, St Mary's University College, Twickenham. Available at http://www.jeanmcniff.com/stmarys/

Jones, C. (2008) 'How Do I Improve my Practice as an Inclusion Officer Working in a Children's Service?'. Draft MA Dissertation, Bath Spa University.

Kafka, F. (2003) *The Metamorphosis, In the Penal Colony, and Other Stories.* New York, Simon & Schuster.

Kelly, V. (1989) *Curriculum Theory and Practice.* London, Paul Chapman Publishing Ltd.

Kipling, R. (1901) *Kim.* London, Macmillan & Co. Ltd.

Kristeva, J. (1986) *The Kristeva Reader* (ed. T. Moi). Oxford, Basil Blackwell.

Kuhn, T. (1962) *The Structure of Scientific Revolutions.* Chicago, University of Chicago Press.

Laidlaw, M. (1996) *How Can I Create my own Living Educational Theory as I Offer You an Account of My Educational Development?.* PhD thesis, University of Bath. Retrieved 20 June 2008 from http://www.actionresearch.net/moira2.shtml

Larter, A. (1987) *An Action Research Approach to Classroom Discussion in the Examination Years*. MPhil., University of Bath. Retrieved 19 June 2008 from http://www.actionresearch.net/andy.shtml

Lather, P. (1991) *Getting Smart: Feminism Research and Pedagogy With/in the Postmodern*. London, Routledge.

Law, J. (2004) *After Method: Mess in Social Science Research*. London, Routledge.

Lillis, S. (2001) *An Inquiry into the Effectiveness of my Practice as a Learning Practitioner-Researcher in Rural Community Development*. PhD thesis, University College Dublin. Retrieved 20 June 2008 from http://www.jeanmcniff.com/seamuslillisabstract.html

Lloyd, G. (2003) 'How Do I/We Help the Students in Key Stage 4 Improve their Learning if They are in Danger of Underperforming?', MA Educational Enquiry assignment, University of Bath. Available at http://www.actionresearch.net/module/glee0203.pdf

Lohr, E. (2006) *Love at Work: What is my Lived Experience of Love, and How May I Become an Instrument of Love's Purpose?*. PhD thesis, University of Bath. Retrieved 20 June 2008 from at http://www.actionresearch.net/lohr.shtml

Lumley, T. (2008) *A Fluid-Dynamical World View*. Victoria, British Columbia, Printorium Bookwork.

Lyotard, J.-F. (1984) *The Postmodern Condition: A Report on Knowledge*. Manchester, Manchester University Press.

Machiavelli, N. (1992) *The Prince*. Mineola, NY, Dover.

MacIntyre, A. (1981) *After Virtue*. London, Duckworth.

Majake, T. (2008a) 'Creating a Dialogical Classroom through a Dialectical Approach'. A paper presented at the American Educational Research Association Annual Meeting, New York, March. Retrieved 20 June 2008 from http://www.jeanmcniff.com/khayelitsha/tsepo_AERA_2008.htm

Majake, T. (2008b) 'Beyond Victimage'. Working paper, St Mary's University College, Twickenham.

Malgas, Z. (2008) Practitioner Research and Knowledge Transfer, Module 6, MA PVP Programme, St Mary's University College, Twickenham.

Marcuse, H. (1964) *One-Dimensional Man*. Boston, MA, Beacon.

Marlin, R. (2002) *Propaganda and the Ethics of Persuasion*. Ontario, Broadview Press.

Mathien, T. and Wright, D.G. (eds) (2006) *Autobiography as Philosophy*. Abingdon, Routledge.

McDonagh, C. (2007) *My Living Theory of Learning to Teach for Social Justice: How Do I Enable Primary School Children with Specific Learning Disability (Dyslexia) and Myself as their Teacher to Realise our Learning Potentials?*. PhD thesis, University of Limerick. Retrieved 19 June 2008 from http://www.jeanmcniff.com/mcdonaghabstract.html

McNiff, J. (2007) 'My story is my living educational theory', in D.J. Clandinin (ed.) *Handbook of Narrative Inquiry: Mapping a Methodology*. Thousand Oaks, CA, Sage. pp. 308–29.

McNiff, J. (2008a) 'Learning With and From People in Townships and Universities: How Do I Exercise my Transformational Educational Influence for Generative Systemic Transformation?'. A paper presented at the American Educational Research Association Annual Meeting as part of the Symposium 'Communicating and Testing the Validity of Claims to Transformational Systemic Influence for Civic Responsibility', March, New York. Retrieved 19 June 2008 from at http://www.jeanmcniff.com/aera08/JM_AERA08_Paper_final.htm

McNiff, J. (2008b) 'I Know How to Set the Caged Bird Free'. Paper presented at a conference at St Mary's College, Twickenham. Modified version in L. Wood (ed.) (2008) *Dealing with HIV & AIDS in the Classroom*. Cape Town, Juta Academic. Retrieved 19 June 2008 from http://www.jeanmcniff.com/cagedbird.htm

McNiff, J. and Whitehead, J. (2005) *Action Research for Teachers*. London, David Fulton.

McNiff, J. and Whitehead, J. (2006) *All You Need to Know about Action Research*. London, Sage.

Mead, G. (2001) *Unlatching the Gate: Realising my Scholarship of Living Inquiry*. PhD thesis, University of Bath. Retrieved 20 June 2008 from http://www.actionresearch.net/mead.shtml

Mellor, N. (1998) 'Notes from a Method', *Educational Action Research* 6(3): 453–70.

Memmi, A. (1974) *The Colonizer and the Colonized*. London, Souvenir.

Midgley, M. (1981) *Heart and Mind: The Varieties of Moral Experience*. Brighton, Harvester.

Milgram, S. (1973) *Obedience to Authority*. London, Tavistock.

Miller, J. (1993) *The Passion of Michel Foucault*. London, HarperCollins.

Mitroff, I. and Linstone, A. (1993) *The Unbounded Mind: Breaking the Chains of Traditional Business Thinking*. New York, Oxford University Press.

Mounter, J. (2007) *Can Children Carry Out Action Research about Learning, Creating their own Learning Theories?*. MA Unit, University of Bath, on Understanding Learners and Learning. Retrieved 19 June 2008 from http://www.jackwhitehead.com/tuesdayma/joymounterull.htm

Moustakim, R. (2008) Academic Paper: Module 7, MA PVP programme, St Mary's University College, Twickenham. Available at http://www.jeanmcniff.com/stmarys/

Murray, R. (2002) *How to Write a Thesis*. Buckingham, Open University Press.

Naidoo, M. (2006) *I Am Because We Are (A Never Ending Story). The Emergence of a Living Theory of Inclusional and Responsive Practice*. PhD thesis, University of Bath. Retrieved 19 May 2008 from http://www.actionresearch.net/naidoo.shtml

Ngugi wa Thiong'o (1993) *Moving the Centre: The Struggle for Cultural Freedoms*. Oxford, James Currey.

Noffke, S. (1997) 'Professional, Personal, and Political Dimensions of Action Research', *Review of Research in Education*, 22: 305–43.

Norris, C. (1989) *The Deconstructive Turn: Essays in the Rhetoric of Philosophy*. London, Routledge.

Olson, G. and Worsham, L. (2003) *Critical Intellectuals on Writing*. Albany, State University of New York Press.

O'Neill, R. (2008) *ICT as Political Action*. PhD thesis, University of Glamorgan. Available at www.ictaspoliticalaction.com

O'Reilly, P. (1994) *Writing for the Market*. Dublin, Mercier Press.

Pearson, J. (2008) *Academic Paper: Module 7*. MA PVP programme, St Mary's University College, Twickenham. Available at http://www.jeanmcniff.com/stmarys/

Perlmutter, D.D. (2000) *Policing the Media: Street Cops and Public Perceptions of Law Enforcement*. London, Sage.

Phillips, E.M. and Pugh, D.S. (2000) *How to Get a PhD: A Handbook for Students and their Supervisors* (3rd edn). Buckingham, Open University Press.

Pithers, K.T. and Soden, R. (2000) 'Critical Thinking in Education: A Review, *Educational Research*, 42(3): 237–49.

Polanyi, M. (1958) *Personal Knowledge*. London, Routledge & Kegan Paul.

Popper, K. (1945) *The Open Society and its Enemies: Volume 1: Plato*. London, Routledge & Kegan Paul.

Pring, R. (2000) *Philosophy of Educational Research*. London, Continuum.

Punia, R. (2004) *My CV is my Curriculum: The Making of an International Educator with Spiritual Values*. PhD thesis, University of Bath. Retrieved 20 June 2008 from http://www.actionresearch.net/punia.shtml

Rawls, J. (1971) *A Theory of Justice*. Oxford, Oxford University Press.

Rayner, A. (2004) 'Inclusionality: The Science, Art and Spirituality of Place, Space and Evolution'. Retrieved 17 August 2008 from http://people.bath.ac.uk/bssadmr/inclusionality/placespaceevolution.html

Rayner, A. (2008) Alan Rayner's home page. Available at http://people.bath.ac.uk/bssadmr/

Raz, J. (2003) *The Practice of Value*. Oxford, Oxford University Press.

Reagan, T. (2005) *Non-Western Educational Traditions* (3rd edn). Mahway, NJ, Lawrence Erlbaum Associates.

Robson, C. (2002) *Real World Research: A Resource for Social Scientists and Practitioner-researchers* (2nd edn). Oxford, Blackwell.

Roche, M. (2007) *Towards a Living Theory of Caring Pedagogy: Interrogating my Practice to Nurture a Critical, Emancipatory and Just Community of Enquiry.* PhD thesis, University of Limerick. Available at http://www.jeanmcniff.com/MaryRoche/index.html

Russell, T. and Korthagen, F. (1995) *Teachers who Teach Teachers to Teach.* New York, Falmer.

Rust, F. and Freidus, H. (eds) (2001) *Guiding School Change: The Role and Work of Change Agents.* New York, Teachers College Press.

Ryle, G. (1949) *The Concept of Mind.* Harmondsworth, Penguin.

Rutter, J. (2006) *Refugee Children in the UK.* Berkshire, Open University Press.

Said, E. (1978) *Orientalism.* London, Routledge & Kegan Paul.

Said, E. (1991) *The World, the Text and the Critic.* London, Vintage.

Said, E. (1994a) *Culture and Imperialism.* London, Vintage.

Said, E. (1994b) *Representations of the Individual: The 1993 Reith Lectures.* London, Vintage.

Said, E. (1997) *Beginnings: Intent and Method.* London, Granta.

Schön, D. (1995) 'Knowing-in-action: The New Scholarship Requires a New Epistemology', *Change*, Nov.–Dec.: 27–32.

Schön, S. (1983) *The Reflective Practitioner: How Professionals Think in Action.* New York, Basic.

Schutz, A. (1972) *The Phenomenology of the Social World.* London, Heinemann.

Sen, A. (1999) *Development as Freedom.* Oxford, Oxford University Press.

Senge, P. (1990) *The Fifth Discipline: The Art & Practice of the Learning Organization.* New York, Doubleday.

Shobbrook, H. (1997) *My Living Educational Theory Grounded in My Life: How Can I Enable my Communication through Correspondence to be Seen as Educational and Worthy of Presentation in its Original Form?.* MPhil disssertation, University of Bath. Retrieved 20 June 2008 from http://www.actionresearch.net/hilary.shtml

Sinclair, A. (2008) *Academic Paper: Module 7.* MA PVP programme, St Mary's University College, Twickenham. Available at http://www.jeanmcniff.com/stmarys/

Slavin, R.E. (2002) 'Evidence-based Education Policies: Transforming Educational Practice and Research', *Educational Researcher*, 31(7): 15–21.

Spiro, J. (2008) *How I have Arrived at a Notion of Knowledge Transformation, Through Understanding the Story of Myself as Creative Writer, Creative Educator, Creative Manager, and Educational Researcher.* PhD thesis, University of Bath. Retrieved 19 June 2008 http://www.actionresearch.net/janespirophd.shtml

Stenhouse, L. (1983) 'Research is Systematic Enquiry Made Public', *British Educational Research Journal*, 9(1): 11–20.

Suderman-Gladwell, G. (2001) 'The Ethics of Personal Subjective Narrative Research'. MA Dissertation, Brock University. Retrieved 5 August 2008 from http://www.actionresearch.net/values/gsgma.PDF

Sullivan, B. (2006) *A Living Theory of a Practice of Social Justice: Realising the Right of Traveller Children to Educational Equality.* PhD thesis, University of Limerick. Retrieved 20th June 2008 from http://www.jeanmcniff.com/bernieabstract.html

Tillich, P. (1973) *The Courage To Be.* London, Fontana.

Todorov, T. (1990) *Genres in Discourse.* Cambridge MA, Cambridge University Press.

Todorov, T. (1999) *Facing the Extreme: Moral Life in the Concentration Camps*. London, Weidenfeld and Nicolson.

University of Bath (2008) *Guidelines for Examiners*. Bath, University of Bath.

University of Limerick (2006) *A Guide for Research Students and Supervisors* (2nd edn). Limerick, University of Limerick.

Vasilyuk, F. (1991) *The Psychology of Experiencing: The Resolution of Life's Critical Situations*. Hemel Hempstead, Harvester Wheatsheaf.

Walsh, D. (2004) 'How do I Improve my Leadership as a Team Leader in Vocational Education in Further Education?'. MA dissertation, University of Bath. Retrieved 27 May 2008 from http://www.actionresearch.net/walsh.shtml

Warren, K. (2001) 'Introduction', in M. Zimmerman, J. Baird Callicott, G. Sessions, K. Warren and J. Clark (eds), *Environmental Philosophy: From Animal Rights to Radical Ecology* (3rd edn). Upper Saddle River, NJ, Prentice Hall.

Wenger, E. (1998) *Communities of Practice: Learning, Meaning, and Identity*. Cambridge, Cambridge University Press.

Wheatley, M. (1994) *Leadership and the New Science: Learning about Organization from an Orderly Universe*. San Francisco, CA, Berrett-Koehler.

Whitehead, J. (1989) 'Creating a Living Educational Theory from Questions of the Kind, "How do I improve my practice"', *Cambridge Journal of Education*, 19(1): 137–53.

Whitehead, J. (1993) *The Growth of Educational Knowledge: Creating your own Living Educational Theories*. Bournemouth, Hyde. Retrieved 20 June 2008 from http://www.actionresearch.net/writings/jwgek93.htm

Whitehead, J. (1999) *How Do I Improve my Practice? Creating a New Discipline of Educational Enquiry*. PhD thesis, University of Bath. Retrieved 20 June 2008 from http://www.actionresearch.net/jack.shtml

Whitehead, J. (2004) 'What Counts as Evidence in the Self-Studies of Teacher Education Practices?', in J.J. Loughran, M.L. Hamilton, V. K. LaBoskey and T. Russell (eds), *International Handbook of Self-Study of Teaching and Teacher Education Practices*. Dordrecht, Kluwer Academic Publishers.

Whitehead, J. (2008a) 'Combining Voices in Living Educational Theories that are Freely Given in Teacher Research'. A keynote presentation to the International Conference on Teacher Research, New York, March. Retrieved 19 June 2008 from http://www.jack whitehead.com/aerictr08/jwictr08key.htm. Streaming video available from mms:// wms.bath.ac.uk/live/education/JackWhitehead_030408/jackkeynoteictr 280308large.wmv

Whitehead, J. (2008b) 'Increasing Inclusion in Educational Research: A Response to Pip Bruce Ferguson', *Research Intelligence*, 103: 16–17. Retrieved 5 August 2008 from http://bera.ac.uk/pdfs/RI102%20for%20Web.pdf

Whitehead, J. (2008c) 'Living Theories of Educational Influences in Teacher Education with Dialogue, Diversity and Self-study', in M.L. Heston, D.L. Tidwell, K.K. East and L.M. Fitzgerald (eds), *Proceedings of The Seventh International Conference on Self-Study of Teacher Education Practices on Pathways to Change in Teacher Education: Dialogue, Diversity and Self-Study*. Iowa, University of Northern Iowa. pp. 308–12.

Whitehead, J. and Huxtable, M. (2008) 'The Catalytic Validity of the Living Educational Theories of Self-study Researchers in Improving Practice and in Creating a New Epistemology of Educational Knowledge', in M.L. Heston, D.L. Tidwell, K.K. East and L.M. Fitzgerald (eds), *Proceedings of The Seventh International Conference on Self-Study of Teacher Education Practices on Pathways to Change in Teacher Education: Dialogue, Diversity and Self-Study*. Iowa, University of Northern Iowa. pp. 313–17.

Whitehead, J. and McNiff, J. (2006) *Action Research: Living Theory*. London, Sage.

Whitty, G. (2005) 'Education(al) Research and Education Policy Making: Is Conflict Inevitable?'. Presidential Address to BERA 2005. Retrieved 13 August 2008 from http://bera.ac.uk/publications/documents/GWBERApresidentialaddress_000.pdf

Winter, R. (1989) *Learning from Experience*. London, Falmer.

Wittgenstein, L. (1953) *Philosophical Investigations*. Oxford, Blackwell.

Wood, L.A., Morar, T. and Mostert, L. (2007) 'From Rhetoric to Reality: The Role of Living Theory Action Research in Transforming Education', *Education as Change*, 11(2): 67–80.

Worsthorne, P. (2004) *Democracy Needs Aristocracy*. London, Harper Perennial.

Young, I.M. (2000) *Inclusion and Democracy*. Oxford, Oxford University Press.

Young, J. (1999) *The Exclusive Society*. London, Sage.

Zimmerman, M.E., Callicott, J.B., Sessions, G., Warren, K.H. and Clark, J. (2001) *Environmental Philosophy: From Animal Rights to Radical Ecology* (3rd edn). Upper Saddle River, NJ, Prentice Hall.

Index

causal relationships 19, 112, 170, 181
Charles, E. 52, 81, 128
China's Experimental Centre for Educational Action Research in Foreign Languages Teaching 16
Chomsky, N. 18, 55, 65, 82, 102, 133, 164, 166, 170, 172, 174, 183
Chopra, D. 39, 165
Church, M. 127, 153
claims to knowledge 12, 17–8, 25, 43; importance of articulating them 15; making them 23; testing the validity of 12–13, 23–4, 30–2, 58, 63, 94; originality of 43–4
Clandinin, D.J. 129
clarity of expression 71
Code, L. 174
Cohen, L. et al. 39–40
communicative action 96–7, 113
communicability 70, 98, 108
communities of enquiry 99, 101
comprehensibility 26, 70–3, 116
conceptual frameworks 89, 90, 95, 122–4, 157
confusion! 55, 65
connectedness 54, 118, 153, 176, 185
content validity 46
contexts: personal 127; importance of 60, 142; locational 128; theoretical 128
Cordery, M. 168
criteria for accreditation: definitions 1; achieving them 3
criteria and standards: definitions of 30, 63, 125; for judging the quality of an action research report 30–2; of practice 23–5, 63, 81, 115; of research 23–7, 115, 135
critical activity theory 131
critical analysis 34–7, 140
critical engagement 30–32, 35–7, 64, 122, 139, 156, 176; with your own thinking 65; with the literatures – see also literatures
critical feedback 78, 107, 114, 149
critical friends 25, 38, 61, 63, 65, 75, 78, 93, 98
critical reflection and thinking 34, 39, 76, 83
critical theory 141
critically reflective accounts: how to create them 37–42
Crossley, N. and Roberts, J.M. 133

cultural transformation 167–8, 175–6, 178, 184
cultures of enquiry 99, 152
cycles of action research 64, 68, 94, 100, 108, 114

Dadds, M. 174
Dadds, M. and Hart, S. 22, 129–30
Dainow, S. 39
data: analysis 62, 112; forms of 61; gathering and techniques 62, 93, 112; relevance of 40, 62, 148; storing 62, 112
decentring 34, 68
deconstructing your own thinking 14, 34, 40, 63, 66, 68, 76, 82, 103
deconstruction 51–4
Delong, J. 16, 151
democratic validity 46
Derrida, J. 2, 3, 21, 40, 52, 72, 82, 123, 165
Deutscher, P. 2, 21, 72
Dewey, J. 132
dialectics 9, 150–1
dialectical critique 25, 34, 40–1, 64, 66, 83, 98, 107, 122–35, 142, 156
disconfirming data and evidence 18, 62–3, 65, 74, 114
dissemination of findings 93–4, 153, 157–8, 175
distinction 3

e–journals 131, 158, 170
Eames, K. 150
editorial capacity, need for 34
educational influence 44, 60, 81–2, 93, 102, 108
educational research 8; and education research 135
educational validity 81–2
Eisner, E. 19, 95, 170
Elliott, J. 166
empathetic validity 174
enhancing professionalism 1
epistemologies: emancipatory 2, 51; inclusional and exclusional 51, 134; living 50, 170; new, for educational knowledge 83, 170; of practice 142, 156; of symbiotic practice (Sinclair); unbounded 185–6
epistemology 8: epistemological base 17; epistemological validity 174; epistemological values 133, 171

complexity 63, 122; differences
    between them 140–1
Lillis, S. 128
linguistic turn 82
literature review 65, 123, 125
literatures, engaging with 27, 31, 33, 39, 60,
    63, 65–6, 71, 75, 95, 122–4
living contradiction, experiencing
    oneself as 43–4, 76, 111, 126
living educational theory 134–5, 143, 148,
    150, 152
living theories of practice 15, 18,
    20–1, 31, 108, 124–5, 127,
    132, 141, 167–8, 174, 180, 184
Lloyd, G. 16
logics: as a form of thinking 71;
    different kinds of 9–10, 167;
    living 135
Lohr, E. 81
Lumley, T. 185
Lyotard, J.–F. 53, 180

Machiavelli, N. 126
MacIntyre, A. 133
Majake, T. 66, 128
Malgas, Z. 66
Marcuse, H. 71
Marlin, R. 76, 171
masters dissertations 121–37;
    criteria for 121–2; achieving
    the criteria 122–35; judging
    their quality 135–7
Mathien, T. and Wright, D.G. 22
McDonagh, C. 45, 67, 127
McNiff, J. 57, 102, 129, 142; McNiff, J.
    and Whitehead, J. 100, 117
Mead, G. 128
medium and message 48;
    see also semiotics
Mellor, N. 55, 130
Memmi, A. 183
meta–reflection (meta–cognition) 34, 41–2,
    98, 140–2
method 8; 'method' and 'methodology'
    93; see also 'How do you do action
    research?' 56–64
methodological rigour 18, 27, 55, 67, 74,
    103, 107, 135, 174
methodological validity 67
Midgley, M. 126
Milgram, S. 76
Miller, J. 166
minimalist forms in writing 71–2, 84
Mitroff, I. and Linstone, A. 185
mixed methods 93
monitoring action and data
    gathering 12, 18, 38, 44,

62, 90, 93, 112,
    129–30, 148
Mounter, J. 32
Moustakim, R. 165
multimedia accounts 36–7, 56,
    95–6
multimedia forms of
    representation 19, 22, 32,
    51, 54, 65, 75, 89,
    93, 105, 114, 127,
    130, 154, 158
Murray, R. 141

Naidoo, M. 143
narrativised accounts 53, 68, 108,
    142–3, 156–7; see also stories
networks of communication 170
new epistemologies 124–5, 175
new scholarship 104, 135,
    136, 170
Ngugi wa Thiong'o 180, 185
Noffke, S. 145
normative assumptions 40, 52, 66,
    82, 103–4, 110, 141, 164,
    173, 175, 180
normative background 70, 84, 116
Norris, C. 52, 82

objectification 10, 129
Olson, G. and Worsham, L. 50
ontology 8; ontological perspectives
    126, 133, 164; ontological
    validity 174
O'Neill, R. 56, 75, 123, 165
O'Reilly, P. 71
original claims to knowledge 121–2,
    139–41, 156, 172
Other and othering 41, 82, 168

participants 61, 89, 92–3, 98
Pearson, J. 165–6, 173
Perlmutter, D.D. 170
permissions 61, 89, 95,
    103, 112, 131
PhD theses 139–58; criteria
    for 139–41; achieving the
    criteria 141–55;
    judging their quality 155–58;
    viva voce examinations
    155–58
Phillips, E.M. and Pugh, D.S. 141
Pithers, K.T. and Soden, R. 132
plagiarism 73, 80
Polanyi, K. 27, 63–5, 118, 125–6,
    132–3, 169, 171, 173–4
politics of educational knowledge
    1–2, 16; of research 8

tacit knowledge 79
textual validity 70
texts, criteria for good quality 69
The Legend of Bagger Vance 119
theoretical validity 63
theory: different forms of 10, 18, 20–1, 28, 126, 131, 156; ownership of 13, 17; propositional forms 19
Tillich, P. 102, 118, 174
Todorov, T. 21, 39, 49–50, 166
transformation, social and cultural 2
transformational forms and processes 10, 20, 22–3, 41, 68, 108, 110, 134, 163, 185; in research 55, 64, 113; texts 49, 108
transformational validity 67
triangulation 75, 93
trust 73; in your action 74; in your research and scholarship 74
truth claims 75, 165, 173–4; *see also* claims to knowledge
truthfulness 26, 70, 75, 116

Ubuntu 52
undergraduate reports 106–99; criteria 106–7; contents 107; form 107–8; achieving the criteria 108–14; making judgements about quality 115–17
University of Bath 27, 43, 122
University of Limerick 101–4

validation groups 25, 61, 63, 75, 93, 114, 122, 134
validity: as the grounds for legitimacy 24, 69, 163, 174; forms of 46, 67, 81–4, 174; ideas about 12, 18, 114, 132; personal 25–6, 116, 132, 174; social 25–6, 63, 69, 116, 133, 174; testing, what is involved 25–8, 63, 152–4
values: as abstractions 9–10, 59, 126, 147; as basis for conceptual frameworks 96; as basis of experience and practice 19, 24–5, 27, 76, 111, 146, 180; as basis for research 90, 113, 132; as criteria and standards of judgement 26–7, 94, 113, 126, 136, 150, 156; as lived experiences 9–10, 44, 59, 64, 73
values and logics in research 8–9, 28, 50, 124
Vasilyuk, F. 95
video data 51, 75; *see also* multimedia forms of representation

video diary 38; *see also* journals
video tapes 130
visual narratives 75, 95, 130, 158, 169; *see also* multimedia forms of representation
voice 21, 53; in different aspects of action research 32–4

Walsh, D. 128
Warren, K. 172
Weber, M. 11
Wenger, E. 99, 103, 124
Winter, R. 24, 34, 39, 83, 113, 156
Wheatley, M. 124
Whitehead, J. 36, 43, 58, 76, 99, 101–2, 111, 126–7, 130, 134–5, 144, 146, 168, 182
Whitehead, J. and Huxtable, M. 83
Whitehead, J. and McNiff, J. 56, 100, 102, 117
Whitty, G. 99
Wittgenstein, L. 82
Wood, L. et al. 99
workbased-learning, accreditation of 1, 106, 121, 183
workplace–university partnerships 17
Worsthorne, P. 126
writerly and readerly texts 49, 70
'writer's block' 79
writing: as a practice 2–3, 157; coping with difficulties 79; critique 78; drafting 78; editing 78–9; genres in 21–2, 79; how to write well 69–83; judging the quality of 81–3; legal issues 80; nature of 21–2; planning 77–8; practicalities of 5; proofreading 79; progression in 54; relationship with practice 2–3; schedules 77, 157; style in 54
writing for a reader 31, 70–1, 109; for publication 158

Young, I.M. 124, 166
Young, J. 51
your contribution: its uniqueness 178–9; to educational knowledge 182; to human wellbeing 184, 186

Zimmerman, M.E. et al. 103, 127

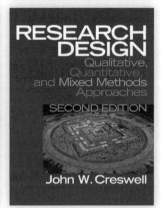